NORTHSTAR 5

READING & WRITING

FOURTH EDITION

Authors	ROBERT F. COHEN
	JUDY L. MILLER
Series Editors	FRANCES BOYD
	CAROL NUMRICH

DEDICATIONS

In loving memory of my mother, Lillian Kumock Cohen,
and my uncle, Julian Kumock.

RFC

To Ariana and Nora.

JLM

NorthStar: Reading & Writing Level 5, Fourth Edition

Copyright © 2015, 2009, 2004, 1998 by Pearson Education, Inc.
All rights reserved.

No part of this publication may be reproduced, stored in a retrieval system, or transmitted in any form or by any means, electronic, mechanical, photocopying, recording, or otherwise, without the prior permission of the publisher.

Pearson Education, 10 Bank Street, White Plains, NY 10606

Staff credits: The people who made up the *NorthStar: Reading & Writing Level 5, Fourth Edition* team, representing editorial, production, design, and manufacturing, are Tracey Cataldo, Kimberly Casey, Rosa Chapinal, Aerin Csigay, Dave Dickey, Mindy DePalma, Niki Lee, Amy McCormick, Mary Perrotta Rich, Robert Ruvo, Christopher Siley, and Debbie Sistino

Text composition: ElectraGraphics, Inc.
Development Editing: Lakeview Editing Services, LLC.

Library of Congress Cataloging-in-Publication Data

Haugnes, Natasha, 1965–
  Northstar 2 : Reading and writing / Authors: Natasha Haugnes, Beth Maher. — Fourth Edition.
      pages cm
  ISBN-13: 978-0-13-338216-7 (Level 2) – ISBN 978-0-13-294039-9 (Level 3) – ISBN 978-0-13-338223-5 (Level 4) – ISBN 978-0-13-338224-2 (Level 5)
1. English language—Textbooks for foreign speakers. 2. Reading comprehension—Problems, exercises, etc. 3. Report writing—Problems, exercises, etc. I. Maher, Beth, 1965- II. Title. III. Title: Northstar two. IV. Title: Reading and writing.
  PE1128.H394 2015
    428.2'4—dc23

                                                                    2013050584

ISBN 10: 0-13-338224-9
ISBN 13: 978-0-13-338224-2

Printed in the United States of America
1 2 3 4 5 6 7 8 9 10—V057—20 19 18 17 16 15 14

CONTENTS

WELCOME TO

NORTHSTAR

A BLENDED-LEARNING COURSE FOR THE 21ST CENTURY

Building on the success of previous editions, *NorthStar* continues to engage and motivate students through new and updated contemporary, authentic topics in a seamless integration of print and online content. Students will achieve their academic as well as language and personal goals in order to meet the challenges of the 21st century.

New for the FOURTH EDITION

★ Fully Blended MyEnglishLab
NorthStar aims to prepare students for academic success and digital literacy with its fully blended online lab. The innovative new MyEnglishLab: *NorthStar* gives learners immediate feedback—anytime, anywhere—as they complete auto-graded language activities online.

★ NEW and UPDATED THEMES
Current and thought-provoking topics presented in a variety of genres promote intellectual stimulation. The authentic content engages students, links them to language use outside of the classroom, and encourages personal expression and critical thinking.

★ EXPLICIT SKILL INSTRUCTION and PRACTICE
Language skills are highlighted in each unit, providing students with systematic and multiple exposures to language forms and structures in a variety of contexts. Concise presentations and targeted practice in print and online prepare students for academic success.

★ LEARNING OUTCOMES and ASSESSMENT
A variety of assessment tools, including online diagnostic, formative and summative assessments, and a flexible gradebook, aligned with clearly identified unit learning outcomes, allow teachers to individualize instruction and track student progress.

THE NORTHSTAR APPROACH TO CRITICAL THINKING

What is critical thinking?

Most textbooks include interesting questions for students to discuss and tasks for students to engage in to develop language skills. Often these questions and tasks are labeled critical thinking. Look at this question as an example:

When you buy fruits and vegetables, do you usually look for the cheapest price? Explain.

The question may inspire a lively discussion with students exploring a variety of viewpoints—but it doesn't necessarily develop critical thinking. Now look at another example:

When people in your neighborhood buy fruits and vegetables, what factors are the most important: the price, the freshness, locally grown, organic (without chemicals)? Make a prediction and explain. How can you find out if your prediction is correct? This question does develop critical thinking. It asks students to make predictions, formulate a hypothesis, and draw a conclusion, all higher-level critical thinking skills. Critical thinking, as philosophers and psychologists suggest, is a sharpening and a broadening of the mind. A critical thinker engages in true problem solving, connects information in novel ways, and challenges assumptions. A critical thinker is a skillful, responsible thinker who is open-minded and has the ability to evaluate information based on evidence. Ultimately, through this process of critical thinking, students are better able to decide what to think, what to say, or what to do.

How do we teach critical thinking?

It is not enough to teach "about" critical thinking. Teaching the theory of critical thinking will not produce critical thinkers. Additionally, it is not enough to simply expose students to good examples of critical thinking without explanation or explicit practice and hope our students will learn by imitation.

Students need to engage in specially designed exercises that aim to improve critical thinking skills. This approach practices skills both implicitly and explicitly and is embedded in thought-provoking content. Some strategies include:

- subject matter that is carefully selected and exploited so that students learn new concepts and encounter new perspectives.
- students identifying their own assumptions about the world and later challenging them.
- activities that are designed in a way that students answer questions and complete language-learning tasks that may not have black-and-white answers. (Finding THE answer is often less valuable than the process by which answers are derived.)
- activities that engage students in logical thinking, where they support their reasoning and resolve differences with their peers.

Infused throughout each unit of each book, *NorthStar* uses the principles and strategies outlined above, including:

- Make Inferences: inference comprehension questions in every unit
- Vocabulary and Comprehension: categorization activities
- Vocabulary and Synthesize: relationship analyses (analogies); comparisons (Venn diagrams)
- Synthesize: synthesis of information from two texts teaches a "multiplicity" approach rather than a "duality" approach to learning; ideas that seem to be in opposition on the surface may actually intersect and reinforce each other
- Focus on the Topic and Preview: identifying assumptions, recognizing attitudes and values, and then re-evaluating them
- Focus on Writing/Speaking: reasoning and argumentation
- Unit Project: judgment; choosing factual, unbiased information for research projects
- Focus on Writing/Speaking and Express Opinions: decision making; proposing solutions

THE NORTHSTAR UNIT

1 FOCUS ON THE TOPIC

* **CT** Each unit begins with a photo that draws students into the topic. Focus questions motivate students and encourage them to make personal connections. Students make inferences about and predict the content of the unit.

UNIT 6

STAYING
Connected

1 FOCUS ON THE TOPIC

1. Do you or does someone you know use social media like Facebook, YouTube, Twitter, Google, LinkedIn, Tumblr? In what way can these sites be useful or interesting?

2. In what way can the use of social media add to or take away from the quality of life in the modern world?

3. What are the dangers associated with online communications?

MyEnglishLab

CT A short self-assessment based on each unit's learning outcomes helps students check what they know and allows teachers to target instruction.

MyEnglishLab

Home | Help | Test student, reallylongname@emailaddress.com | Sign out

NORTHSTAR 5 READING & WRITING

1   Unit 1

Check What You Know

Look at the list of skills. You may already know how to do some of these. Don't worry if you don't know how to do some or all of these skills. You will learn and practice them in Unit 6.
Check the skills that you already know. Put an *X* by the number.

Vocabulary

1. Infer word meaning from context
2. Categorize vocabulary
3. Recognize and use idiomatic expressions

Reading

4. Identify the main ideas in a reading
5. Identify different types of supporting details, examples and reasons
6. Scan a text to locate specific information
7. Infer and understand an argument made by analogy
8. Create subheadings for note-taking and summarizing
9. Summarize problems and solutions using information from two texts

Writing

10. Use various graphic organizers to organize ideas
11. Support a main idea with reasons, facts,

Vocabulary
1.
2.
3.
Reading
4.
5.
6.
7.
8.
9.

ALWAYS LEARNING

PEARSON

---

*indicates Critical Thinking

2 FOCUS ON READING

Two contrasting, thought-provoking readings, from a variety of authentic genres, stimulate students intellectually.

CT Students predict content, verify their predictions, and follow up with a variety of tasks that ensure comprehension.

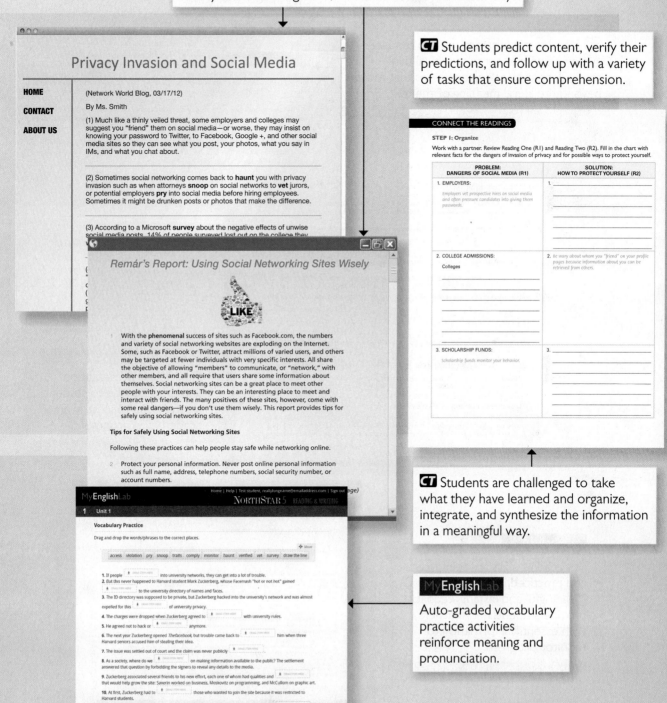

Privacy Invasion and Social Media

HOME

CONTACT

ABOUT US

(Network World Blog, 03/17/12)

By Ms. Smith

(1) Much like a thinly veiled threat, some employers and colleges may suggest you "friend" them on social media—or worse, they may insist on knowing your password to Twitter, to Facebook, Google +, and other social media sites so they can see what you post, your photos, what you say in IMs, and what you chat about.

(2) Sometimes social networking comes back to **haunt** you with privacy invasion such as when attorneys **snoop** on social networks to **vet** jurors, or potential employers **pry** into social media before hiring employees. Sometimes it might be drunken posts or photos that make the difference.

(3) According to a Microsoft **survey** about the negative effects of unwise social media posts, 14% of people surveyed lost out on the college they

Remár's Report: Using Social Networking Sites Wisely

LIKE

With the **phenomenal** success of sites such as Facebook.com, the numbers and variety of social networking websites are exploding on the Internet. Some, such as Facebook or Twitter, attract millions of varied users, and others may be targeted at fewer individuals with very specific interests. All share the objective of allowing "members" to communicate, or "network," with other members, and all require that users share some information about themselves. Social networking sites can be a great place to meet other people with your interests. They can be an interesting place to meet and interact with friends. The many positives of these sites, however, come with some real dangers—if you don't use them wisely. This report provides tips for safely using social networking sites.

Tips for Safely Using Social Networking Sites

Following these practices can help people stay safe while networking online.

2 Protect your personal information. Never post online personal information such as full name, address, telephone numbers, social security number, or account numbers.

CONNECT THE READINGS

STEP 1: Organize

Work with a partner. Review Reading One (R1) and Reading Two (R2). Fill in the chart with relevant facts for the dangers of invasion of privacy and for possible ways to protect yourself.

PROBLEM: DANGERS OF SOCIAL MEDIA (R1)	SOLUTION: HOW TO PROTECT YOURSELF (R2)
1. EMPLOYERS: *Employers vet prospective hires on social media and often pressure candidates into giving them passwords.*	1.
2. COLLEGE ADMISSIONS: Colleges	2. *Be wary about whom you "friend" on your profile pages because information about you can be retrieved from others.*
3. SCHOLARSHIP FUNDS: *Scholarship funds monitor your behavior.*	3.

CT Students are challenged to take what they have learned and organize, integrate, and synthesize the information in a meaningful way.

MyEnglishLab

Auto-graded vocabulary practice activities reinforce meaning and pronunciation.

MyEnglishLab

NORTHSTAR 5 READING & WRITING

Home | Help | Test student, reallylongname@emailaddress.com | Sign out

1 Unit 1

Vocabulary Practice

Drag and drop the words/phrases to the correct places.

access   violation   pry   snoop   traits   comply   monitor   haunt   verified   vet   survey   draw the line

1. If people _____ into university networks, they can get into a lot of trouble.
2. But this never happened to Harvard student Mark Zuckerberg, whose Facemash "hot or not hot" gained _____ to the university directory of names and faces.
3. The ID directory was supposed to be private, but Zuckerberg hacked into the university's network and was almost expelled for this _____ of university privacy.
4. The charges were dropped when Zuckerberg agreed to _____ with university rules.
5. He agreed not to hack or _____ anymore.
6. The next year Zuckerberg opened *Thefacebook* but trouble came back to _____ him when three Harvard seniors accused him of stealing their idea.
7. The issue was settled out of court and the claim was never publicly _____.
8. As a society, where do we _____ on making information available to the public? The settlement answered that question by forbidding the signers to reveal any details to the media.
9. Zuckerberg associated several friends to his new effort, each one of whom had qualities and _____ that would help grow the site: Saverin worked on business, Moskovitz on programming, and McCollum on graphic art.
10. At first, Zuckerberg had to _____ those who wanted to join the site because it was restricted to Harvard students.

ALWAYS LEARNING

PEARSON

Welcome to *NorthStar*   vii

EXPLICIT SKILL INSTRUCTION AND PRACTICE

MAKE INFERENCES

ARGUMENT BY ANALOGY

An analogy compares one thing to another, saying they are related or similar.

Look at the example and read the explanation.

"A person can treat [social media] almost like a diary." *(paragraph 4)*

What comparison is the writer making here? What point is made by the comparison?

Analogy: social media = a diary

Just as we wouldn't read personal information in someone else's diary, we shouldn't spy on social media.

With this analogy, the author emphasizes the dangers of social media: People treat it as a diary, but it can be made public. Ms. Smith is highlighting the importance of the problem she is warning about. She wants the reader to realize that if the contents of an individual's most private document—his or her diary—are made public, the most intimate details of a person's life cannot remain private. The analogy therefore shows the danger of losing our right to privacy.

There are several analogies in the reading. For each analogy below, describe what is being compared. Then explain the meaning in the context of the blog article. Check your answers with a partner.

1. "Much like a thinly veiled threat, some employers and colleges may suggest you 'friend' them on social media—or worse, they may insist on your password to Twitter, to ... +, and other social media sites so they can see what you post, your ... say in IMs, and what you chat about." *(paragraph 1)*

...from reading people's Facebook posts to reading their email."

(continued on next page)

CT Step-by-step instructions and practice guide students to exercise critical thinking and to dig deeper by asking questions that move beyond the literal meaning of the text.

COMPREHENSION

Read each statement. Decide if it is **T** (true) or **F** (false) according to the reading. If it is false, change it to make it true. Discuss your answers with a partner.

_____ 1. Never meet anyone in person that you have chatted with online.

_____ 2. Post where you go to school or work, but never where you live.

_____ 3. Don't use your own name as your screen name.

_____ 4. Posting photos of your favorite meeting place is OK as long as there are no names.

▪▪▪▪▪▪▪▪▪▪▪▪▪▪▪▪▪▪▪▪▪▪▪▪▪▪▪▪▪▪▪ GO TO MyEnglishLab *FOR MORE VOCABULARY PRACTICE.*

READING SKILL

1 Reread Reading Two. Group paragraphs together with common ideas. How would you label or categorize them?

CREATING SUBHEADINGS FOR NOTE-TAKING AND SUMMARIZING

Subheadings can help you take notes on the important points of a reading because they regroup information on the same topic in a clear way. Once you have taken notes under particular categories, it is easier to summarize the information.

Look at the example and read the information.

"Identity Theft" could be one possible **subheading** for paragraphs 2–4 because all the information in these paragraphs is about protecting your identity: names, addresses, screen names, and so on. To go from note-taking under this subheading to **summarizing**, you would be able to write the following **summary**:

Make sure you don't put anything online that can lead back to you: not your name, your address, the places you frequent, or your screen name. Be careful about photos or any information about your school life.

Explicit skill presentation and practice lead to student mastery and success in an academic environment.

MyEnglishLab

Key reading skills are reinforced and practiced in new contexts. Meaningful and instant feedback provide students and teachers with essential information to monitor progress.

3 FOCUS ON WRITING

Productive vocabulary targeted in the unit is reviewed, expanded upon, and used creatively in this section and in the final writing task. Grammar structures useful for the final writing task are presented and practiced. A concise grammar skills box serves as an excellent reference.

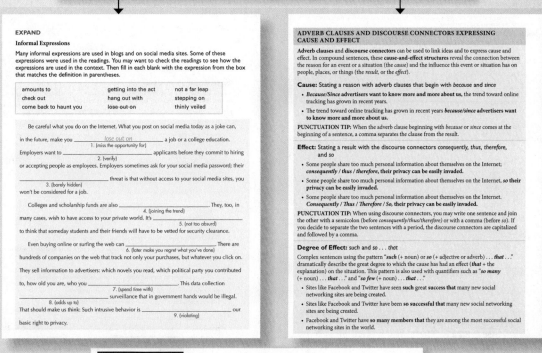

EXPAND

Informal Expressions

Many informal expressions are used in blogs and on social media sites. Some of these expressions were used in the readings. You may want to check the readings to see how the expressions are used in the context. Then fill in each blank with the expression from the box that matches the definition in parentheses.

amounts to	getting into the act	not a far leap
check out	hang out with	stepping on
come back to haunt you	lose out on	thinly veiled

Be careful what you do on the Internet. What you post on social media today as a joke can, in the future, make you ___lose out on___ a job or a college education.
1. (miss the opportunity for)
Employers want to _____ applicants before they commit to hiring
2. (verify)
or accepting people as employees. Employers sometimes ask for your social media password; their
_____ threat is that without access to your social media sites, you
3. (barely hidden)
won't be considered for a job.

Colleges and scholarship funds are also _____. They, too, in
4. (joining the trend)
many cases, wish to have access to your private world. It's _____
5. (not too absurd)
to think that someday students and their friends will have to be vetted for security clearance.

Even buying online or surfing the web can _____. There are
6. (later make you regret what you've done)
hundreds of companies on the web that track not only your purchases, but whatever you click on.
They sell information to advertisers: which novels you read, which political party you contributed
to, how old you are, who you _____. This data collection
7. (spend time with)
_____ surveillance that in government hands would be illegal.
8. (odds up to)
That should make us think: Such intrusive behavior is _____ our
9. (violating)
basic right to privacy.

ADVERB CLAUSES AND DISCOURSE CONNECTORS EXPRESSING CAUSE AND EFFECT

Adverb clauses and **discourse connectors** can be used to link ideas and to express cause and effect. In compound sentences, these **cause-and-effect structures** reveal the connection between the reason for an event or a situation (the *cause*) and the influence this event or situation has on people, places, or things (the *result*, or the *effect*).

Cause: Stating a reason with adverb clauses that begin with *because* and *since*
- *Because/Since* advertisers want to know more and more about us, the trend toward online tracking has grown in recent years.
- The trend toward online tracking has grown in recent years *because/since* advertisers want to know more and more about us.

PUNCTUATION TIP: When the adverb clause beginning with *because* or *since* comes at the beginning of a sentence, a comma separates the clause from the result.

Effect: Stating a result with the discourse connectors *consequently, thus, therefore,* and *so*
- Some people share too much personal information about themselves on the Internet; *consequently / thus / therefore,* their privacy can be easily invaded.
- Some people share too much personal information about themselves on the Internet, *so their privacy can be easily invaded.*
- Some people share too much personal information about themselves on the Internet. *Consequently / Thus / Therefore / So,* their privacy can be easily invaded.

PUNCTUATION TIP: When using discourse connectors, you may write one sentence and join the other with a semicolon (before *consequently/thus/therefore*) or with a comma (before *so*). If you decide to separate the two sentences with a period, the discourse connectors are capitalized and followed by a comma.

Degree of Effect: *such* and *so . . . that*
Complex sentences using the pattern "*such* (+ noun) or *so* (+ adjective or adverb) . . . *that* . . ." dramatically describe the great degree to which the cause has had an effect (*that* + the explanation) on the situation. This pattern is also used with quantifiers such as "*so many* (+ noun) . . . *that* . . ." and "*so few* (+ noun) . . . *that* . . ."
- Sites like Facebook and Twitter have seen *such* great success *that* many new social networking sites are being created.
- Sites like Facebook and Twitter have been *so* successful *that* many new social networking sites are being created.
- Facebook and Twitter have *so many members that* they are among the most successful social networking sites in the world.

MyEnglishLab

Auto-graded vocabulary and grammar practice activities with feedback reinforce meaning, form, and function.

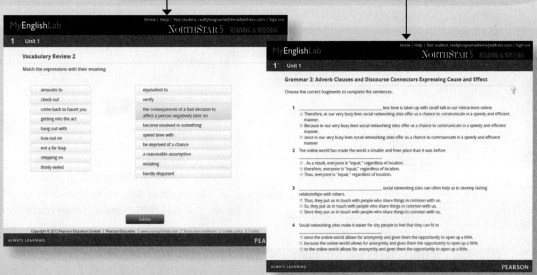

A TASK-BASED APPROACH TO PROCESS WRITING

FINAL WRITING TASK

In this unit, you read Ms. Smith's blog "Privacy Invasion and Social Media" and "Remar's Report: Using Social Networking Sites Wisely."

You will write a short cause-and-effect essay. Focus on either the positive or negative effects of the Internet and social media. Use the vocabulary and grammar from the unit.*

PREPARE TO WRITE: Listing

1 From the readings and your own experience, write notes about the positive and negative effects of the Internet and social media.

Positive Effects   **Negative Effects**

_____   _____

_____   _____

_____   _____

_____   _____

_____   _____

_____   _____

2 Decide whether you are going to write about the positive effects or negative effects.

---

* For Alternative Writing Topics, see page 187. These topics can be used in place of the writing topic for this unit or as homework. The alternative topics relate to the theme of the unit, but may not target the same grammar or rhetorical structure taught in the unit.

> **CT** A final writing task gives students an opportunity to integrate ideas, vocabulary, and grammar presented in the unit.

> **CT** Students organize their ideas for writing using a particular structural or rhetorical pattern.

WRITE: A Cause-and-Effect Essay

A cause-and-effect essay most often focuses on either the causes or the effects of an event or a situation. This focus is reflected in the thesis statement of the introductory paragraph.

1 Work with a partner. Read the introductory paragraph of an essay and discuss the questions.

As a result of the development of the online world of the Internet and social media, our lives have changed for the better. No matter where we are, regardless of the time of day, we can attend to many of our personal needs online. As long as we carry a device that gives us online access, we can do our banking, pay our bills, shop for groceries or clothes, buy tickets for all kinds of events, plan vacations, and, sometimes, even meet the love of our life! In addition to convenience, because the Internet and social media make it easy to connect with family and friends and enrich the experience of globalization all over the world, they have had a positive effect on the present generation.

1. Underline the topic sentence. Does it tell you whether this is an essay about causes or about effects?

2. The first effect concerns convenience. What is the second effect? The third?

3. Underline the thesis statement that will guide the rest of the essay. Will this be an essay about positive or negative effects?

2 The thesis statement gives an idea of the argumentation that is to follow in more detail in the body paragraphs. For each thesis statement, decide whether the essay will be about the positive or negative effects of the Internet and social media. With a partner, discuss the topics that will be developed in the body paragraphs.

1. Social media makes people-to-people contact all the easier: from individuals caught in natural disasters, to support groups bringing people together to help others, to the thousands of people in many countries working for social change.

2. Social media are reducing children's attention span to nanoseconds, creating a platform for immature behavior and exposing young people to online predators.

3. Far from its beginnings as a collection of individual homepages with very little cash, the Internet has become the playground of corporate interests: Consumerism and spyware have created the largest global advertising platform in the history of the world.

4. Social media is a force that can change history: With focused pressure from the Internet and social media, people can change minds and hearts, and all but the most isolated countries are forced to confront the modern world.

> **My English Lab**
>
> Key writing skills and strategies are reinforced and practiced in new contexts. Immediate feedback allows students and teachers to monitor progress and identify areas that need improvement.

Students continue through the writing process to learn revising techniques that help them move toward coherence and unity in their writing. Finally, students edit their work with the aid of a checklist that focuses on essential outcomes.

3 Read the information in the box and then complete the exercises.

ESSAY ORGANIZATION

Essays about causes or effects must follow a logical pattern of organization. Some common ways of organizing cause-and-effect essays are:

1. From the personal to the general: The essay will go from personal experiences to more general and universal statements.

Thesis statement 1 in Exercise 2 on page 181 introduces an essay that will use this pattern.

2. Immediate versus long-term: You may want to begin with immediate effects and go on to consider long-range results.

For example, the immediate reaction to social media was great enthusiasm, but now people are concerned about the long-term effects on privacy.

3. A coherent order of importance: You may want to begin with the least important causes or effects of an event and work up to the most important. Thesis statement 2 uses this pattern.

Or you may need to begin with the historical background of a situation and then go on to the present-day situation. Thesis statement 3 follows this pattern.

4. Order of familiarity or interest: You may want to work from what your readers know or would be most interested in, to what is new and different from what they expect.

The thesis statement of the sample introductory paragraph on page 181 goes from conveniences of the Internet and social media that everyone understands to their more unusual link with globalization.

4 Based on your decision about the focus of your essay, write your thesis statement.

_____

_____

_____

5 Based on what you have read in the Essay Organization box, discuss with your partner the writing strategy you will use in your essay. Will your method of organization be based on "the personal to the general," "immediate versus long-term," "a coherent order of importance," or "order of familiarity or interest"?

2 Look at the first draft of your essay. Are your supporting details effective? Do they include some reasons, facts, examples, and explanations that make your ideas clear? Make any changes needed to improve your supporting details.

▪▪▪▪▪▪▪▪▪▪▪▪▪▪▪▪▪▪▪▪▪▪▪▪▪▪▪▪▪▪▪▪▪▪▪▪ GO TO MyEnglishLab FOR MORE SKILL PRACTICE.

EDIT: Writing the Final Draft

Go to MyEnglishLab and write the final draft of your essay. Carefully edit it for grammatical and mechanical errors, such as spelling, capitalization, and punctuation. Make sure you use some of the grammar and vocabulary from the unit. Use the checklist to help you write your final draft. Then submit your essay to your teacher.

FINAL DRAFT CHECKLIST

❑ Does your thesis statement prepare the reader adequately for the focus of the essay, the positive or the negative effects?

❑ Does the thesis statement give the reader a clear idea of the topics that will be discussed in the body paragraphs in support of the thesis?

❑ Do your body paragraphs provide the reader with sufficient supporting details?

❑ Are the adverb clauses and discourse connectors expressing cause and effect used correctly in the essay?

❑ Have you used new vocabulary and expressions in the essay?

REVISE: Providing Sufficient Supporting Details

The supporting details in your body paragraphs should give the reader complete information about the points you are making. Without the necessary examples, explanations, facts, or reasons, your arguments will not be compelling and the essay will not convince the reader.

1 Read the body paragraph from an essay on social media. Below are supporting details that should be integrated with the paragraph to make it fuller and more complete. Read the supporting details and decide where they should be placed.

(1) Revealing too much about yourself online can lead to serious consequences. (2) Others may steal your identity and rob you of your money and your good reputation. (3) Some photos or posts may at first seem all in fun, but they can become embarrassing all too soon. (4) The information may not even be true, but people neglect to consider social media's lasting "memory." (5) Because of the fast-paced nature of online communications, people can express themselves so quickly and easily on social media that they sometimes do not think before they respond to posts. (6) Unfortunately, these regrettable exchanges may never be totally erased. (7) Evidence of these exchanges can come back to haunt us at the most unexpected moments. (8) Of course, the ultimate danger people face when they sacrifice their privacy goes beyond protecting their identity and personal reputation to putting their physical safety at risk. (9) It stands to reason that we should all be responsible in online media.

1. This embarrassing information can be harmful especially when potential employers or college administrators have access to it.
   BETWEEN SENTENCES ____ AND ____
2. Such "identity theft" can easily occur when people are careless and give their real names, home addresses, and telephone numbers to the strangers that they meet online.
   BETWEEN SENTENCES ____ AND ____
3. This happens when potential predators learn where they live and go to their homes.
   BETWEEN SENTENCES ____ AND ____
4. Even when people cancel their memberships in online communities and delete the contents on their screens, such embarrassing information remains online permanently because it has already appeared on many other people's screens, whether they realize it or not.
   BETWEEN SENTENCES ____ AND ____

INNOVATIVE TEACHING TOOLS

With instant access to a wide range of online content and diagnostic tools, teachers can customize learning environments to meet the needs of every student.

USING MyEnglishLab, NORTHSTAR TEACHERS CAN:

Deliver rich online content to engage and motivate students, including:

- student audio to support listening and speaking skills.
- engaging, authentic video clips, including reports adapted from ABC, NBC, and CBS newscasts, tied to the unit themes.
- opportunities for written and recorded reactions to be submitted by students.

Use a powerful selection of diagnostic reports to:

- view student scores by unit, skill, and activity.
- monitor student progress on any activity or test as often as needed.
- analyze class data to determine steps for remediation and support.

Use Teacher Resource eText* to access:

- a digital copy of the student book for whole-class instruction.
- downloadable achievement and placement tests.
- printable resources including lesson planners, videoscripts, and video activities.
- classroom audio.
- unit teaching notes and answer keys.

*Teacher Resource eText is accessible through MyEnglishLab: NorthStar.

Reading and Writing 5
Unit 1 Achievement Test

Name: _____
Date: _____

PART 1: READING SKILLS
Read the article. Then use the information to complete the activities that follow.

The Benefits of Empathy

1   Most of us have the capacity to show empathy toward others, even in experimental simulations where we feel skeptical or untrusting. But is there any benefit to being empathetic? And why do some people seem to live in a vacuum and have no empathy toward others? Studies of the brain region associated with empathy, called the right supramarginal gyrus, indicate why empathy is so important and hail the idea of developing it.

2   Recent studies helped to confirm the positive impact of empathy. In the studies conducted, participants were tested in pairs. They were told whether they were likely to receive a mild shock or no shock at all. Then their brains were scanned in MRI machines for display. Not surprisingly, the brain's threat response transmitted activity when people were told that they might get a shock. The interesting part of the study was that the threat response was almost just as active when a friend was about to receive the shock. The response was not active at all when a stranger was to receive the shock. This confirms that we show more empathy for people we know and love.

3   The *benefits* of empathy were revealed through the brain activity of the person receiving the shock. The study showed that when a spouse was about to receive a shock, he or she had *less* of a threat response when the husband or wife was there to give support. The better the relationship between the spouses, the lower the threat response in the brain—highlighting the power of empathy in helping those

COMPONENTS   PRINT or eTEXT

STUDENT BOOK and MyEnglishLab

★ Student Book with MyEnglishLab

The two strands, Reading & Writing and Listening & Speaking, for each of the five levels, provide a fully blended approach with the seamless integration of print and online content. Students use MyEnglishLab to access additional practice online, view videos, listen to audio selections, and receive instant feedback on their work.

eTEXT and MyEnglishLab

★ eText with MyEnglishLab

Offering maximum flexibility for different learning styles and needs, a digital version of the student book can be used on iPad® and Android® devices.

★ Instructor Access: Teacher Resource eText and MyEnglishLab (Reading & Writing 1–5)

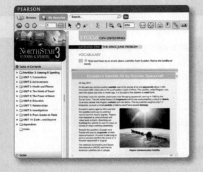

Teacher Resource eText

Each level and strand of *NorthStar* has an accompanying Teacher Resource eText that includes: a digital student book, unit teaching notes, answer keys, downloadable achievement tests, classroom audio, lesson planners, video activities, videoscripts, and a downloadable placement test.

MyEnglishLab

Teachers assign MyEnglishLab activities to reinforce the skills students learn in class and monitor progress through an online gradebook. The automatically-graded exercises in MyEnglishLab *NorthStar* support and build on academic skills and vocabulary presented and practiced in the Student Book/eText. The teacher-graded activities include pronunciation, speaking, and writing, and are assigned by the instructor.

★ Classroom Audio CD

The Listening & Speaking audio contains the recordings and activities, as well as audio for the achievement tests. The Reading & Writing strand contains the readings on audio.

SCOPE AND SEQUENCE

UNIT OUTCOMES	1 THE BRAIN NEUROSCIENCE AND EMPATHY pages 2–31 *Reading 1: Do Mirror Neurons Give Us Empathy?* *Reading 2: From The Kindness of Strangers: Penniless Across America*	2 LYING LIES AND TRUTH pages 32–59 *Reading 1: Looking for the Lie* *Reading 2: On the River*
READING	• Make and confirm predictions • Identify the main ideas in a reading • Identify different types of supporting details • Scan a text to locate specific information • Create timelines to enhance note-taking skills • Summarize information from a text MyEnglishLab Vocabulary and Reading Skill Practice	• Make and confirm predictions • Identify the main ideas in a reading • Identify different types of supporting details • Scan a text to locate specific information • Recognize irony in a text MyEnglishLab Vocabulary and Reading Skill Practice
WRITING	• Organize events using a life map • Understand the elements of a clear narrative (character, technique, and theme) • Use quotes appropriately for interest and authenticity • Edit and revise writing for content, language, and conventions **Task:** Write an autobiographical narrative MyEnglishLab Writing Skill Practice and Writing Task	• Complete a summary of a text • Organize ideas using a chart • Understand the elements and structure of an effective introduction • Recognize a good thesis statement • Edit and revise writing for content, language, and conventions **Task:** Write an introductory paragraph with a thesis statement MyEnglishLab Writing Skill Practice and Writing Task
INFERENCE	• Infer and measure an author's degree of certainty	• Interpret the author's words to understand intention
VOCABULARY	• Infer word meaning from context • Recognize and use word forms (nouns, verbs, adjectives, and adverbs) MyEnglishLab Vocabulary Practice	• Infer word meaning from context • Identify negative and positive connotations of words MyEnglishLab Vocabulary Practice
GRAMMAR	• Recognize, form, and use past unreal conditionals MyEnglishLab Grammar Practice	• Identify and use double comparatives for emphasis and to focus readers' attention MyEnglishLab Grammar Practice
VIDEO	MyEnglishLab *Memory Boost,* ABC News, Video Activity	MyEnglishLab *Why Do Kids Lie?* ABC News, Video Activity
ASSESSMENTS	MyEnglishLab Check What You Know, Checkpoints 1 and 2, Unit 1 Achievement Test	MyEnglishLab Check What You Know, Checkpoints 1 and 2, Unit 2 Achievement Test

3 PERSONALITY
THE ROAD TO SUCCESS
pages 60–87

Reading 1: Gotta Dance
Reading 2: Kids Learn Poise Through Dance

4 CROSS-CULTURAL INSIGHTS
WHAT IS LOST IN TRANSLATION?
pages 88–125

Reading 1: Lost in Translation and The Struggle to Be an All-American Girl
Reading 2: From Bayamon to Brooklyn

• Make and confirm predictions • Summarize the main ideas in a reading • Identify different types of supporting details • Scan a text to locate specific information • Identify and categorize keywords to aid comprehension • Identify connecting themes between two texts **MyEnglishLab** Vocabulary and Reading Skill Practice	• Make and confirm predictions • Identify the main ideas in a reading • Identify different types of supporting details • Scan a text to locate specific information • Compare, contrast, and categorize information in two readings • Create an outline and take effective notes while reading **MyEnglishLab** Vocabulary and Reading Skill Practice
• Identify paragraph structure including a strong topic sentence, illustration, and conclusion • Write a unified paragraph • Edit and revise writing for content, language, and conventions **Task:** Write a topic sentence, illustration, and conclusion **MyEnglishLab** Writing Skill Practice and Writing Task	• Complete a summary • Organize information using an outline and various graphic organizers • Identify organizational structures and elements of comparison-and-contrast essays • Combine sentences and ideas to improve clarity and eliminate repetition • Edit and revise writing for content, language, and conventions **Task:** Write a comparison-and-contrast essay **MyEnglishLab** Writing Skill Practice and Writing Task
• Make inferences to understand someone's character	• Infer a character's meaning
• Infer word meaning from context • Identify and use synonyms • Identify and create noun and verb collocations • Identify and create hyphenated adjectives **MyEnglishLab** Vocabulary Practice	• Infer word meaning from context • Identify and use synonyms • Recognize suffixes to create related word forms **MyEnglishLab** Vocabulary Practice
• Distinguish between and use identifying and nonidentifying adjective clauses **MyEnglishLab** Grammar Practice	• Recognize and use adverb clauses of comparison and contrast **MyEnglishLab** Grammar Practice
MyEnglishLab *Dale Carnegie Training Institute,* Video Activity	**MyEnglishLab** *Japanese Gardens,* Video Activity
MyEnglishLab Check What You Know, Checkpoints 1 and 2, Unit 3 Achievement Test	**MyEnglishLab** Check What You Know, Checkpoints 1 and 2, Unit 4 Achievement Test

SCOPE AND SEQUENCE

UNIT OUTCOMES	5 BUSINESS **SIZE MATTERS IN BUSINESS** pages 126–157 *Reading 1: Howard Schultz's Formula for Starbucks®* *Reading 2: Swiping at Industry*	6 SOCIAL MEDIA **STAYING CONNECTED** pages 158–187 *Reading 1: Privacy Invasion and Social Media* *Reading 2: Using Social Networking Sites Wisely*
READING	• Make and confirm predictions • Identify the main idea in a reading • Identify different types of supporting details • Scan a text to locate specific information • Take effective notes that compare positive and negative ideas • Categorize information from texts MyEnglishLab Vocabulary and Reading Skill Practice	• Make and confirm predictions • Identify the main ideas in a reading • Identify different types of supporting details, examples, and reasons • Scan a text to locate specific information • Create subheadings for note-taking and summarizing • Summarize problems and solutions using information from two texts MyEnglishLab Vocabulary and Reading Skill Practice
WRITING	• Organize information into categories • Use transitional sentences to connect ideas within and between paragraphs • Edit and revise writing for content, language, and conventions **Task:** Write an essay describing advantages and disadvantages MyEnglishLab Writing Skill Practice and Writing Task	• Organize ideas using a list • Support a main idea with reasons, facts, examples, and explanations • Identify organizational structures and elements of cause-and-effect essays • Edit and revise writing for content, language, and conventions **Task:** Write a cause-and-effect essay MyEnglishLab Writing Skill Practice and Writing Task
INFERENCE	• Interpret the author's intention to provide information or express an opinion	• Infer and understand an argument made by analogy
VOCABULARY	• Infer word meaning from context • Identify synonyms • Recognize and use idiomatic expressions MyEnglishLab Vocabulary Practice	• Infer word meaning from context • Categorize vocabulary • Recognize and use idiomatic expressions MyEnglishLab Vocabulary Practice
GRAMMAR	• Distinguish between and use infinitives and gerunds MyEnglishLab Grammar Practice	• Recognize and use adverb clauses and discourse connectors to express cause and effect MyEnglishLab Grammar Practice
VIDEO	MyEnglishLab *Giving Back*, ABC News, Video Activity	MyEnglishLab *Making the Grade*, ABC News, Video Activity
ASSESSMENTS	MyEnglishLab Check What You Know, Checkpoints 1 and 2, Unit 5 Achievement Test	MyEnglishLab Check What You Know, Checkpoints 1 and 2, Unit 6 Achievement Test

7 THE ARTS
THE CELLIST OF SARAJEVO
pages 188–217

Reading 1: The Cellist of Sarajevo
Reading 2: The Soloist

8 POVERTY
THE END OF POVERTY
pages 218–253

Reading 1: Can Extreme Poverty Be Eliminated?
Reading 2: Making Ends Meet

• Make and confirm predictions • Identify the main ideas in a reading • Identify different types of supporting details • Scan a text to locate specific information • Identify and analyze figurative language • Categorize information from two texts **MyEnglishLab** Vocabulary and Reading Skill Practice	• Make and confirm predictions • Identify and summarize the main ideas in a reading • Identify different types of supporting details • Scan a text to locate specific information • Summarize problems and solutions using information from two texts **MyEnglishLab** Vocabulary and Reading Skill Practice
• Analyze the various organizational structures for narrative essays • Develop an outline to organize ideas and structure for an essay • Use descriptive language to add depth to writing • Edit and revise writing for content, language, and conventions **Task:** Write a descriptive, narrative essay **MyEnglishLab** Writing Skill Practice and Writing Task	• Analyze the structure of an argumentative essay • Create an outline to organize ideas • Develop arguments, counterarguments, and refutations • Compose statements of concession • Edit and revise writing for content, language, and conventions **Task:** Write an argumentative essay **MyEnglishLab** Writing Skill Practice and Writing Task
• Understand characters' motivations through close reading of descriptions	• Infer the author's purpose
• Infer word meaning from context • Identify connotations of words • Use participles as adjectives **MyEnglishLab** Vocabulary Practice	• Infer word meaning from context • Identify synonyms • Identify negative and positive connotations of words **MyEnglishLab** Vocabulary Practice
• Recognize and use the passive voice **MyEnglishLab** Grammar Practice	• Recognize and use noun clauses in apposition **MyEnglishLab** Grammar Practice
MyEnglishLab *Interlochen Arts Academy,* Video Activity	**MyEnglishLab** *Young Innovators,* CBS News, Video Activity
MyEnglishLab Check What You Know, Checkpoints 1 and 2, Unit 7 Achievement Test	**MyEnglishLab** Check What You Know, Checkpoints 1 and 2, Unit 8 Achievement Test

ACKNOWLEDGMENTS

This project would never have come to fruition without the kind support and sincere dedication of many people.

As in the past, our greatest debt is to our wonderful editor and friend, Carol Numrich, whose expertise, optimism, and creative insight have guided us throughout every stage of the writing process. We are also grateful to Frances Boyd, whose expression of confidence in our work has continued to be a great source of encouragement.

In addition, we would like to thank Debbie Sistino for her expert coordination of this effort and for her unflagging support and invaluable guidance every step of the way, Kathleen Smith for her meticulous and insightful work in the development phase of this edition, and Robert Ruvo for his contribution as project manager.

Finally, our heartfelt thanks go to our colleagues at the Department of Language and Cognition at Eugenio María de Hostos Community College and the American Language Program at Columbia University, and to our students, who are our true inspiration.

Robert F. Cohen and Judy L. Miller

REVIEWERS

Chris Antonellis, Boston University – CELOP; Gail August, Hostos; Aegina Barnes, York College; Kim Bayer, Hunter College; Mine Bellikli, Atilim University; Allison Blechman, Embassy CES; Paul Blomquist, Kaplan; Helena Botros, FLS; James Branchick, FLS; Chris Bruffee, Embassy CES; Nese Cakli, Duzce University; María Cordani Tourinho Dantas, Colégio Rainha De Paz; Jason Davis, ASC English; Lindsay Donigan, Fullerton College; Bina Dugan, BCCC; Sibel Ece Izmir, Atilim University; Érica Ferrer, Universidad del Norte; María Irma Gallegos Peláez, Universidad del Valle de México; Jeff Gano, ASA College; Juan Garcia, FLS; María Genovev a Chávez Bazán, Universidad del Valle de México; Heidi Gramlich, The New England School of English; Phillip Grayson, Kaplan; Rebecca Gross, The New England School of English; Rick Guadiana, FLS; Sebnem Guzel, Tobb University; Esra Hatipoglu, Ufuk University; Brian Henry, FLS; Josephine Horna, BCCC; Arthur Hui, Fullerton College; Zoe Isaacson, Hunter College; Kathy Johnson, Fullerton College; Marcelo Juica, Urban College of Boston; Tom Justice, North Shore Community College; Lisa Karakas, Berkeley College; Eva Kopernacki, Embassy CES; Drew Larimore, Kaplan; Heidi Lieb, BCCC; Patricia Martins, Ibeu; Cecilia Mora Espejo, Universidad del Valle de México; Kate Nyhan, The New England School of English; Julie Oni, FLS; Willard Osman, The New England School of English; Olga Pagieva, ASA College; Manish Patel, FLS; Paige Poole, Universidad del Norte; Claudia Rebello, Ibeu; Lourdes Rey, Universidad del Norte; Michelle Reynolds, FLS International Boston Commons; Mary Ritter, NYU; Minerva Santos, Hostos; Sezer Sarioz, Saint Benoit PLS; Ebru Sinar, Tobb University; Beth Soll, NYU (Columbia); Christopher Stobart, Universidad del Norte; Guliz Uludag, Ufuk University; Debra Un, NYU; Hilal Unlusu, Saint Benoit PLS; María del Carmen Viruega Trejo, Universidad del Valle de México; Reda Vural, Atilim University; Douglas Waters, Universidad del Norte; Leyla Yucklik, Duzce University; Jorge Zepeda Porras, Universidad del Valle de México

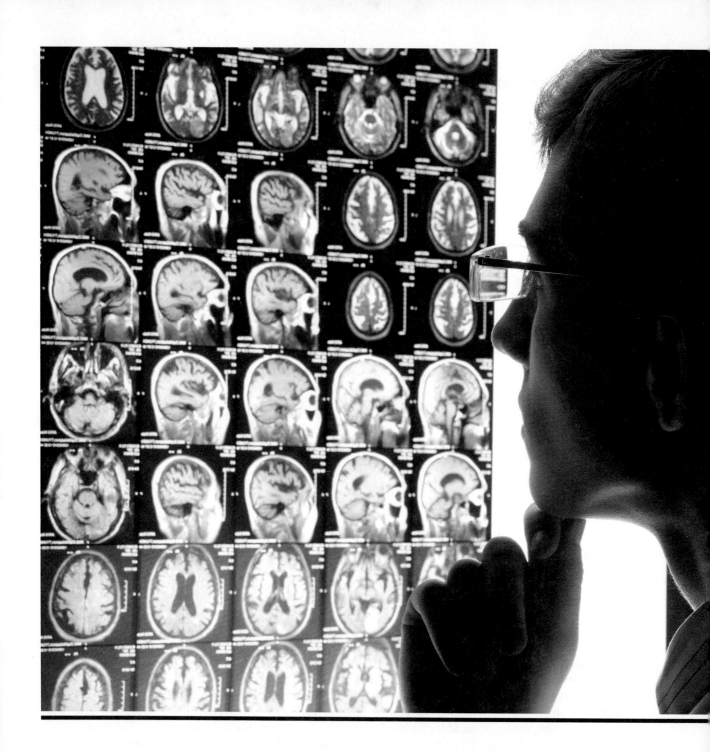

NEUROSCIENCE AND
Empathy

1 FOCUS ON THE TOPIC

1. Neuroscience is the study of the brain and the nervous system. What are the functions of the brain?

2. How is the brain related to our emotions?

3. Do you believe it is important for us to be able to "tune into" other people's feelings? Why or why not?

GO TO MyEnglishLab *TO CHECK WHAT YOU KNOW.*

VOCABULARY

Work with a partner. Read the sentences and circle the correct synonyms for the boldfaced words. Use the context of the sentences to help determine the meaning of the words. Then use a dictionary to check your work.

1. We humans are good at reading faces and bodies. We can look at someone and feel what the other person is feeling. **Empathy** is one of our finer traits, and it may be because we have some special wiring in our brains.

   a. compassion   **b.** indifference

2. In the past, studying brain functions was difficult because we couldn't look into a living brain. The invention of functional MRIs (fMRIs), **hailed** as a major scientific breakthrough, changed all that.

   a. celebrated   **b.** began

3. Now scientists can **conduct** research on how the different parts of the brain work.

   a. predict   **b.** perform

4. Neurons, or nerve cells, **orchestrate** the relaying of chemical signals from one neuron to the next.

   a. coordinate   **b.** obey

5. Digital computer programs can show **simulations** of how large groups of nerve cells operate so that scientists don't have to use live cells.

   a. substitutions   **b.** imitations

6. Oxytocin is a molecule found in mammals that causes changes in the **affective** domain. For example, it contributes to the bond between parents and children and increases feelings of trust between people.

   a. emotional   **b.** intellectual

7. Experiments done in several countries have **validated** the notion that when oxytocin floods the brain, most people feel empathy for others. This is now an accepted view in scientific research.

   a. rejected   **b.** confirmed

8. Though the public is **skeptical**, most scientists seem to agree that human beings, as well as some animals, have a biological basis for moral behavior.

   a. confident   **b.** doubtful

9. Scientific discoveries need to be verified, and, until that happens, people should not **go overboard about** their significance or assume their absolute truth.

   a. underestimate   **b.** exaggerate

10. Once findings have been confirmed, universities and other scientific institutions begin **transmitting** the results of the research to colleagues and students.

   a. spreading   **b.** criticizing

GO TO MyEnglishLab *FOR MORE VOCABULARY PRACTICE.*

PREVIEW

You are going to read an article about mirror neurons and the role they play in empathy. Discuss the questions with a partner.

1. What does it mean to "put yourself in another person's shoes"?

2. How do you feel when you see someone cry or suffer?

Keep your responses in mind as you read "Do Motor Neurons Give Us Empathy?"—an interview with a neuroscientist from the University of California.

DO MIRROR NEURONS GIVE US EMPATHY?
(*Greater Good Magazine,* Berkeley; March 29, 2012)
By Jason Marsh

1   Did you ever have that sensation where you're watching someone do something— serve a tennis ball, say, or get pricked by a needle—and you can just feel exactly what they must be feeling, as if you were in their shoes? Scientists have long wondered why we get that feeling, and more than two decades ago, a team of Italian researchers thought they stumbled on an answer. While observing monkeys' brains, they noticed that certain cells activated both when a monkey performed an action and when that monkey watched another monkey perform the same action. "Mirror neurons" were discovered.

2   Since that time, mirror neurons have been **hailed** as a key to human **empathy**, language, and other vital processes. But there has also been something of a mirror neuron backlash,[1] with some scientists suggesting that the importance of mirror neurons has been exaggerated.

---
[1] **backlash:** a reaction against recent events or trends

(continued on next page)

3   V.S. Ramachandran has been one of mirror neurons' most ardent scientific champions. Ramachandran (known as "Rama" to friends and colleagues), a distinguished professor of neuroscience at the University of California, San Diego, **conducted** early research on mirror neurons; he has since called them "the basis of civilization" in a TED[2] talk and defended their significance in his recent book *The Tell-Tale Brain*. "I don't think they're being exaggerated," he said a few days ago. "I think they're being played down, actually."

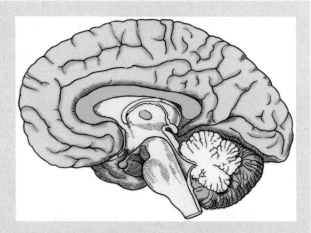

4   **Jason Marsh:** First, could you explain a little bit about what mirror neurons are and how they were discovered?

5   **V.S. Ramachandran:** Well, basically Giacomo Rizzolatti and Vittorio Gallese and some of their colleagues in Italy discovered mirror neurons. They found these neurons in the frontal lobes of the brain—the pre-frontal areas of the brain—among what were originally found as motor command neurons. These neurons fire when I reach out and grab a peanut; there is another set of neurons which fire when I reach out and pull a lever, and other neurons when I'm pushing something, or hitting something. These are regular motor command neurons, **orchestrating** a sequence of muscle twitches that allow me to reach out and grab something or do some other action. A subset[3] of these neurons also fires when I simply watch another person—watch you reach out and do exactly the same action. So, these neurons are performing a virtual reality **simulation** of your mind, your brain. Therefore, they're constructing a theory of your mind—of your intention—which is important for all kinds of social interaction.

6   **JM:** So you've talked about the role of mirror neurons in motor skills. I wonder if you could elaborate on the role of mirror neurons in **affective** experiences, in emotional experiences.

7   **VR:** All I know is they are involved in empathy for, say, touch or a gentle caress or pain. For example, pretend somebody pokes my left thumb with a needle. We know that the insular cortex fires cells, and we experience a painful sensation. The agony of pain is probably experienced in a region called the anterior cingulate, where there are cells that respond to pain. The next stage in pain processing, we experience the agony, the painfulness, the affective quality of pain.

8   It turns out these anterior cingulate neurons that respond to my thumb being poked will also fire when I watch you being poked— but only a subset of them. So, these mirror neurons are probably involved in empathy for pain. If I really and truly empathize with your pain, I need to experience it myself. That's what the mirror neurons are doing, allowing me to empathize with your pain—saying, in

---

[2] **TED (TED.com):** a website run by a non-profit organization offering free viewing of talks on "ideas worth spreading" by well-known innovative thinkers

[3] **subset:** a set that is part of a larger set

effect, that person is experiencing the same agony and excruciating pain as you would if somebody were to poke you with a needle directly. That's the basis of all empathy.

9   **JM:** From your perspective, what do you think are some of the biggest misconceptions around mirror neurons—speculations that have yet to actually be **validated** by science?

10   **VR:** Well, I think as with any new scientific discovery, initially people are very **skeptical.** When people discovered that these neurons do exist, and that they exist in humans, then people **went overboard** and said they do everything.

11   One of the things I argue, and others have argued, is that mirror neurons are important in **transmitting** skills from generation to generation. I need to put myself in your shoes to observe what you're doing and to imitate it accurately. Mirror neurons are important in that.

12   **JM:** Right, and that's what culture's about—the transmission of those learned skills.

13   **VR:** Exactly. That's one of the proposals I made. But if that were true, if they were responsible for all that transmission of skills and culture, monkeys should be very good at those things because they have mirror neurons. So, clearly mirror neurons provide the substrate[4] for those skills, and maybe there are more sophisticated mirror neurons in humans than in monkeys, but they're not responsible by themselves. Those kinds of errors are quite common, but that's okay.

14   **JM:** Why do you say it's okay?

15   **VR:** It's how science progresses. People make overstatements and then correct them.

---

[4] **substrate:** a layer under another layer

MAIN IDEAS

1 Look again at the Preview on page 5. How did your answers help you understand the article?

2 Work with a partner. Read all the statements and circle the three that represent the main ideas of Reading One. Discuss the reasons for your choices.

1. Mirror neurons are a biological basis for empathy.

2. Some scientists feel that the role of mirror neurons has been exaggerated.

3. Mirror neurons are responsible for the transmission of culture.

4. Mirror neurons help us transmit motor skills by imitation.

5. It is inevitable that when a new discovery is made scientists can underestimate or overestimate its significance.

DETAILS

Work with a partner. Write the letter of the phrase from the box that completes each sentence.

> a. you have affective experiences
>
> b. researchers make errors and correct them
>
> c. they were working with monkeys in Italy
>
> d. the brain seems to reflect the movement or feeling it sees
>
> e. monkeys also have mirror neurons but do not transmit culture
>
> f. you see someone else do the same thing
>
> g. they can "feel" the other person's pain

1. Motor neurons fire when you perform an action yourself; some neurons (called "mirror" neurons) fire when _____

2. They are called mirror neurons because _____

3. Scientists first discovered mirror neurons when _____

4. Mirror neurons have a role when you observe motor skills and _____

5. When most people see someone experience pain, their mirror neurons fire and _____

6. Mirror neurons do not tell the whole story of cultural transmission across generations because _____

7. Science makes progress as _____

MAKE INFERENCES

MEASURING THE AUTHOR'S DEGREE OF CERTAINTY

As we see in Reading One, scientists are not always 100% sure of their findings. They may be "positively certain," "somewhat certain," or "not certain" of the results of their research. As V.S. Ramachandran explains, progress is often made by correcting what may turn out to be "overstatements."

Look at the example and read the explanation.

- How certain is Professor Ramachandran about the role of mirror neurons? Based on what is written in the interview, try to determine his degree of certainty. Place an "X" under "Positively certain," "Somewhat certain," or "Not certain."

MIRROR NEURONS . . .	POSITIVELY CERTAIN	SOMEWHAT CERTAIN	NOT CERTAIN
cause us to feel someone's physical pain. *(paragraphs 7 and 8)*	X		

Based on the information in Paragraphs 7 and 8, Ramachandran is "positively certain" that mirror neurons cause us to feel someone else's pain.

Work with a partner. Read each phrase that completes the sentence "Mirror neurons . . . ." Indicate how certain Professor Ramachandran is of the statement by placing an "X" under "Positively certain," "Somewhat certain," or "Not certain."

MIRROR NEURONS . . .	POSITIVELY CERTAIN	SOMEWHAT CERTAIN	NOT CERTAIN
1. are important for social interaction. *(paragraph 5)*			
2. do everything. *(paragraph 10)*			
3. allow people to experience empathy for other people's pain. *(paragraph 8)*			
4. transmit culture. *(paragraph 11–13)*			
5. are exaggerated in terms of importance. *(paragraphs 2 and 15)*			

EXPRESS OPINIONS

Discuss the questions in a small group. Then share your opinions with the class.

1. In Reading One, mirror neurons are credited with allowing people who observe others participating in a particular activity to feel the pain or excitement of the participants. Could mirror neurons play a role in making people who know how to play a sport get very emotionally involved while watching the sport on TV or in a stadium? Can you think of other times in entertainment or the arts when mirror neurons might play a role?

2. According to Professor Ramachandran, mirror neurons are "the basis of civilization." What does he mean? Do you agree?

3. According to the article, motor neurons are the biological basis of empathy. Do you think culture and family upbringing also play a role in empathy and kindness? Why do you think some people lack empathy despite the influence of biology?

■■■■■■■■■■■■■■■■■■■■■■■■ *GO TO* MyEnglishLab *TO GIVE YOUR OPINION ABOUT ANOTHER QUESTION.*

READD

1 Look at the boldfaced words and phrases in the reading and think about the questions.

1. Which words and phrases do you know the meanings of?

2. Can you use any of the words or phrases in a sentence?

2 Read this passage from the book *The Kindness of Strangers: Penniless Across America.* As you read, notice the boldfaced vocabulary. Try to guess the meanings of the words through the context.

FROM *THE KINDNESS OF STRANGERS: PENNILESS ACROSS AMERICA*
By Mike McIntyre

1   I drive up to Lake Tahoe to say goodbye to my family and tell them the logic behind chucking a perfectly good job in the middle of a recession. It's a spiritual journey, I say. I'm making a leap of faith a continent wide. I'll go from the Pacific to the Atlantic without a penny: a cashless journey through the land of the almighty dollar. I'll accept only rides, food, and a place to rest my head. Wait and see—it'll work.

The Baxter farm

2   I've been amazed on this trip by the stubborn capacity of Americans to help a stranger, even when it seems to run contrary to their own best interests. I think of all the families who take me in. I arrive with nothing but my pack, while they expose their homes, their possessions, their children. As scared as I am to trust them, they must be doubly afraid to trust me. Then again, what might truly frighten them is the idea of not trusting anybody. They help me in ways they aren't even aware of. It's always a comfort to meet an honest man, and I'm always sad to say goodbye.

Baxter's Farm, Tennessee

3   The entrance to Baxter's farm is marked by a harvest **display** of pumpkins, gourds, and corn, wrapped with an orange bow. Sam, a rottweiler-boxer mix, bounds up and nearly knocks me over. He holds himself up against my chest and licks my face.

4   Baxter says come in. I follow him along a porch that wraps clear around the two-story house. There isn't a barn in sight. I realize he has just invited me to spend the night. The bed in the guest room belonged to Baxter's great-grandparents. Confederate soldiers commandeered their house during the Civil War. A Union bullet is still lodged in the bed's headboard.

5   Carol is cooking pot roast when we walk into the kitchen. Baxter dons[1] an apron and makes a sheet of biscuits from scratch, using a chilled wine bottle for a rolling pin. He and Carol have been married 35 years but seem like newlyweds. Carol is a seventh-grade science teacher. The family is an **anomaly** in these parts. Both Baxter and Carol have college degrees. The only television allowed on in the house is the *McNeil-Lehrer News Hour.*

6   This fall, Baxter took 29 local youths to a Tennessee Tech football game in Cookesville, an hour south. Only four of the boys had ever been out of the county before—all of them with Baxter to a previous game.

7   Baxter calls folks around here "mountain stay-at-home people." He considers himself one of them. "We rarely entertain in our house," he says. "When we do, it's usually kin."[2] The **revelation** makes my night here all the more special.

8   I ask Baxter what he likes best about his part of the country. "The people," he says. "If you come here and say you are the King of Siam, that's who you are—'til you mess up."

9   After dinner, we go for a walk in the woods with Carol's sister and her husband. The night is clear and crisp. The bright stars look close enough to grab and put in my pocket: the simple pleasures of country living.

10   When I come downstairs in the morning, Baxter is frying sausages and eggs while Carol grades papers at the kitchen table. Carol asks if I'll come to school today and tell her class about my trip. I'm worried I'll give her students the wrong message. I don't want to prompt seventh-graders to hitchhike across the United States.

11   But Carol says the kids should be exposed to what else is out there. "They need to know." She wants me to tell them the good and the bad. She teaches at the elementary school in Allardt, an old German community outside of Jamestown. Before long, I've agreed to talk to every class in the school.

12   The questions keep coming. Where are people the kindest? How many pairs of shoes do I have? Am I carrying a gun? Has anybody tried to run me over? Is there racism in other states? Are the pigs' feet as good in other parts of the country? Have I fallen in love with anyone? What am I most afraid of? And my favorite question, from a meek little girl with glasses and freckles, who raises her hand and says, "Yew wanna eat lunch with us?"

13   The women in the cafeteria load me up with a huge tray of chicken strips, macaroni and cheese, two rolls, Jell-O with whipped cream, green beans, milk, and an ice cream sandwich. Carol tells me that one of the kids I spoke to is slightly retarded.[3] He's ordinarily quite shy. But she says he came up to her in the cafeteria and said, "I want to grow up to be a journalist and go all the places he's been."

14   When I left San Francisco, I was thinking only of myself. I never thought this trip would **impact** a child in Allardt, Tennessee. I'm reminded that no matter how hard we try, nothing we do is **in a vacuum**. All at once a realization hits me. It's so simple. It took giving up money to have the richest experience of my life. At the end of the day, kids press around me. They wish me luck.

---

[1] **dons (an apron):** puts on a piece of clothing

[2] **kin:** family

[3] **retarded:** When the book was written, "retarded" was acceptable language. Today it is more acceptable to say "slow" instead.

COMPREHENSION

Read each statement. Decide if it is **T** (true) or **F** (false), according to the reading. If it is false, change it to make it true. Discuss your answers with a partner.

_____ **1.** McIntyre wants to prove that Americans don't think only about money.

_____ **2.** The Baxters are a typical family from their town in Tennessee.

_____ **3.** The Baxters are used to taking in visitors.

_____ **4.** McIntyre is an inspiration for the children.

_____ **5.** McIntyre is disillusioned about kindness in America.

GO TO MyEnglishLab *FOR MORE VOCABULARY PRACTICE.*

READING SKILL

1 Reread Reading Two. Pay special attention to the different events that are part of the narrator's story.

MAKING TIMELINES TO ENHANCE NOTE-TAKING SKILLS

Timelines display information from a reading in visual form. This is especially important because readers often have difficulty remembering the sequence of events and appreciating the connection between one event and another.

Using a timeline as the structure for a note-taking activity can be very effective.

Look at the example and read the explanation.

If you planned to write a summary of Reading Two, you could take notes according to these "time sequence markers":

- Before setting out
- The next morning
- Arriving at Baxter's Farm
- During the day
- In the evening
- During the next day

By writing notes under each category, you would be able to summarize the main events of the reading according to the chronological time sequence these categories provide.

2 Work with a partner. Read the events from McIntyre's story, which are described in the list below. Then put their numbers in chronological order in the timeline.

Before setting out	☐	During the day	☐	The next morning	☐

☐   Arriving at Baxter's Farm   ☐   In the evening   ☐   During the next day

1. Going to see the students at school

2. Being greeted by the family dog

3. Getting lunch in the cafeteria

4. Explaining his idea about kindness to his family

5. Seeing the Civil War bedroom

6. Eating fried eggs and sausages

7. Taking a walk under the stars

8. Husband and wife preparing dinner

GO TO MyEnglishLab *FOR MORE SKILL PRACTICE.*

CONNECT THE READINGS

STEP 1: Organize

Review Reading One (R1) and Reading Two (R2). Complete the summary of information about empathy in each reading.

EMPATHY	
SCIENTIFIC RESEARCH (R1)	A PERSONAL EXPERIENCE (R2)
1. Mirror neurons _____ _____ _____ _____ _____ _____	1. McIntyre wants to prove _____ _____ _____ _____ _____
2. Mirror neurons were first discovered in animals, but then researchers realized that they were also essential in humans.	2. Mirror neurons are important in human emotions; people open their homes to a stranger and feed and shelter him just because _____ _____ _____ _____ _____
3. Mirror neurons are a basis for _____ _____ _____ _____ _____	3. McIntyre encounters a family that spends their money to help poor students in their area.

STEP 2: Synthesize

Work with a partner. Write a letter from McIntyre to Professor Ramachandran about empathy. Using the information from the chart in Step 1, complete the letter to show how the insights about the brain in Reading One shed light on the experiences of Mike McIntyre in Reading Two.

Dear Professor Ramachandran,

    I listened to your lecture on mirror neurons, and I read your book. It is amazing that things like kindness and empathy could be encoded in our brains.

    I'd like to tell you about my adventure across America because _____

_____

_____

    I read how scientists found mirror neurons first in animals, and then I realized _____

_____

_____

    I thought about your observations when I was traveling in Tennessee. _____

_____

_____

    It certainly seems to me that our capacity for empathy forms the basis of community ties and culture. Thank you for your fascinating work on the human brain.

Best wishes,
Mike McIntyre

GO TO MyEnglishLab TO CHECK WHAT YOU LEARNED.

3 FOCUS ON WRITING

VOCABULARY

REVIEW

Read the paragraph. Fill in each blank with the word from the box that matches the definition in parentheses. Check your answers with a partner's.

affective	display	impact	transmitted
anomaly	empathy	in a vacuum	validate
conduct	hailed	skeptical	

It took a leap of faith for Mike McIntyre to leave his job and travel penniless across America

in order to _____ an experiment on the generosity and kindness of the American
      1. (carry out)

people. He was able to _____ his thinking about the kindness of strangers because
          2. (confirm)

he often saw true _____ in people's interactions with one another as he traveled
          3. (compassion)

from town to town. He _____ these _____ experiences as proof of
            4. (praised)   5. (emotional)

the inherent goodness of human beings.

McIntyre's assessment of human character is in direct contrast with that of people who

are _____ about human goodness and believe that a _____
        6. (doubtful)   7. (show)

of compassion and understanding is more a(n) _____ than a characteristic of
                  8. (exception)

ordinary behavior. However, if we consider scientists' revelations about the way mirror neurons

work in the human brain, we may be justified in taking a more optimistic view. Since we do

not live _____ and what we do can _____ others, we have the
      9. (in isolation)   10. (have an effect on)

power to influence the future with our actions. According to scientists' research findings, it is

possible that the benefits of living in a culture of kindness will be _____ to future
                                11. (passed on)

generations if we learn to be a more compassionate society.

EXPAND

1 Work in a small group. Fill in the chart with the correct forms of the words. Use your dictionary if necessary. An X indicates that there is no commonly used word for that form.

	NOUN	VERB	ADJECTIVE	ADVERB
1.			affective	
2.	anomaly	X		X
3.	display			X
4.	empathy			
5.		impact	X	X
6.		orchestrate		X
7.	revelation			
8.		simulate		X
9.	skepticism	X		
10.		validate		X

2 Complete the sentences with the information from the chart in Exercise 1. Then check your answers with a partner's.

1. Research conducted by James Fallon, a neuroscientist at the University of California, **r**_____ some hidden truths. His **r**_____ on National Public Radio were very surprising.

2. Fallon studied brain scans that **d**_____ the inner workings of the minds of serial killers.

3. When his mother told him there were killers among his father's ancestors, he was **sk**_____. His **sk**_____ changed when he had his own brain scanned.

4. The brain **si**_____ showed that he had the same brain **an**_____ as the serial killers he studied.

5. The results of his PET scan* seemed to **v**_____ his mother's comment about his ancestry.

6. Then after he voluntarily agreed to look at his genes, especially 12 genes related to violence and aggression, he **o**_____ the testing of his whole family. It turned out that he alone has the "warrior gene" shared by many serial killers.

(continued on next page)

---

* **PET scan:** positron emission tomography (PET) produces a three-dimensional image of body processes.

7. How does he explain not becoming a killer like the ones he studies? The **af**_____ domain is his answer: He had a wonderful, loving childhood, unlike that of most serial killers who had suffered abuse.

8. A biological substrate is not enough. There must be traumatic experiences that cut off a person's capacity for **e**_____

9. In other words, we do not grow up in a vacuum, and the love and care we receive in our childhood have a positive **i**_____ on our future development.

CREATE

On a separate piece of paper, write a paragraph to someone who is skeptical about the potential of human kindness. In your paragraph, pretend you are one of the students who heard McIntyre speak at school or that you are one of the Baxters who opened their home to him. Use at least eight vocabulary words.

GO TO MyEnglishLab FOR MORE VOCABULARY PRACTICE.

GRAMMAR

1 Examine the sentence and discuss the questions with a partner.

If Mike McIntyre had not quit his job, he would not have been able to go on a spiritual journey across America.

1. Did Mike McIntyre quit his job?

2. Was he able to go on a spiritual journey across America?

3. How are these two ideas connected?

USING PAST UNREAL CONDITIONALS

A **past unreal conditional** is used to express past untrue or past imagined situations and their result. A past unreal conditional statement can be used to explain why things happened the way they did or to express a regret about the past. A past unreal conditional statement is formed by combining an *if*-clause and a **result clause**. Both clauses have to be stated in terms that are opposite to what really happened.

Reality

Mike McIntyre quit his job, so he was able to go on a spiritual journey across America.

Past Unreal Conditional

If Mike McIntyre had not quit his job, he would not have been able to go on a spiritual journey across America.

Mike McIntyre would not have been able to go on a spiritual journey across America *if* he had not quit his job.

Formation

To form a past unreal conditional statement, use **had** (not) + past participle in the *if*-clause and **would**, **might**, **could** (not) + **have** + past participle in the result clause.

1. If-clause   *If* Mike McIntyre **had not quit** his job,

    Result clause   he **would not have been able** to go on a spiritual journey across America.

2. Result clause   Mike McIntyre probably **would not have been able** to learn so much about the kindness of strangers

    if-clause   *if* he **had walked** across America with a wallet full of money.

GRAMMAR TIP: The *if*-clause can come first or second in the sentence. When it comes second, no comma is required between the two clauses (see example 2). For clarity, the subject should be identified in the first clause in the sentence.

In example 1, "Mike McIntyre" is used in the *if*-clause, and "he" replaces "Mike McIntyre" in the result clause.

In example 2, "Mike McIntyre" is used in the result clause, which comes first in the sentence, and "he" replaces "Mike McIntyre" in the *if*-clause.

GRAMMAR TIP: Using *could have* or *might have* in the result clause shows more doubt about the conclusion.

---

2 Combine the ideas in the sentences using the past unreal conditional. Remember that the sentences must express the opposite of what really happened.

1. The Italian research team stumbled on the reason why humans can empathize with someone who is in pain.
They discovered mirror neurons.

> *If the Italian research team had not stumbled on the reason why humans*
>
> *can empathize with someone who is in pain, they would not have*
>
> *discovered mirror neurons.*

2. The Italian researchers studied monkeys' brains.
Based on these observations, they located mirror neurons in humans.

_____

_____

_____

(continued on next page)

3. Mike McIntyre took a leap of faith to travel penniless across America.
His belief in the inherent goodness of strangers was confirmed.

_____

_____

_____

4. Carol told Mike about the school.
He had such a wonderful time sharing with the children.

_____

_____

_____

5. Baxter told Mike that they opened their home only to other family members.
Mike understood how special their hospitality towards him was.

_____

_____

_____

6. Mike gave up the money he earned at his job to travel across America.
He had the richest experience of his life.

_____

_____

_____

3 Write three statements that show how an event or a person in your life inspired you to become who you are today. Then change the statements into past unreal conditional sentences. When you have finished, share your sentences with a partner.

1. I became a compassionate person because my mother taught me how to pay attention to the needs of others.

Past Unreal Conditional:

If my mother had not taught me how to pay attention to the needs of

others, I might (may) not have become a compassionate person.

2. When I visited a poverty-stricken country, I understood the true impact of poverty.

Past Unreal Conditional:

I would probably not have understood the true impact of poverty if I had

not visited a poverty-stricken country.

3.

_____

_____

Past Unreal Conditional:

_____

_____

4.

_____

_____

Past Unreal Conditional:

_____

_____

5.

_____

_____

Past Unreal Conditional:

_____

_____

■■■■■■■■■■■ *GO TO* MyEnglishLab *FOR MORE GRAMMAR PRACTICE AND TO CHECK WHAT YOU LEARNED.*

FINAL WRITING TASK

In this unit, you read an excerpt from an autobiographical narrative by journalist Mike McIntyre about kindness in America.

*You will **write an autobiographical narrative telling how someone taught you a valuable lesson about life**. You may have learned this lesson in a series of events over time or in one particular event. Use the vocabulary and grammar from the unit.**

PREPARE TO WRITE: Creating a Life Map

As a brainstorming activity, you will create a life map. With a life map, you can write down dates that represent important periods or events in your life. Next to each date, you can write personal symbols that reflect your emotional state (e.g., happy, sad, optimistic, pessimistic, lonely, etc.) at the time. Then next to each symbol, you can include the names and pictures of people who were important to you during each period and notes about what happened.

1 On a separate piece of paper, create a life map similar to the one below. Write freely about the different times in your life that people made an impression on you (they can be family members, teachers, or others) and how certain events were significant in your personal development.

DATE	SYMBOL	NAMES AND EVENTS

2 Now think about how these people made an impression on you. Write answers to the following questions:

1. Did they behave in a special way?

2. Did they say something that you would never have said in the same situation?

3. What impact did they have on your behavior or your attitude toward key issues in life?

4. Did you try to "mirror" their actions in your own life situations?

5. Who made the greatest impression on you?

6. How would your life have been different if you had not known this person?

As you write your notes, do not worry about grammar or formal structure. Just express your ideas as they occur to you.

---

* For Alternative Writing Topics, see page 31. These topics can be used in place of the writing topic for this unit or as homework. The alternative topics relate to the theme of the unit, but may not target the same grammar or rhetorical structures taught in the unit.

3 Share your answers with a partner. Compare insights and decide which particular experience would be the best one to write about in an autobiographical narrative.

WRITE: An Autobiographical Narrative

1 Work with a partner. Reread the excerpt from *The Kindness of Strangers: Penniless Across America*. Then answer the questions.

Excerpt 1

After dinner, we go for a walk in the woods with Carol's sister and her husband. The night is clear and crisp. The bright stars look close enough to grab and put in my pocket: the simple pleasures of country living.

When I come downstairs in the morning, Baxter is frying sausages and eggs while Carol grades papers at the kitchen table. Carol asks if I'll come to school today and tell her class about my trip. I'm worried I'll give her students the wrong message. I don't want to prompt seventh-graders to hitchhike across the United States.

But Carol says the kids should be exposed to what else is out there. "They need to know." She wants me to tell them the good and the bad. She teaches at the elementary school in Allardt, an old German community outside of Jamestown. Before long, I've agreed to talk to every class in the school.

1. Whose actions are being described here?
2. Who is the narrator (the person who is telling the story)?
3. What time period in the narrator's visit to Jamestown does it cover?
4. What verb tenses are used?

2 Read the explanations for the questions and discuss them with a partner.

In Excerpt 1, the actions of Baxter, Carol, Carol's sister, and her husband are being described, but the main focus of the excerpt is on the conversation between Carol and the narrator. Because the passage is written in the first-person narrative (as shown by the use of the pronoun *I,* the possessive adjective *my,* and the direct object pronoun *me*), it is clear to the reader that the narrator is Mike McIntyre.

Although the action reveals a past experience—one that happened only once during the narrator's journey across America (an overnight stay at Baxter's Farm, including a walk after dinner in the evening and breakfast in the morning)—Mike McIntyre gives his account of the action in the present tense ("we <u>go</u> for a walk") and the future tense ("Carol asks if <u>I'll</u> come to school today") rather than in the past tense (e.g., "we <u>went</u> for a walk"/"Carol <u>asked</u> if <u>I'd</u> come to school today"). The author has probably made this choice in order to make his narrative more "immediate" and to give his readers the sense that they are right there with him experiencing the situation at the same time it is happening.

3 Now reread this excerpt from *The Kindness of Strangers: Penniless Across America,* and discuss the questions with your partner.

Excerpt 2

When I left San Francisco, I was thinking only of myself. I never thought this trip would impact a child in Allardt, Tennessee. I'm reminded that no matter how hard we try, nothing we do is in a vacuum. All at once a realization hits me. It's so simple. It took giving up money to have the richest experience of my life. At the end of the day, kids press around me. They wish me luck.

1. Who is the narrator?

2. How is the content of Excerpt 2 different from the content of Excerpt 1?

3. What verb tenses are used?

4 Read the explanations for the questions and discuss them with your partner.

In this excerpt, which is the **conclusion** of the narrative, the author, Mike McIntyre ("I"), assesses the value of the lesson he learned from his experience in Jamestown and the school in Allardt, and he uses the simple past and past progressive forms ("When I <u>left</u> San Francisco, I <u>was thinking</u> only of myself").

5 Character, **technique**, and **theme** are three major elements of autobiographical writing. Read the information in the boxes and complete the exercises that follow.

CHARACTER

Authors of autobiographies provide details about themselves and people around them, and about their reactions to the events in their lives. The narrators create self-portraits and portraits of people who have played important roles in their lives. These people can be family members, close friends, teachers, colleagues, or even individuals the narrator may have met briefly, at a particular time and place.

Through the portraits, we discover each writer's character or system of values. We learn how the writer views various character traits (such as generosity, sensitivity, meanness, happiness, and sadness) by examining how such traits were reflected in his and others' behavior.

For example, in Excerpt 1, the narrator quotes Carol as saying, "They need to know." Because he himself is in search of knowledge, he agrees to go to Carol's school and speak not only to her students but to all the students in the school. This interest in "honesty" and communication with others is a value that he shares with Carol. Accepting her invitation allows him to experience the wonderful "realization" that comes to him in the end.

6 Write short answers to the questions and discuss your answers with a partner.

1. Sharing knowledge with others is one of the positive values highlighted in Excerpt 1. Where else in the reading is this value reflected?

2. What other positive value does the narrator embrace in Excerpt 1 that was difficult for him to appreciate in his life in San Francisco?

3. Look at the rest of *The Kindness of Strangers: Penniless Across America*. What other values are reflected in the narrative? Find evidence in the text that shows a value being placed on cooperation, family closeness, trust, hospitality, and education.

TECHNIQUE

Autobiographers' portraits are effective when they are set in a picture of the past (no matter which verb tense—present or past—the narrator uses), and they are told in the first-person narrative. At the same time, writers must use interesting language and imagery to tell their story. For example, when the narrator says, "The bright stars look close enough to grab and put in my pocket," he gives us the image of a visual experience. If he had said, "The bright stars looked close and not as far away as I knew they were," his description would not have been as effective. Writers may also use other stylistic devices (such as direct quotations, indirect quotations, or questions) to attract readers to their writing.

7 Discuss the questions with a partner.

1. What other interesting images can you find in Excerpt 1?

2. Suppose that in Excerpt 1, Mike McIntyre had written, "Baxter is preparing breakfast," instead of "Baxter is frying sausages and eggs." Why is "Baxter is frying sausages and eggs" more appealing to the reader?

(continued on next page)

3. Find at least three other descriptive details in the narrative that give you a real picture of what the narrator saw and understood when he visited Baxter's Farm. Would the narrative be as interesting without these details? Why or why not?

4. Excerpt 1 has one direct quotation ("They need to know") and several indirect quotations (for example, "Carol asks if I'll come to school today and tell her class about my trip"). Find the other indirect quotations in the excerpt. In what way do the quotations (both direct and indirect) give life to the narrative? How do they help us understand the communication between the narrator and Carol?

5. Look at the rest of the narrative and underline the direct and indirect quotations you find.

6. Look at the rest of the narrative and underline the questions you find. Suppose the narrator had simply said, "The children asked a lot of questions, and I answered them to the best of my ability." Why is it better that the narrator gave real examples of the questions the children asked? How do these questions bring to the surface the issues that most likely ran through the narrator's mind throughout his journey across America?

THEME

Autobiographers must create an intimate bond with readers by making them aware of the issues or problems that have shaped their lives and that continue to be a major concern to them. For example, one of the themes that surfaces in *The Kindness of Strangers: Penniless Across America* is people's generosity.

8 Write short answers to the questions. Compare your answers with a partner's.

1. What is the main theme of Excerpt 1? Underline the sentence(s) that you think are the most significant.

2. What is the main theme of Excerpt 2, the conclusion of the reading? How does this theme relate to the "spiritual journey" the narrator describes in paragraph 1 (the introduction) of the reading?

3. How does the narrator create "an intimate bond" with the reader?

9 Write a first draft. Show how an individual taught you a valuable lesson about life—one you learned through a series of events over time or through one particular event. The individual could be a parent, a family member, a teacher, or someone else you knew. Use the first-person narrative and the present or past tense as you write about the experience. In the conclusion, you may want to use the past unreal conditional as you assess the value of the experience. Express yourself in interesting and descriptive language. Pay careful attention to the main elements of an autobiographical narrative—character, technique, and theme.

You can:

1. describe your personality as it was during a particular period or at the time of a special event in your life;

2. consider how that period or special event affected you and how it may have changed or strengthened your value system;

3. describe the person (or people) who had a great influence on you at the time;

4. share with the reader the issue that was most on your mind at that time;

5. tell whether there was anything you should have done differently.

REVISE: Using Quotes for Interest and Authenticity

THE IMPORTANCE OF QUOTES IN AN AUTOBIOGRAPHICAL NARRATIVE

Direct quotations attract the reader to the writing in an autobiographical narrative. Without direct quotations, the writing may seem dull and unreal.

You must use quotation marks when you use the exact words that a person has said or written. You place the second quotation mark after a period, comma, question mark, or exclamation point.

Mike McIntyre wrote, "The night is clear and crisp."

"The night is clear and crisp," wrote Mike McIntyre.

1 Work with a partner. Rewrite the direct quotations with the correct punctuation.

1. You know we don't work in a vacuum. People talk, and sometimes the truth comes out she said.

   "You know we don't work in a vacuum. People talk, and sometimes the

   truth comes out," she said.

2. I will have to drop out of school if I don't find the money to pay my tuition he said sadly.

   _____

3. You will never believe me when I tell you what Professor Chandler has done. He has paid the balance of a student's tuition so that the student will be able to register next semester she exclaimed.

   _____

(continued on next page)

4. I whispered it's like a ripple effect.

_____

5. Professor, I don't know who did this for me. But a kind stranger gave a gift on my behalf and paid my debt. I will now be eligible for financial aid for the rest of my college career he said with total joy.

_____

6. The young man told me that when he is a successful businessman, he will set up a scholarship fund for students in need she declared.

_____

7. If I hadn't been the beneficiary of such an act of generosity, I would have never learned how to be charitable she quoted him as saying.

_____

2 Read this excerpt from an autobiographical narrative. Working with a partner, decide where each of the quotations in Exercise 1 should be inserted in the paragraphs. Write the number of each sentence on the appropriate line.

My colleague was impressed with the story she had just heard about another teacher's kindness. _____ Although the professor had donated the money anonymously, somehow his gesture of kindness had leaked out. _____ Nevertheless, she went on to tell me that a student of hers had come to her practically in tears a week ago, telling her about his financial problems. _____ However, when he came back to see her yesterday, the student had the look of good news on his face. _____

I thought to myself that there are more acts of kindness out there than we can possibly imagine and that one act of kindness can lead to many others. _____ Almost as if she knew what I was thinking, my colleague agreed with me when she described the impact this act of generosity would have on her student's future behavior. _____ However, she wanted to be as precise as possible when describing the student's newfound sense of compassion. _____ I learned something so important from this story: The next time you hear someone say "Charity begins at home," tell him, "Home is everywhere!"

After you have finished, reread the paragraph with the direct quotations in place. Discuss with your partner why the paragraph is now better than it was without the quotations.

3 Look at the first draft of your narrative. Have you used direct quotations correctly? Have you also used other effective stylistic devices, such as questions, interesting language, and imagery?

GO TO MyEnglishLab FOR MORE SKILL PRACTICE.

EDIT: Writing the Final Draft

Go to MyEnglishLab and write the final draft of your autobiographical narrative. Carefully edit it for grammatical and mechanical errors, such as spelling, capitalization, and punctuation. Make sure you use some of the grammar and vocabulary from the unit. Use the checklist to help you write your final draft. Then submit your narrative essay to your teacher.

FINAL DRAFT CHECKLIST

❏ Does your narrative give a clear picture of the situation?

❏ Are the three main elements of autobiographical narratives—character, technique, and theme—properly addressed?

❏ Do you use correct punctuation for the direct quotations that are included?

❏ Is the past unreal conditional used correctly to evaluate the consequence of past actions on your life?

❏ Have you used vocabulary from the unit?

UNIT PROJECT

As we have learned in Reading One, scientists discovered mirror neurons in humans because of the work they were doing with monkeys' brains. You are going to do some research on empathy in animals. You will try to find out if there is a biological basis for empathy in animal behavior and if animals are capable of experiencing true empathy. If so, how is it expressed? Follow these steps:

STEP 1: Start your project by doing Internet research to identify five animals whose behavior scientists have studied for signs of empathy.

1. _____

2. _____

3. _____

4. _____

5. _____

STEP 2: Select one of the animals you identified in Step 1 and focus on this animal's "empathic behavior." Take notes on the following:

- why scientists believe (or do not believe) that this animal feels empathy

- what kinds of experiments scientists have conducted to reach their conclusion

- how the animal expresses empathy

- what further work scientists need to do in order to learn more about this animal's behavior

- what impact scientists' research findings about this animal's behavior may have on current research in regard to human behavior

STEP 3: Write a report summarizing your findings. Prepare to share your results with your class in an oral presentation.

ALTERNATIVE WRITING TOPICS

Write an essay about one of the topics. Use the vocabulary and grammar from the unit.

1. Write a letter to someone who has been very important to you in your life. If you hadn't had that person in your life, what would have happened to you? Would you have been more or less capable of empathizing with others? How would your life have been different?

2. Years after he wrote *The Kindness of Strangers: Penniless Across America*, Mike McIntyre explained that he did not tell most of the people he met on his journey that he was a journalist writing a book. Most people believed that he was a "down-and-out drifter," someone who is always moving from one job or place to another because he has no luck or money.

   First of all, do you believe McIntyre was right to lie about being homeless? Is it acceptable for researchers or journalists to act this way?

   Second, do you believe McIntyre's findings would have been as authentic if people had known he was a journalist? Do you believe people would have treated him in the same caring and compassionate manner if they had known this? Why or why not?

3. The work done by scientists on mirror neurons points to a biological basis for empathy.

   What do you believe is the value of this research? Do you think that as we learn more about mirror neurons, we may eventually find ways to make people become more compassionate? What do you think also plays a role in empathy: family upbringing, education, religious or spiritual beliefs? Will a better understanding of the brain help us to become a more compassionate society?

■■■■■■■■■■■■■■■■■■■■■■■■■■■■ *GO TO* MyEnglishLab *TO WRITE ABOUT ONE OF THE ALTERNATIVE TOPICS, WATCH A VIDEO ABOUT TRAINING YOUR BRAIN, AND TAKE THE UNIT 1 ACHIEVEMENT TEST.* ■■■■■■■■■■■

LIES AND
Truth

1. What is happening in the photo?

2. Why do people lie? Should we be honest all the time?

3. What would happen to a society if no one ever told a lie?

GO TO MyEnglishLab *TO CHECK WHAT YOU KNOW.*

VOCABULARY

Write your own synonym for the boldfaced words. Use the context of the sentences to help determine the meaning of the words. Compare your answers with a partner's. Then use a dictionary to check your work.

1. Many psychological experiments have been conducted to see if there are ways that

   people can successfully **spot** liars. _____

2. As children, we are taught to tell the truth and not to use **deception** with other people.

   _____

3. In everyday life, people may feel a sense of **betrayal** when someone lies to them and

   breaks their trust. _____

4. People sometimes tell "white lies" to be kind, not to be **malicious**. _____

5. According to a study published in the *Journal for Business Ethics,* people are more

   likely to engage in **outright** lying when texting than when using any other form

   of communication, including video chats, audio chats, or face-to-face discussions.

   _____

6. The man was a cold and **cunning** liar who took advantage of lonely people by tricking

   them out of their money. _____

7. **Empirical** evidence from brain scans indicates that lying leads to more brain activity

   than telling the truth, although there is no accepted theory to explain these results.

   _____

8. The **quest** for the perfect way to detect liars has been unsuccessful so far.

   _____

9. Severe mental illness creates **delusions** that seem completely real to the patient; in this case, the patient may not be aware that he is lying. _____

10. There is no completely accurate way of detecting lies, and even lie detectors are not **foolproof**. _____

11. Some people regret that we are **plagued by** liars who refuse to speak the truth, but others feel that certain types of lying may be necessary. _____

GO TO MyEnglishLab FOR MORE VOCABULARY PRACTICE.

PREVIEW

You are going to read an article about lying and the role it plays in our lives. Discuss the questions with a partner.

1. Do you know when someone is lying to you?

2. Is there a way to accurately tell whether someone is lying or telling the truth?

Keep your responses in mind as you read "Looking for the Lie" by Robin Marantz Henig.

LOOKING FOR THE LIE
(New York Times Magazine)
By Robin Marantz Henig

1   When people hear that I'm writing an article about deception, they're quick to tell me how to catch a liar. Liars always look to the left, several friends say; liars always cover their mouths, says a man sitting next to me on a plane. Beliefs about lying are plentiful and often contradictory: depending on whom you choose to believe, liars can be detected because they fidget a lot, hold very still, cross their legs, cross their arms, look up, look down, make eye contact, or fail to make eye contact. Freud thought anyone could **spot deception** by paying close enough attention, since the liar, he wrote, "chatters with his fingertips;

betrayal oozes out of him at every pore." Nietzsche wrote that "the mouth may lie, but the face it makes nonetheless tells the truth."

2   The idea that liars are easy to spot is still with us. Just last month, Charles Bond, a psychologist at Texas Christian University, reported that among 2,520 adults surveyed in 63 countries, more than 70 percent believe that liars avert their gazes.[1] The majority believe that liars squirm, stutter, touch or scratch themselves or tell longer stories than usual. The liar stereotype exists in just about every culture, Bond wrote, and its persistence "would be less puzzling if we had more reason

_____
[1] **avert their gazes:** look away

(continued on next page)

to imagine that it was true." What is true, instead, is that there are as many ways to lie as there are liars; there's no such thing as a dead giveaway.[2]

3   Most people think they're good at spotting liars, but studies show otherwise. A very small minority of people, probably fewer than 5 percent, seem to have some innate ability to sniff out deception with accuracy. But, in general, even professional lie-catchers, like judges and customs officials, perform, when tested, at a level not much better than chance. In other words, even the experts would have been right almost as often if they had just flipped a coin. Most of the mechanical devices now available, like the polygraph, detect not the lie but anxiety about the lie. The polygraph measures physiological responses to stress, like increases in blood pressure, respiration rate and electrodermal skin response. So it can miss the most dangerous liars: the ones who don't care that they're lying or have been trained to lie. It can also miss liars with nothing to lose if they're detected, the true believers willing to die for the cause.

4   Serious lies can have a range of motives and implications. They can be **malicious**, like lying about a rival's behavior in order to get him fired, or merely strategic, like not telling your wife about your mistress. Not every one of them is a lie that needs to be uncovered. "We humans are active, creative mammals who can represent what exists as if it did not and what doesn't exist as if it did," wrote David Nyberg, a visiting scholar at Bowdoin College, in *The Varnished Truth*. "Concealment, obliqueness, silence, **outright** lying—all help to keep Nemesis at bay[3]; all help us abide too-large helpings of reality." Learning to lie is an important part of maturation. What makes a child able to tell lies, usually at about age 3 or 4, is that he has begun developing a theory of mind, the idea that what goes on in his head is different from what goes on in other people's heads.

5   Deception is, after all, one trait associated with the evolution of higher intelligence. According to the Machiavellian[4] Intelligence Hypothesis, developed by Richard Byrne and Andrew Whiten, two Scottish primatologists at the University of St. Andrews in Fife, the more social a species, the more intelligent it is. This hypothesis holds that as social interactions became more and more complex, our primate ancestors evolved so they could engage in the trickery, manipulation, skullduggery,[5] and sleight of hand[6] needed to live in larger social groups, which helped them to avoid predators and survive.

6   "All of a sudden, the idea that intelligence began in social manipulation, deceit, and

---

[2] **dead giveaway:** something that reveals you have lied or done something wrong

[3] **keep Nemesis at bay:** escape revenge (Nemesis was the ancient Greek goddess of rightful punishment)

[4] **Machiavellian:** named after Niccolo Machiavelli (1469–1527), an Italian political philosopher; in common language, we call something Machiavellian when it uses deceitful methods for selfish reasons

[5] **skullduggery:** dishonest behavior

[6] **sleight of hand:** the use of tricks and lies to achieve something

cunning cooperation seems to explain everything we had always puzzled about," Byrne and Whiten wrote. In 2004, Byrne and another colleague, Nadia Corp, looked at the brains and behavior of 18 primate species and found **empirical** support for the hypothesis: the bigger the neocortex, the more deceptive the behavior.

7   "Lying is just so ordinary, so much a part of our everyday lives and everyday conversations, that we hardly notice it," said Bella DePaulo, a psychologist at the University of California, Santa Barbara. "And in many cases it would be more difficult, challenging and stressful for people to tell the truth than to lie."

8   DePaulo said that her research led her to believe that not all lying is bad, that it often serves a perfectly respectable purpose; in fact, it is sometimes a nobler, or at least kinder, option than telling the truth. "I call them kindhearted lies, the lies you tell to protect someone else's life or feelings," DePaulo said. A kindhearted lie is when a genetic counselor says nothing when she happens to find out, during a straightforward test for birth defects, that a man could not have possibly fathered his wife's new baby. It's when a neighbor lies about hiding a Jewish family in Nazi-occupied Poland. It's when a doctor tells a terminally ill patient that the new chemotherapy might work. And it's when a mother tells her daughter that nothing bad will ever happen to her.

9   The Federal government has been supporting research recently to look for machines that detect the brain tracings of deception. But the **quest** might be doomed to failure, since it might turn out to be all but impossible to tell which tracings are signatures of truly dangerous lies, and which are the images of lies that are harmless and kindhearted, or self-serving without being dangerous. Alternatively, the quest could turn out to be more successful than we really want, generating instruments that can detect deception not only as an antiterrorism device but also in situations that have little to do with national security: job interviews, tax audits, classrooms, boardrooms, bedrooms.

10   But it would be destabilizing indeed to be stripped of the half-truths and **delusions** on which social life depends. As the great physician-essayist Lewis Thomas once wrote, a **foolproof** lie-detection device would turn our quotidian lives upside down: "Before long, we would stop speaking to each other, television would be abolished as a habitual felon, politicians would be confined by house arrest and civilization would come to a standstill." It would be a mistake to bring such a device too rapidly to market, before considering what might happen not only if it didn't work—which is the kind of risk we are accustomed to thinking about—but also what might happen if it did. Worse than living in a world **plagued by** uncertainty, in which we can never know for sure who is lying to whom, might be to live in a world plagued by its opposite: certainty about where the lies are, thus forcing us to tell one another nothing but the truth.

MAIN IDEAS

1 Look again at the Preview on page 35. How did your ideas help you understand the article?

2 Underline three sentences in the article that express the main points the author is presenting. Share your answers with a partner.

DETAILS

Read each statement. Decide if it is **T** (true) or **F** (false) according to the reading. If it is false, change it to make it true. Discuss your answers with a partner.

_____ 1. Most people believe that liars avert their glances.

_____ 2. About 20% of people have a natural ability to detect liars.

_____ 3. Psychologists are better than ordinary people at detecting liars.

_____ 4. Polygraphs can detect lies.

_____ 5. Some experts like David Nyberg and Bella DePaulo think that lying is a necessary way for us to cope with reality.

_____ 6. According to the Machiavellian Intelligence Hypothesis, intelligence evolved in order to increase the ability to deceive.

_____ 7. Learning to lie is a sign that something has gone wrong in a child's development.

_____ 8. Many experts believe that people would feel more secure if everyday lies were uncovered.

_____ 9. According to the article, doctors shouldn't lie to their patients and parents should never lie to their children.

_____ 10. An antiterrorism device could also detect lies told at work, school, and home.

_____ 11. Lewis Thomas was an advocate for a foolproof lie-detection device.

MAKE INFERENCES

INTERPRETING THE AUTHOR'S WORDS

When we interpret an author's words, we practice "reading between the lines" to understand the author's intention, even when it is not stated openly or explicitly. Being able to read between the lines is an important comprehension skill.

Look at the example and read the explanation.

"The liar stereotype exists in just about every culture . . . and its persistence 'would be less puzzling if we had more reason to imagine that it was true.'" *(paragraph 2)*

 a. The liar stereotype is widespread and true.

 b. The liar stereotype is widespread and false.

The Answer is **b**: The use of the present unreal conditional ("would be less puzzling if we had more reason to imagine") makes it clear that the liar stereotype, although widely believed, is, in fact, not true.

Work with a partner. Read the quotes from Reading One and go back to the paragraphs in which they appear. Choose *a* or *b* to explain what the author means by the quotes.

1. "We humans are active, creative mammals who can represent what exists as if it did not and what doesn't exist as if it did." *(paragraph 4)*

   a. Humans are able to use rational thought.

   b. Humans have imagination.

2. "Concealment, obliqueness, silence, outright lying—all help to keep Nemesis at bay; all help us abide too-large helpings of reality." *(paragraph 4)*

   a. Too much reality is bad for us.

   b. Too much lying is bad for us.

3. "Before long, we would stop speaking to each other, television would be abolished as a habitual felon, politicians would be confined by house arrest and civilization would come to a standstill." *(paragraph 10)*

   a. Social interaction is built on truth.

   b. Social interaction is built on lies.

EXPRESS OPINIONS

Discuss the questions in a small group. Share your group's conclusions with the rest of the class.

1. Robin Marantz Henig categorizes these lies as "kindhearted lies" *(paragraph 8)*:

   • a doctor telling a terminally ill patient that the new chemotherapy might work

   • a researcher not telling a man that his wife's baby is not his

   • a husband not telling his wife about his mistress

   Are these really kindhearted lies, or are they strategic lies to protect the feelings of the doctor, researcher, or husband? Don't people have a right to the truth?

2. Henig writes that "it would be destabilizing indeed to be stripped of the half-truths and delusions on which social life depends" *(paragraph 10)*. Explain what she means. Do you agree or disagree with her? Why?

■■■■■■■■■■■■■■■■■■■■■■■■■■■■■ *GO TO* MyEnglishLab *TO GIVE YOUR OPINION ABOUT ANOTHER QUESTION.*

READ

1 Look at the boldfaced words and phrases in the reading and think about the questions.

1. Which words and phrases do you know the meanings of?

2. Can you use any of the words or phrases in a sentence?

2 Read the passage from *The Adventures of Huckleberry Finn*. As you read, notice the boldfaced vocabulary. Try to guess the meanings of the words through the context.

"ON THE RIVER"

From *The Adventures of Huckleberry Finn*

By Mark Twain

The story you are about to read takes place in the United States before the Civil War (1861–1865). In the South, 4 million black people were slaves. Many wanted to get to the North to live freely, but any white person who helped them was committing a crime. Mark Twain, the famous American writer, wrote this story twenty years after the end of slavery. Although he deals with his story in a humorous way, he tries to make a more general point about social customs and morality, about lies and deeper truth.

Huck and Jim are on a raft floating down the Mississippi River. Both of them are runaways. Huck, age 14, has run away from his drunk and abusive father, and Jim, a slave, has run away from his owner to reach a town in the North where he can be free.

1   There wasn't anything to do now but to look out for the town and not pass it without seeing it. Jim said he'd be very sure to see it because he'd be a free man the minute he saw it.

Jim said it made him feel all trembly and **feverish** to be so close to freedom.
5   Well, I can tell you it made me all over trembly and feverish, too, because I'd just realized that he was almost a free man and who was to blame for it? Why, me. I couldn't get that out of my **conscience**. I tried to tell myself that I wasn't to

blame because I didn't take Jim from his rightful owner. But it wasn't any use. Conscience comes and says every time, "But you knew he was running for his freedom and you could have told somebody." That was true. I couldn't **get around** that. What had poor Miss Watson done to me that I could see her slave go off right under my eyes and never say one single word? I felt so mean and miserable I wished I were dead.

Jim talked out loud all the time while I was talking to myself. He was saying how as soon as he got to a free State he would save up money and never spend a single cent and when he got enough, he would buy his wife, who was owned on a farm close to where Miss Watson lived. And then they would both work to buy the two children and if their master wouldn't sell them, he'd get an Abolitionist[1] to go and steal them. It almost froze me to hear such talk. He wouldn't ever have dared to talk such talk in his life before. Just see what a difference it made in him the minute he judged he was about free.

"Old Jim won't ever forget you, Huck. You're the best friend Jim's ever had and you're the only friend he has now."

I was paddling off, all in a sweat to tell on him, but when he said this, it seemed to take all the tuck out of me.[2]

"That's you. The only white gentleman who ever kept his promise to old Jim."

Well, I just felt sick.

Right then, along comes a small skiff with two men in it, with guns, and they stopped and I stopped. One of them says: "Any men on that raft?"

"Only one, sir."

"Well, five slaves ran off tonight. Is your man white or black?"

I didn't answer **promptly**. I tried to, but the words wouldn't come. I tried, for a second or two, to brace up and out with it, but I wasn't man enough. I hadn't the spunk[3] of a rabbit. I saw I was weakening so I just gave up trying, and said,

"He's white."

"I guess we'll go and see for ourselves."

"I wish you would," I said, "because it's pop that's there, and maybe you'd help me tow the raft ashore where the light is. He's sick and so is mom and Mary Ann."

"Say, boy, what's the matter with your father?"

"It's the- a- the- well, it isn't anything, much."

"Your pop's got smallpox,[4] and you know it! Why didn't you just say so? Do you want to spread it to everyone?"

(continued on next page)

---

[1] **abolitionist:** a white or black man or woman who worked to end slavery
[2] **take the tuck out of me:** take the fight out of me
[3] **spunk:** courage or spirit
[4] **smallpox:** a deadly disease eliminated from the world in the twentieth century

"Well," says I, **pretending** to cry, "I've told everybody before, and then they just went away and left us."

45 "Here- I'll put a twenty dollar gold piece on this board, and you get it when it floats by. I feel mighty mean to leave you, but it won't do to fool with smallpox, don't you see?"

They went off, and I got back on board the raft, feeling awful because I knew for certain that what I'd just done was wrong. I saw that it was no use for me to 50 try and do the right thing.

Then I thought a minute and said to myself, now, hold on; suppose you had done what was right and given Jim up? Would you feel better than you do now? No, I said, I'd feel bad—I'd feel just about as bad as I do right now. Well then, I said to myself, what's the use in trying to learn to do the right thing? I couldn't 55 answer my own question. So I decided not to worry about it anymore. From then on, I'd just do whatever seemed easiest at the time.

COMPREHENSION

Work with a partner. Complete each sentence with a word or phrase from the box.

buy	freedom	in the North	saved
conscience	friend	lied	smallpox

1. The most important goal for Jim and Huck was to get to a town _____ so

   that Jim could be free.

2. Huck had a guilty _____ for two reasons: He had not done anything to

   tell Jim's owner that Jim was escaping, and he was also thinking of turning Jim in.

3. Being so close to _____ made Jim speak more openly than he had ever

   spoken before.

4. Jim said that once he was free, he would do anything he could to _____

   the freedom of his wife and children.

5. Jim regarded Huck as his best _____.

6. Huck _____ to the men looking for the runaway slaves by saying that his

sick father was the white man on the raft in the distance.

7. The men believed Huck. They were afraid to catch _____, so they didn't

go to check the raft on their own. Instead, they gave him a twenty-dollar gold piece to

help him out.

8. Huck _____ Jim's life as a result.

■■■■■■■■■■■■■■■■■■■■■■■■■■■■■■■■■■ *GO TO* MyEnglishLab *FOR MORE VOCABULARY PRACTICE.*

READING SKILL

1 Reread Reading Two. Underline what Huck thinks to himself and does not say.

RECOGNIZING IRONY

Irony is a device an author uses to say the opposite of what he or she really means. It is usually done for humorous effect, but it often has a serious purpose as well. Often the readers understand what is really going on in a story, but the characters in the story do not.

Look at the example and read the explanation.

Jim says: "That's you. The only white gentleman who ever kept his promise to old Jim."

Huck thinks to himself: "Well, I just felt sick.'" (*lines 26–27*)

The reader knows that Huck is thinking of turning Jim over to the authorities, but Jim doesn't know it; he's thanking Huck for being a real friend.

2 Work with a partner. Read each excerpt. Answer the question by choosing 1, 2, 3, or 4 from the box.

EXPLANATIONS OF IRONY

1. How to "do the right thing" in his situation is very unclear to Huck, so he decides to forget about morality altogether. The author may believe that an unjust society is incapable of teaching morality to young people, who have to rely on their own instinctive sense of friendship and fairness.

2. It's true that by running away, Jim is "stealing himself" from his owner, but human beings should not be property. Whoever makes others into slaves should feel guilty, not Huck.

3. Jim talks about Huck being his best friend now, while Huck is really thinking of betraying him. Jim's trust makes Huck stop thinking of betrayal.

4. Huck is shocked that Jim would speak so forcefully, but the irony is that when Jim thinks he will soon be free, he starts asserting himself like any free man would in order to get back his family.

1. "Conscience comes and says every time, 'But you knew he was running for his freedom and you could have told somebody.' That was true. I couldn't get around that. What had poor Miss Watson done to me that I could see her slave go off right under my eyes and never say one single word? I felt so mean and miserable I wished I were dead." *(lines 9–13)*

What is the irony? _____

2. "He was saying how as soon as he got to a free State he would save up money and never spend a single cent and when he got enough, he would buy his wife, who was owned on a farm close to where Miss Watson lived. And then they would both work to buy the two children and if their master wouldn't sell them, he'd get an Abolitionist to go and steal them. It almost froze me to hear such talk. He wouldn't ever have dared to talk such talk in his life before. Just see what a difference it made in him the minute he judged he was about free." *(lines 14–21)*

What is the irony? _____

3. "'Old Jim won't ever forget you, Huck. You're the best friend Jim's ever had and you're the only friend he has now.'

I was paddling off, all in a sweat to tell on him, but when he said this, it seemed to take all the tuck out of me." *(lines 24–25)*

What is the irony? _____

4. "They went off, and I got back on board the raft, feeling awful because I knew for certain that what I'd just done was wrong. I saw that it was no use for me to try and do the right thing.

Then I thought a minute and said to myself, now, hold on; suppose you had done what was right and given Jim up? Would you feel better than you do now? No, I said, I'd feel bad—I'd feel just about as bad as I do right now. Well then, I said to myself, what's the use in trying to learn to do the right thing? I couldn't answer my own question. So I decided not to worry about it anymore. From then on, I'd just do whatever seemed easiest at the time." *(lines 48–56)*

What is the irony? _____

■■ GO TO MyEnglishLab *FOR MORE SKILL PRACTICE.*

CONNECT THE READINGS

STEP 1: Organize

Complete the chart. Decide **YES** or **NO** if the main ideas of Reading One (R1) are expressed in Reading Two (R2). Then explain how these main ideas are expressed in the second reading. Compare your answers with a partner's.

"LOOKING FOR THE LIE" (R1)	"ON THE RIVER" (R2)
1. Only a very small number of people can sniff out lies. *(paragraph 3)*	YES. The men on the boat don't recognize Huck's lies. (lines 41–47)
2. There are malicious lies. *(paragraph 4)*	
3. Intelligence began in social manipulation and deceit. *(paragraph 6)*	
4. Lying is sometimes a nobler, kinder option than telling the truth. *(paragraph 8)*	
5. "[A] foolproof lie-detection device would turn our quotidian lives upside down." *(paragraph 10)*	YES. There would be no moral decisions. Huck would have had no choice; he would have had to turn over the slave. (lines 51–56)

STEP 2: Synthesize

Show how the main ideas of Reading One are supported in Reading Two. Complete the summary with the words and phrases in the box.

intelligence	malicious	moral	possibility of lying	save his friend

In "Looking for the Lie," Robin Marantz Henig asserts that most people do not know when someone is lying to them. It seems that Mark Twain agrees because the men searching for slaves are totally taken in by Huck's lies. Of course, Huck is a very resourceful liar: He knows just what to say to turn the men away and just the right way to say it—not too obviously. This proves what Henig has been saying: Lying is a sign of _____. Huck's behavior is not
1.
_____, however. He is being noble and trying to _____.
2. 3.
As Henig points out, there would be no _____ choices, no free will, if there were
4.
no _____.
5.

GO TO MyEnglishLab TO CHECK WHAT YOU LEARNED.

3 FOCUS ON WRITING

VOCABULARY

REVIEW

Read the selection. Fill in each blank on the next page with the word from the box that matches the definition in parentheses.

betrayal	delusions	get around	pretending
conscience	empirical	outright	quest
deception	foolproof	plagued by	

Truth and History

Strangely, a nation first has to remember something before it can begin to forget it. Only

when nations turn away from their subjective _____ about the past can they
1. (false beliefs)

join with others in peaceful union. The European Union is a convincing example. The nations of

Europe fought against each other in two worldwide conflicts in the twentieth century. Only after

Germans faced the enormity of their past could they stop being _____ it. Until
2. (tormented by)

the French understood their role in World War II, they could not move on. There is no way to

_____ this process. In fact, each nation in Europe, to one degree or another, had
3. (avoid)

to overcome obstacles of its own past in order to build a strong European Union. Confronting the

past was a big challenge.

The instrument used in this _____ for truth was not personal memory but
4. (search)

history: the _____, professional study of the past, based on facts, proof, and
5. (objective)

evidence. Historians believe in the pursuit of truth no matter how complex it may be. But history

does not make comfortable reading because it shows how we may be _____
6. (fooling ourselves)

about the past. It reveals the myths and even _____ lies we invent about
7. (complete)

our countries to be a _____ of the truth. But without a powerful desire for
8. (breach)

truth among ordinary citizens, history books can become a simple instrument for political

_____.
9. (trickery)

The new Europe, "bound together," as the historian Tony Judt has written, "by the signs and

symbols of its terrible past, is a remarkable achievement," but there is no _____
10. (sure and certain)

way to keep the lessons of the past alive in our _____ unless they are taught to the
11. (moral sense)

coming generations.

EXPAND

Negative and Positive Connotations of Words

1 The two words in each pair are related in meaning. However, one word has a more positive meaning (or connotation), while the other has a more negative meaning (or connotation). Put a **P** next to the word with the more positive connotation and an **N** next to the word with the more negative connotation.

1. __N__ **a.** manipulate   __P__ **b.** persuade

2. _____ **a.** pretend   _____ **b.** lie

3. _____ **a.** creativity   _____ **b.** trickery

4. _____ **a.** sleight of hand   _____ **b.** magic

5. _____ **a.** artful   _____ **b.** deceptive

6. _____ **a.** false stories   _____ **b.** tall tales

7. _____ **a.** cover up   _____ **b.** throw a veil over (something)

2 Circle the word or phrase that best completes each sentence.

1. Using reason, facts, and proof, professional historians try to (*manipulate / persuade*) people to recognize unpopular truths.

2. Some political leaders (*manipulate / persuade*) others by playing on their fears and ignorance.

3. Sometimes children like to (*pretend / lie*) and say they are princes and princesses.

4. People often (*pretend / lie*) on their tax returns to minimize their contribution.

5. Computer animators use their (*creativity / trickery*) to make the writers' stories come alive.

6. A leader used lies and (*creativity / trickery*) to convince us to follow his plan.

7. The performance ends with a (*magic / sleight of hand*) trick: A man saws a lady in half.

8. The gambler used (*magic / sleight of hand*) to cheat at cards.

9. Teachers have to be very (*deceptive / artful*) in devising history lessons that are interesting to their students.

10. Truth be told, many students dislike discussing history because politicians can be very (*deceptive / artful*) in changing history to suit their purposes.

11. At bedtime, parents read their children many (*tall tales / false stories*) about mythical creatures and animals that talk.

12. A man came into the police station and told a (*tall tale / false story*) to the police to hide his crime.

13. Some people prefer to (*throw a veil over / cover up*) the past for selfish reasons because they have a vested interest in keeping silent about their own role.

14. Victims may also keep silent and (*throw a veil over / cover up*) the past, but for them, it's because the past is too painful and heartbreaking to discuss.

CREATE

On a separate piece of paper, write two paragraphs about an example of truth and lies in your own life, or choose an example from the history of your country. Use at least eight vocabulary words from the unit and three words with either negative or positive connotations.

■■■■■■■■■■■■■■■■■■■■■■■■■■■■■■■ *GO TO* MyEnglishLab *FOR MORE VOCABULARY PRACTICE.*

GRAMMAR

1 Examine the sentence and discuss the questions with a partner.

The <u>bigger</u> the neocortex, <u>the more deceptive</u> the behavior.

1. How many clauses are in this sentence?

2. What grammatical structure is underlined?

3. Why does the author put the two clauses in juxtaposition in the same sentence?

USING DOUBLE COMPARATIVES

Double comparatives are sentences that have two clauses, each of which starts with a comparative adjective, noun, or adverb structure. The clauses are separated by a comma and define the logical relationship between ideas with variations of **"the more . . . , the more," "the less . . . , the less," "the more . . . , the less,"** or **"the less . . . , the more."** In most cases, the second clause explains the "effect" of the first. Here are some rules to follow:

1. For a good "balanced" writing style, it is preferable when both sides of the double comparative are "parallel," or written with the same word order.

   The more social scientists study human behavior, the more we understand our social interactions.

   The + comparative + subject + verb + object = *The* + comparative + subject + verb + object.

   The experts agreed that **the more social scientists study human behavior, the more we understand our social interactions.**

   (continued on next page)

Lies and Truth   **49**

2. Sometimes the verb in one clause can be left out.

The more social the species, the more intelligent it is.

The more social the species (is), the more intelligent it is.

3. Sometimes both verbs can be left out when the meaning is clear from the sentences that went before.

Psychological research is not a waste of money. The university should fund more studies of human behavior. In this field, there can't be too many studies. **The more, the better.**

4. Notice that a double comparative can never be correct unless the definite article **"the"** accompanies the comparatives in both clauses of the sentence.

Double comparatives are a stylistic tool that writers use to focus the reader's attention more closely on key concepts and the connection between them. However, be careful not to overuse this form.

2 Work with a partner. Write **C** next to the sentences that are correct and **I** next to those that are incorrect. Revise the incorrect sentences.

_____ **1.** The most informed we are, the more we can protect ourselves.

_____ **2.** The more we investigate a problem, the closer we come to finding the solution.

_____ **3.** The more I think about it, the least sure I become.

_____ **4.** The bigger the deception, the greatest the challenge.

3 The following refers to the story of Erin Brockovich, who became famous for uncovering the truth of a company's lie about pollution in the biggest class action lawsuit in American history. Use the cues to rewrite the underlined sentences or parts of sentences with a double comparative. You may have to change the word order and leave out or change some words.

Erin Brockovich

1. Pacific Gas and Electric Company was anxious to buy up the property of residents in Hinkley, California. Many residents did not want to sell their property, but the company insisted that <u>they sell very soon. Otherwise, they would receive less money.</u>

Cue: *the longer . . . the less* OR *the sooner . . . the more*

The company insisted that <u>the longer they waited to sell, the less money they</u>
<u>would receive.</u> or <u>The sooner they sold their land to the company, the more</u>
<u>money they would receive.</u>

2. Working as a file clerk for the law firm of Masry and Vititoe, Erin Brockovich examined many documents. <u>After reading document after document, she found proof</u> that the company had been lying about the pollution of the town's drinking water.

Cue: *The more . . . the more*

_____

_____

that the company had been lying about the pollution of the town's drinking water.

3. The company told the people that only harmless chromium 3 leaked from their factory into the water. In fact, it was harmful chromium 6. Based on scientific evidence, it was clear that <u>there was a direct relationship between frequent exposure to chromium 6 and harm to people's health.</u>

Cue: *the greater / the more . . . the more*

Based on scientific evidence, it was clear that _____

_____

_____

4. Unfortunately, as <u>Hinkley residents continued to drink the water, their health became worse.</u>

Cue: *the more . . . the sicker*

Unfortunately, _____

_____

_____

5. At first, people hesitated to file the legal papers against the company because they depended on it for a lot of financial assistance. Obviously, <u>when people depend a lot on others for money, they are not so willing</u> to displease them.

Cue: *the more . . . the less*

Obviously, _____

_____

_____ to displease them.

(continued on next page)

6. However, Erin Brockovich eventually convinced them. <u>As people got to know her better, they trusted her.</u>

Cue: *The more / The better . . . the more*

_____

_____

_____

7. The result was that Erin Brockovich and Ed Masry were able to win a settlement of over $333 million for more than 630 families. Now, with her own consulting company, Erin Brockovich continues to fight for the disadvantaged. She is convinced that <u>when we dig more and more for the truth, we are able to uncover the lies</u> that prevent us from living quality lives.

Cue: *the more . . . the more*

She is convinced that _____

_____

_____ that prevent us from living quality lives.

▪▪▪▪▪▪▪▪▪▪▪▪▪▪▪▪▪▪▪ *GO TO* MyEnglishLab *FOR MORE GRAMMAR PRACTICE AND TO CHECK WHAT YOU LEARNED.*

FINAL WRITING TASK

In this unit, you read "Looking for the Lie," an essay which deals with the place lies have in our lives, and "On the River," an excerpt from *Huckleberry Finn,* which shows the main character's conflict about lying to save his friend's life.

*You will **write an introductory paragraph to an opinion essay in response to this question:** **Should we always tell the truth?** Use the vocabulary and grammar from the unit.** *

---

* For Alternative Writing Topics, see page 59. These topics can be used in place of the writing topic for this unit or as homework. The alternative topics relate to the theme of the unit, but may not target the same grammar or rhetorical structures taught in the unit.

PREPARE TO WRITE: Brainstorming

Working in a small group, brainstorm some advantages and disadvantages of always telling the truth.

ADVANTAGES OF ALWAYS TELLING THE TRUTH	DISADVANTAGES OF ALWAYS TELLING THE TRUTH
1.	1.
2.	2.
3.	3.
4.	4.
5.	5.

WRITE: An Introductory Paragraph with a Thesis Statement

1 Work with a partner. Read the introductory paragraph and discuss the questions.

Is honesty the best policy? We are taught that it is when we are little. However, most of us soon learn that social life is full of lies. Telling the truth all the time just doesn't seem possible. Some people, like Robin Marantz Henig in her article "Looking for the Lie," believe that if we told the truth all the time the whole structure of our social relationships would crumble. Others would perhaps disagree and would point out that we always have a duty to discover the truth and that ignoring "lies" may cause great harm. Indeed, we are often tempted to tell "kindhearted" lies either because we want to avoid hurting others or because we do not like confrontation or conflict. However, this is just taking the easy way out. It is important for us to be honest with others because, by being truthful, we stop living a lie in our own life, we show respect for others, and we create the conditions for meaningful relationships.

1. How does the writer attract the reader's attention in the first sentence?
2. How do you think the ideas develop throughout the paragraph: from the general to the specific? From the specific to the general?
3. Which sentence tells the reader what the writer will focus on in the body of the essay?

2 Read the information in the box and then complete the exercises that follow.

INTRODUCTORY PARAGRAPHS AND THESIS STATEMENTS

Introductory Paragraphs

An essay is composed of an introduction, a body, and a conclusion. In the **introductory paragraph**, the author writes a statement to attract the reader's attention. This statement, known as "the hook," is the first of the paragraph's general statements, which introduce the general topic of the essay. There are many ways the writer can spark the reader's interest: with a question, a humorous remark, a shocking statement, a quotation, or an anecdote.

The flow of ideas in the paragraph goes from the general (large, broad ideas) to the specific (details, examples, particular cases). The most specific statement is the thesis statement, which is usually the last statement of the paragraph.

Thesis Statement

The **thesis statement** communicates the main idea of the essay. It reflects the writer's narrow focus and point of view, attitude, or opinion, and it also forecasts which aspects of the subject the writer will discuss to support the thesis in the body of the essay. A good thesis statement should have all of these criteria.

The thesis statement is not a statement of fact, nor is it a statement that simply announces the general topic of the essay.

Lies are distortions of the truth.	THIS IS NOT A THESIS STATEMENT. It states a fact. No point of view is given.
This essay is about the role of truth and lies in our life.	THIS IS NOT A THESIS STATEMENT. It only announces the topic.
Telling the truth in our life is important.	THIS IS NOT A THESIS STATEMENT. Although it gives us the writer's point of view, there is no focus here. Why exactly is telling the truth at all times "important"?
It is important for us to be honest with others because by being truthful, we stop living a lie in our own life, we show respect for others, and we create the conditions for meaningful relationships.	THIS IS A THESIS STATEMENT. It explains why the writer believes it is important for us to tell the truth. The three body paragraphs will deal with: 1. not living a lie in our own life 2. showing respect for others 3. creating the conditions for meaningful relationships

3 Read the sentences from the introduction to an essay. Work with a partner to put the sentences in order. Using **1** for the first sentence and **7** for the last sentence (the thesis statement), write the numbers in the blanks.

_____ We may say this because there are so many miraculous coincidences in our life that seem so unreal.

_____ That is why even my brothers, who grew up under the same roof as I, tell different stories about the same events that took place in our childhood.

_____ We often say that "truth is stranger than fiction."

_____ Another aspect of this may be that we can never completely trust the accuracy of anyone's story, given the fact that we all see the world through different eyes.

_____ In my opinion, thinking that truth is relative and that everyone has his or her own truth can be a very liberating force in our lives, allowing us to be more creative and spontaneous.

  6 All this leads me to say that we have to accept the potential "lie" in the truth and, in so doing, disagree with those who argue that the truth is not relative.

_____ One day when I was visiting Norway, I wrote a postcard telling a friend how lonely I was, and, as I looked up, I saw my cousin miraculously sitting on the next bench in the park.

4 Work with a partner. Evaluate the statements and put a check (✓) next to the ones that are good thesis statements. Do not automatically think that the longer the statement, the better the thesis statement. For the statements you choose, discuss how you think the writer could develop each of them in the body of the essay.

_____ **1.** Learning to lie during childhood prepares us for our adult lives in higher education, the workplace, and society.

_____ **2.** Primatologists believe that deception is a trait associated with the development of higher intelligence.

_____ **3.** In this essay, the writer will discuss truth and lying.

_____ **4.** More than 70 percent of adults interviewed in 63 countries believe that liars avert people's gazes.

_____ **5.** A country that cannot confront the truth of its past can never move forward into the future.

5 Using what you have learned about writing introductory paragraphs, write an introduction to an essay that responds to the question "Should we always tell the truth?" Refer to the work you did in Prepare to Write and Write, pages 53–55, to write your first draft.

REVISE: Writing Introductory Hooks and General Statements

1 Read the student's introduction to an essay. Then discuss the questions with a partner.

In "Looking for the Lie," Robin Marantz Henig expresses doubt about the possibility of living a healthy life in a world without lies. In "On the River," Mark Twain gives support for Henig's view that it is not always best to tell the truth. Twain's story shows that, in an unjust world, it is sometimes necessary to lie in the service of humanity. Twain would have agreed with the reasons for telling Henig's "kindhearted lies." The more Huck lies, the worse he feels, but he is doing a good deed in saving his friend. It would seem, therefore, that telling a lie is not always a morally objectionable option. Lies can serve a higher truth.

1. Does the writer spark the reader's interest at the very beginning?

2. Does the writer go from broad general statements to specific statements?

3. Does the writer have a thesis statement?

The writer of this introduction starts with specific statements and goes from the specific statements right to the thesis statement, which is the last sentence of the paragraph. However, the writer does not do anything to spark the reader's interest. There is no "hook," and there are no general statements "flowing" from the hook that make the reader understand the subject's general importance and inspire the reader to continue reading.

For instance, at the beginning of Reading One, Robin Marantz Henig attracts the reader's attention by discussing all the different ways people believe they can detect liars. Although it is not an essay, but an excerpt from a novel, Reading Two starts with a sentence that makes the reader want to read more in order to find out if Huck and Jim actually find the town that will make Jim a free man. In both cases, the reader is "hooked."

2 Work with a partner. Read the statements and write **YES** next to the ones that would be good "hooks" and would serve as inspiration for general statements. Write **NO** next to the ones that would not.

_____**1.** I'll never forget how terrible I felt in that moment of truth.

_____**2.** All through history people have told lies.

_____**3.** Did you ever think what life would be like if all our lies were broadcast on a huge video screen for everyone to see?

_____ **4.** Only 1 out of every 20 people has a natural ability to recognize liars.

_____ **5.** "A liar chatters with his fingertips, betrayal oozes out of him at every pore," said Freud.

3 With your partner, start the student's introduction with one of the good hooks from Exercise 2. Then write the general statements that would naturally connect with what the student has already written (i.e., the portion that is not underlined in the box below). Before you proceed, see the general statements (i.e., the underlined portion in the box below) that another student has written to improve the paragraph. Use a separate piece of paper.

I'll never forget how terrible I felt in that moment of truth. When my friend asked me why the others didn't like her, I couldn't stop myself. I said, "You're too fat and you don't look good." I wish I had held my tongue. Whatever good I thought I was doing evaporated as my friend's face showed her pain. This experience had a great impact on me. Since then, I have been plagued by the idea that kindness is not always served by frankness. That is why this discussion about truth and lying, in response to the writing of Robin Marantz Henig and Mark Twain, interests me. In "Looking for the Lie," Robin Marantz Henig expresses doubt about the possibility of living a healthy life in a world without lies. In "On the River," Mark Twain gives support for Henig's view that it is not always best to tell the truth. Twain's story shows that, in an unjust world, it is sometimes necessary to lie in the service of humanity. Twain would have agreed with the reasons for telling Henig's "kindhearted lies." The more Huck lies, the worse he feels, but he is doing a good deed in saving his friend. It would seem, therefore, that telling a lie is not always a morally objectionable option. Lies can serve a higher truth.

Answer the questions. Compare your answers with a partner's.

1. What happened in the "moment of truth" mentioned in the hook?

2. How did it make the writer feel?

3. What is the link between these general statements and the specific opinions of Henig and Twain?

4. More specifically, how does the writer compare Henig and Twain?

5. What is the thesis statement?

4 Now use what you have learned to write the introductory paragraph to an opinion essay.

5 Look at the draft of your introductory paragraph. Is it a good one? If not, decide what you can do to improve it.

■■■ *GO TO* MyEnglishLab *FOR MORE SKILL PRACTICE.*

EDIT: Writing the Final Draft

Go to MyEnglishLab and write the final draft of your introductory paragraph. Carefully edit it for grammatical and mechanical errors, such as spelling, capitalization, and punctuation. Make sure you use some of the grammar and vocabulary from the unit. Use the checklist to help you write your final draft. Then submit your paragraph to your teacher.

FINAL DRAFT CHECKLIST

❏ Does the introductory paragraph have a hook and go from general statements to specific statements, ending in a thesis statement?

❏ Is it clear from the thesis statement what the focus will be in the body paragraphs?

❏ Have you tried to use at least one double comparative to pinpoint the main issues of an argument?

❏ Have you used new vocabulary and expressions (including negative and positive connotations) in the essay?

UNIT PROJECT

Because security has become such an important issue all over the world, inventors have been struggling to develop technology that can uncover the "lies" that may leave us in great danger. To understand how we should apply such technology in the future, it is important to learn about the history of lie detectors, to know who their inventors are and how they have succeeded or failed. Follow these steps:

STEP 1: Do research on the Internet about the history of lie detectors. Who are the most famous inventors? What were their motives? How did they succeed, and how did they fail in inventing these protective devices? What are the developments in lie detection today?

To proceed with your research, do the following:

1. Go to a search engine (for example, www.google.com, www.yahoo.com).

2. Use key words: "lie detector inventors."

3. Read the entries that are of interest to you.

4. Take notes as you find the answers to the questions in Step 1.

STEP 2: Write a summary of your research findings in a report that you will give to the class.

ALTERNATIVE WRITING TOPICS

Write about one of the topics. Use the vocabulary and grammar from the unit.

1. Should high school students be taught everything, whether good or bad, about their country's history? Or, is it better to conceal some aspects of the truth from young people, such as the grave errors committed in the past? Can a country go forward if it does not teach its young citizens the truth about its past?

2. A whistleblower is an individual who tries to make the management of a company aware of a problem in its operation that can affect the health or safety of employees and the neighboring community. When management refuses to do anything, the individual "blows the whistle" and reveals the company's dangerous practices, often with great risk to his or her job and personal safety.

   The following films are all about this kind of situation: *Enron, The Smartest Guys in the Room* (a documentary); *Network; A Civil Action;* and *The Insider.* See one or more of these films. Then write a review, commenting on the effort to uncover the truth in business practices.

■■■■■■■■■■■■■■■■■■■■■■■■■■■ *GO TO* MyEnglishLab *TO WRITE ABOUT ONE OF THE ALTERNATIVE TOPICS, WATCH A VIDEO ABOUT WHY KIDS LIE, AND TAKE THE UNIT 2 ACHIEVEMENT TEST.* ■■■■■■■■■■■■■■■

THE ROAD TO
Success

1 FOCUS ON THE TOPIC

1. In what ways does the photo suggest "success" to you?

2. What is your definition of success? Is it happiness? Love? Money? Being able to help others? Pursuing a dream?

GO TO MyEnglishLab *TO CHECK WHAT YOU KNOW.*

READING ONE   GOTTA DANCE

VOCABULARY

Katie from Reading One (page 63) took a Self-Discovery Quiz. Fill in the form with the correct words from the box to see how she answered the questions.

back: support	**miss a beat:** hesitate and	**spare (something):** afford to
come together: make sense	show surprise or shock	give (time, money) to others
dim: gloomy, dark	**pace:** the speed of events	**take it out of me:** exhaust
discretion: good judgment	**reluctant:** unwilling	(me)

SELF-DISCOVERY QUIZ

Achieving success has a lot to do with how you look at yourself.

1. Write down three things that you like about yourself.

   I know how to keep a secret; people can trust me. _____ is my middle name.

   When I encounter difficulties or make a mistake, I never give up; I never _____. I just keep going.

   I am a generous person. I can always _____ a little money for people in need.

2. Write down a goal that you would like to achieve.

   I would like to have all the different parts of my life _____ so I could feel like a whole person with no regrets. For this, I need to find someone to _____ me in my dancing career: a helper and mentor.

3. What is your target date for achieving it?

   I am _____ to set a date for success because I believe life should follow its own _____, but I would like to join a major dance company in five years.

4. What obstacles or opposition to your goal might you encounter?

   Sometimes I get discouraged at night. I sit alone in the _____ light of my room and worry. Depression can _____, but I always remember my dreams.

5. What are some first steps you could take toward your goal?

   I am going to New York to apply to dance school.

GO TO MyEnglishLab FOR MORE VOCABULARY PRACTICE.

You are going to read a story about Katie, a young girl who leaves her home and everything that is familiar to her to pursue her dream. Discuss the questions with a partner.

1. What do you think drives Katie to leave home?

2. What consequences might leaving home have for her or her family?

Keep your responses in mind as you read Jackson Jodie Daviss's short story.

GOTTA DANCE[1]
BY JACKSON JODIE DAVISS

1   Maybe I shouldn't have mentioned it to anyone. Before I knew it, it was all through the family, and they'd all made it their business to challenge me. I wouldn't tell them my plan, other than to say I was leaving, but that was enough to set them off. Uncle Mike called from Oregon to say, "Katie, don't do it," and I wouldn't have hung up on him except that he added, "Haven't you caused enough disappointment?" That did it. Nine people had already told me no, and Uncle Mike lit the fire under me[2] when he made it ten. Nine-eight-seven-six-five-four-three-two-one. Kaboom.

2   On my way to the bus station, I stopped by the old house. I still had my key, and I knew no one was home. After ducking my head into each room, including my old one, just to be sure I was alone, I went into my brother's room and set my duffel bag and myself on his bed.

3   The blinds were shut so the room was **dim**, but I looked around at all the things I knew by heart and welcomed the softening effect of the low light. I sat there a very long time in the silence until I began to think I might never rise from that bed or come out of that gray

light, so I pushed myself to my feet. I eased off my sneakers and pushed the rug aside so I could have some polished floor, then I pulled the door shut.

4   Anyone passing in the hall outside might've heard a soft sound, a gentle sweeping sound, maybe a creak of the floor, but not much more as I danced a very soft shoe[3] in my stocking feet. Arms outstretched but loose and swaying, head laid back and to one side, like falling asleep, eyes very nearly closed in that room like twilight, I danced to the beat of my heart.

5   After a while, I straightened the rug, opened the blinds to the bright day, and walked out of what was now just another room without him in it. He was the only one I said good-bye to, and the only one I asked to come with me, if he could.

6   At the bus station, I asked the guy for a ticket to the nearest city of some size. Most of them are far apart in the Midwest, and I liked the idea of those long rides with time to think. I like buses—the long-haul kind, anyway—because they're so public that they're private. I also like the **pace**, easing you out of one place

(continued on next page)

---

[1] **gotta dance:** slang expression for "I have got to dance," "I must dance"

[2] **lit the fire under me:** slang expression for "made me angry," "made me finally take action"

[3] **a soft shoe:** tap dance steps but without taps (metal caps) on the shoes; a silent dance

before easing you into[4] the next, no big jolts to your system.[5]

7   My bus had very few people in it and the long ride was uneventful, except when the little boy threw his hat out the window. The mother got upset, but the kid was happy. He clearly hated that hat; I'd seen him come close to launching it twice before he finally let fly. The thing sailed in a beautiful arc, then settled on a fence post, a ringer, just the way you never can do it when you try. The woman asked the driver if he'd mind going back for the hat. He said he'd mind. So the woman stayed upset and the kid stayed happy. I liked her well enough, but the boy was maybe the most annoying kid I've come across, so I didn't offer him the money to buy a hat he and his mother could agree on. Money would have been no problem. Money has never been my problem.

8   There are some who say money is precisely my problem, in that I give it so little thought. I don't own much. I lose things all the time. I'm told I dress lousy. I'm told, too, that I have no appreciation of money because I've never had to do without it. That may be true. But even if it is, it's not all there is to say about a person.

9   There is one thing I do well, and money didn't buy it, couldn't have bought it for me. I am one fine dancer. I can dance like nobody you've ever seen. Heck, I can dance like everybody you've ever seen. I didn't take lessons, not the usual kind, because I'm a natural, but I've worn out a few sets of tapes and a VCR. I'd watch Gene Kelly and practice until I had his steps. Watch Fred Astaire, practice, get his steps. I practice all the time. Bill Robinson. Eleanor Powell. Donald O'Connor. Ginger Rogers. You know, movie dancers. I'm a movie dancer. I don't dance in the movies though. Never have. Who does, anymore? I dance where and when I can.

10   My many and vocal relatives don't think much, have never thought much, of my dancing—largely, I believe, because they are not dancers themselves. To be honest, they don't think much of anything I do, not since I left the path they'd set for me, and that's been most of my 23 years. These people, critical of achievement they don't understand, without praise for talents and dreams or the elegant risk, are terrified of being left behind but haven't the grace to come along in spirit.

11   Mutts and I talked a lot about that. He was a family exception, as I am, and he thought whatever I did was more than fine. He was my brother, and I **backed** everything he did, too. He played blues harmonica. He told bad jokes. We did have plans. His name was Ronald, but everyone's called him Mutts since he was a baby. No one remembers why. He never got his chance to fly, and I figure if I don't do this now, I maybe never will. I need to do it for both of us.

12   The bus depot was crowded and crummy, like most city depots seem to be. I stored my bag in a locker, bought a paper, and headed for where the bright lights would be. I carried my tap shoes and tape player.

13   When I reached the area I wanted, it was still early, so I looked for a place to wait. I

---

[4] **easing you out . . . easing you into:** taking you gently from one place to another
[5] **no big jolts to your system:** smoothly and carefully

found a clean diner, with a big front window, where I could read the paper and watch for the lines to form. I told the waitress I wanted a large cup of coffee before ordering. After half an hour or so, she brought another refill and asked if I was ready. She was kind and patient, and I wondered what she was doing in the job. It seems like nothing **takes it out of you** like waitress work. She was young; maybe that was it. I asked her what was good, and she recommended the baked chicken special and said it was what she had on her break. That's what I had, and she was right, but I only picked at[6] it. I wanted something for energy, but I didn't want to court a side-ache, so the only thing I really ate was the salad. She brought an extra dinner roll and stayed as pleasant the whole time I was there, which was the better part of two hours, so I put down a good tip when I left.

14   While I was in the diner, a truly gaunt[7] young man came in. He ordered only soup, but he ate it like he'd been hungry a long time. He asked politely for extra crackers, and the waitress gave them to him. When he left, he was full of baked chicken special with an extra dinner roll. He wouldn't take a loan. Pride, maybe, or maybe he didn't believe I could **spare** it, and I didn't want to be sitting in a public place pushing the idea that I had plenty of money. Maybe I don't know the value of money, but I do know what **discretion** is worth. The guy was **reluctant** even to take the chicken dinner, but I convinced him that if he didn't eat it, nobody would. He reminded me of Mutts, except that Mutts had never been hungry like that.

15   When the lines were forming, I started on over. While I waited, I watched the people. There were some kids on the street, dressed a lot like me in my worn jeans, faded turtleneck, and jersey warm-up jacket. They were working the crowd like their hopes amounted to spare change.[8] The theater patrons waiting in line were dressed to the nines,[9] as they say. There is something that makes the well-dressed not look at the shabby. Maybe it's guilt. Maybe it's embarrassment because, relatively, they're overdressed. I don't know. I do know it makes it easy to study them in detail. Probably makes them easy marks[10] for pickpockets, too. The smell of them was rich: warm wool, sweet spice and alcohol, peppermint and shoe polish. I thought I saw Mutts at the other edge of the crowd, just for a moment, but I remembered he couldn't be.

16   I was wearing my sneakers, carrying my taps. They're slickery[11] black shoes that answer me back. They're among the few things I've bought for myself, and I keep them shiny. I sat on the curb and changed my shoes. I tied the sneakers together and draped them over my shoulder.

17   I turned on my tape player, and the first of my favorite show tunes began as I got to my feet. I waited a few beats, but no one paid attention until I started to dance. My first taps rang off the concrete clear and clean, measured, a telegraphed message: Takkatakka-takka-tak! Takka-takka-takka-tak! Takkatakka-takka-tak-tak-tak! I paused; everyone turned.

18   I tapped an oh-so-easy, wait-a-minute time-step while I lifted the sneakers from around

(continued on next page)

---

[6] **picked at:** ate very little with no appetite

[7] **gaunt:** very thin

[8] **their hopes amounted to spare change:** extra coins; "their hopes were very small"

[9] **dressed to the nines:** dressed in expensive clothes

[10] **easy marks:** easy victims

[11] **slickery:** patent leather, shiny and smooth

my neck. I gripped the laces in my right hand and gave the shoes a couple of overhead, bola-style swings, tossing them to land beside the tape player, neat as you please. I didn't **miss a beat.** The audience liked it. I knew they would. Then I let the rhythm take me, and I started to fly. Everything **came together.** I had no weight, no worries, just the sweet, solid beat. Feets, do your stuff.[12]

19   Didn't I dance. And wasn't I smooth. Quick taps and slow-rolling, jazz it, swing it, on the beat, off the beat, out of one tune right into the next and the next, and I never took one break. It was a chill of a night, but didn't I sweat, didn't that jacket just have to come off. Didn't I feel the solid jar to the backbone from the heavy heel steps, and the pump of my heart on the beat on the beat.

20   Time passed. I danced. A sandy-haired man came out of the theater. He looked confused. He said, "Ladies and Gentlemen, curtain in five minutes." I'm sure that's what he said. Didn't I dance and didn't they all stay. The sandy-haired man, he was tall and slim and he looked like a dancer. Didn't he stay, too.

21   Every move I knew, I made, every step I learned, I took, until the tape had run out,

until they set my rhythm with the clap of their hands, until the sweet sound of the overture drifted out, until I knew for certain they had held the curtain for want of an audience. Then I did my knock-down, drag-out, could-you-just-die, great big Broadway-baby finish.

22   Didn't they applaud, oh honey, didn't they yell, and didn't they throw money. I dug coins from my own pockets and dropped them, too, leaving it all for the street kids. Wasn't the slender man with the sandy hair saying, "See me after the show"? I'm almost sure that's what he said as I gripped my tape recorder, grabbed my sneakers, my jacket, and ran away, ran with a plan and a purpose, farther with each step from my beginnings and into the world, truly heading home.

23   The blood that drummed in my ears set the rhythm as I ran, ran easy, taps ringing off the pavement, on the beat, on the beat, on the beat. Everything was pounding, but I had to make the next bus, that I knew, catch that bus and get on to the next town, and the next, and the next, and the next. Funeral tomorrow, but Mutts will not be there, no, and neither will I. I'm on tour.

---

[12] **Feets, do your stuff:** Feet, start dancing.

MAIN IDEAS

1   Look again at the Preview on page 63. How did your ideas help you understand the story?

2   "Gotta Dance" can be divided into three parts. Write a sentence that summarizes the main idea of each part of the story. Use your own words.

Part I: Saying Good-bye *(paragraphs 1–5)*

   After saying good-bye to her childhood home and the memory of her brother, Katie

   decides to change her life.

Part II: On the Road *(paragraphs 6–14)*

_____

_____

_____

Part III: Meeting the Challenge *(paragraphs 15–23)*

_____

_____

_____

DETAILS

Circle the correct answer to each question. Then compare your answers with a partner's.

1. How would you describe the attitude of the majority of Katie's family?

   a. They were critical of Katie's desire to be a dancer.

   b. They encouraged her risk-taking.

   c. They were very supportive of all her plans.

2. Which statement is <u>not</u> true of Mutts's life and death?

   a. He loved playing the blues.

   b. He died before he could realize his dream.

   c. His sister was very upset at his funeral.

3. Which of the following did Katie do before setting out for the bus depot?

   a. She went straight to her brother's room after entering her old house.

   b. She danced a soft shoe in her brother's room to the beat of a jazz album.

   c. She danced with a lot of emotion in her brother's room knowing full well that no one else was in the house.

4. Which one of Katie's ideas must she re-evaluate as a result of her experiences?

   a. The pace of a long bus trip allows her time for reflection.

   b. Waiters and waitresses are generally impatient and unkind.

   c. Bus depots are usually dirty and packed with a lot of people.

(continued on next page)

5. What did Katie observe when she was in the bus?

    a. On his third attempt, the boy succeeded in throwing his hat out the window.

    b. The boy showed his perfect aim when his hat landed on a fence post.

    c. The bus driver responded to the mother with a great deal of compassion.

6. Why did Katie go to the diner?

    a. She needed to be in a quiet place to think more about her brother and what his life meant to her.

    b. She needed to wait for her audience to arrive and to mentally and physically prepare for her performance.

    c. She needed to sit down for a while to take care of a pain in her side that she got from dancing.

7. What thoughts did Katie have when she was watching the lines form in front of the theater?

    a. She considered how differences in dress can cause people to be uncomfortable with each other.

    b. She realized that one should dress up when going to the theater to show respect to the entertainers.

    c. She thought the street kids would be chased away by the police because they would be begging.

8. Which of the following is true about Katie's performance?

    a. The theatergoers liked it so much that they missed the first five minutes of the show they had been waiting in line to see.

    b. Katie was offered a job after she performed her dance so well in the street in front of the theater.

    c. Katie was satisfied with her performance.

MAKE INFERENCES

UNDERSTANDING SOMEONE'S CHARACTER

A person's character can be understood through the remarks that are made and actions that are taken by that person in a story.

Look at the example and read the explanation.

Statement: Katie was a very private person. **T** (true) or **F** (false)?

Answer: T

Support: Paragraphs 1, 5, 6

Katie was a very private person because she didn't enjoy sharing her thoughts or feelings. She "shouldn't have mentioned [her reasons for leaving] to anyone" *(paragraph 1)*. Once she told her family, everyone had an opinion that she was not interested in hearing. In the end, she "wouldn't tell them [her] plan other than to say [she] was leaving." In paragraph 5, Katie went into the family house alone to dance a "good-bye" to her brother. She also showed her concern for privacy when she thought about buses as being "so public that they're private" *(paragraph 6)*.

Work with a partner as you answer the questions. Based on your understanding of the story, discuss whether the statements are **T** (true) or **F** (false). Refer to the paragraphs in the story where you find support for your interpretation. Write **T** or **F** on the line. Then explain in one or more sentences how the information leads you to this conclusion.

_____ **1.** Family was important to Katie.

Support: *(paragraphs 1–5, 10, 11, 15)*

_____

_____

_____ **2.** Dancing came easily to Katie.

Support: *(paragraph 9)*

_____

_____

_____ **3.** Katie was ambitious.

Support: *(paragraph 9)*

_____

_____

(continued on next page)

The Road to Success 69

_____ **4.** Katie sympathized with children who rebel against their families.

Support: *(paragraph 7)*

_____

_____

_____ **5.** Katie was careless with money.

Support: *(paragraphs 7–8, 13–14, 22)*

_____

_____

_____ **6.** To Katie, being home was important.

Support: *(paragraph 22)*

_____

_____

EXPRESS OPINIONS

Discuss the questions in a small group. Share your group's conclusions with the rest of the class.

1. Katie's Uncle Mike told her: "Katie, don't do it. . . . Haven't you caused enough disappointment?" *(paragraph 1)* If one of your relatives said something like that to you, how would you feel? What would you do? Would you react the same way Katie did? Why or why not?

2. Do you think rebelling against the family is part of growing up? Is it necessary or dangerous, or both?

3. How did Katie's feelings about her brother Mutts affect her decisions? Do you think it is good for siblings to have such a close relationship? Why or why not?

4. In the story, Katie left the money people gave her for the street kids who had been begging from the theatergoers. Do you do the same thing when strangers ask you for money? Why or why not?

■■■■■■■■■■■■■■■■■■■■■■■■■■■ *GO TO* MyEnglishLab *TO GIVE YOUR OPINION ABOUT ANOTHER QUESTION.*

READ

1 Look at the boldfaced words and phrases in the reading and think about the questions.

1. Which words or phrases do you know the meanings of?

2. Can you use any of the words or phrases in a sentence?

2 Read the passage "Kids Learn Poise Through Dance." As you read, notice the boldfaced vocabulary. Try to guess the meanings of the words through the context.

KIDS LEARN POISE THROUGH DANCE

1   You might think that the only music kids today are dancing to is rap. But for *The Early Show*'s Study Hall report, correspondent Melinda Murphy found that New York City's public schools are using classic dance tunes to teach kids manners and **civility**.

2   The fact that a New York elementary school is located in one of the city's poorest neighborhoods doesn't mean that its fifth graders will lack **poise** or **social graces**. They are learning them on the dance floor. Dance instructor Daniel Ponickly notes, "They don't yet know how to be ladies and gentlemen. But I say to them, 'You are going to become ladies and gentlemen' and all of a sudden, when they come to class, their shirts are tucked in. They stand up straighter." Ponickly is one of more than 30 ballroom instructors teaching dances like the foxtrot and swing in New York City's inner city schools. "We're teaching them that they matter, and that they can show it," Ponickly says.

3   This program was started by Pierre Dulaine, a four-time British exhibition dance champion. Eleven years ago, Dulaine offered to teach ballroom in one school. Today, his instructors teach in more than 60 schools. Dulaine says, "It has developed into an arts and education program where the children learn about ballroom dancing and dances from different countries. But most important,

(continued on next page)

they learn teamwork, having to work with another human being. It's not easy for a young boy and girl, lady and gentleman, to work with each other." For Rosemary Tejada, the course had an added benefit. She says, "I've gotten to be better friends with a boy. I've known my partner since first grade, but we didn't really communicate a lot. But now, with ballroom dancing, we've communicated more." At the end of every course, all the schools compete in a series of competitions.

4   Tejada and her partner, Julian Perez, have made it to the semifinals. "At the competition, I'm really excited, but I'm also nervous," Tejada says. To compete, teams must be **proficient** in five dances: swing, rumba, foxtrot, tango, and merengue. But each couple also has a specialty, and Tejada's is swing. She says, "In swing, you really move a lot, and you feel in a happy mood. I get to express my feelings when I dance."

5   It is wonderful to see the students getting excited about something as old-fashioned as ballroom dance. Dulaine notes, "There is a **camaraderie** that develops between them, and it's a camaraderie to excel." He adds, "Quite honestly, I'm not interested in whether they remember every single step. Learning to touch someone with respect is the key to all of ballroom dancing."

6   In this competition, Tejada and her teammates won a silver trophy. But Dulaine hopes that they've also gained an interest in a pastime that promotes grace, manners, and civility. He says, "All those children love to dance. They have their imagination, and this is what we need to **nurture**." If you'd like to learn more, there is a documentary movie about the program entitled "Mad Hot Ballroom."

COMPREHENSION

Circle the correct answer(s) to the questions below. There may be more than one correct answer. Compare your answers with a partner's.

1. What is true about this arts and education program?

   a. It began this year.

   b. It includes 11 schools.

   c. The teachers are experts.

2. Why must the students in the program dress correctly?

   a. to develop good manners

   b. to show respect for each other

   c. to pay attention in class

3. What is the significance of the international aspect of this program?

    a. Children learn about manners in other countries.

    b. Children learn dances from different countries.

    c. Children compete with dancers from other countries.

4. What does competing in a ballroom dance contest teach the 10- and 11-year-old children who represent their schools?

    a. to do the best they can

    b. to get along with children of the opposite sex

    c. to appreciate school spirit

GO TO MyEnglishLab *FOR MORE VOCABULARY PRACTICE.*

READING SKILL

1 Reread Reading Two. Circle the "keywords" that are important examples or details about what happened to the students in ballroom dancing.

USING KEYWORDS

Keywords are the most important details or examples in a reading. By circling or highlighting keywords and then reviewing them, you will better understand and remember the information in the reading. This process will also help you see the way the various parts of a reading fit together.

For example, the keywords "poise" and "social graces" appear in paragraph 2 because this paragraph is about qualities that students learn on the dance floor.

2 Work with a partner. Put the keywords in the correct category. You can add some of your own.

Keywords

- nervous
- silver trophy
- teamwork
- respect
- excited
- dances from different countries
- poise and social graces
- semi-finalists
- ~~love to dance~~
- camaraderie
- manners

STUDENTS' FEELINGS	SKILLS LEARNED	ACCOMPLISHMENTS
love to dance		

3 With a partner, summarize how the students felt, what they learned, and what they accomplished.

GO TO MyEnglishLab *FOR MORE SKILL PRACTICE.*

CONNECT THE READINGS

STEP 1: Organize

Fill in the Venn diagram. Where the circles overlap, write the similar things Katie (Reading One) and Rosemary Tejada (Reading Two) learned or felt in their dance experiences. In Katie's circle, write what only Katie learned or felt from the experience and in Rosemary's circle, write what only Rosemary learned or felt. Share your answers with a partner.

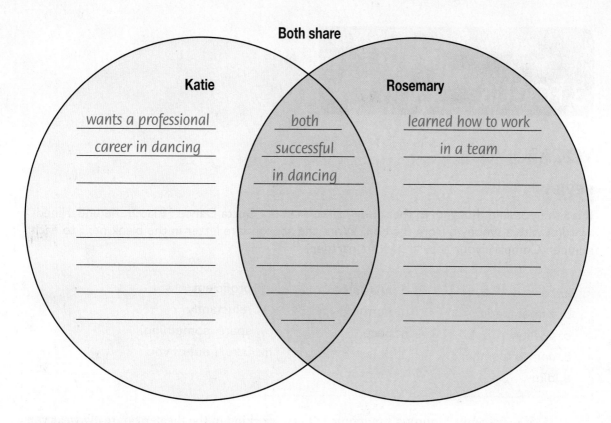

Both share

Katie

wants a professional
career in dancing

_____
_____
_____
_____
_____

both
successful
in dancing

_____
_____
_____
_____
_____

Rosemary

learned how to work
in a team

_____
_____
_____
_____
_____

STEP 2: Synthesize

Work with a partner. Write a dialogue between Katie and Rosemary Tejada, in which they explain their feelings about dancing and what they learned from their experiences. You can use this sample beginning or create your own. Use a separate piece of paper or go to MyEnglishLab.

KATIE: I saw your school dance in the competition. You were great. I also love to dance for the public, but I do tap dancing, not ballroom dancing.

ROSEMARY: Do you dance with a partner? I would be scared to get up there alone.

■■■■■■■■■■■■■■■■■■■■■■■■■■■■■■■■■■■■ *GO TO* MyEnglishLab *TO CHECK WHAT YOU LEARNED.*

3 FOCUS ON WRITING

VOCABULARY

REVIEW

Read the possible thoughts of the sandy-haired man in "Gotta Dance." Match the underlined word(s) with a synonym from the box. Write the appropriate letter in the blank next to each number. Compare your answers with a partner's.

a. backed	f. miss a beat	j. proficient
b. camaraderie	g. nurtured	k. reluctantly
c. civility	h. pace	l. spare (something)
d. comes together	i. poise	m. take it out of you
e. dim		

_____ **1.** It may seem glamorous, but let me tell you, working in the theater can really <u>wear you out.</u> I've been a dancer, singer, ticket taker, scenery painter, and everything else you can think of. It's not an easy life and my sandy hair is turning gray.

_____ **2.** Of course, show business can surprise you, and then one night, all of a sudden, it all <u>makes sense</u>.

_____ **3.** I remember one night we were on tour in a shabby little theater in a small city in the Midwest. Despite the theater's lack of elegance, the people who were waiting outside in the <u>fading</u> light for the show to begin were all dressed to the nines.

_____ **4.** They seemed to understand the meaning of <u>courtesy and good manners</u>.

_____ **5.** But when we opened the doors, no one came in! No one! We couldn't understand it. All we could hear was music from the street. <u>With unwilling steps</u>, I went outside to announce the curtain and saw a young woman in jeans and tap shoes dancing for the crowd.

_____ **6.** She didn't <u>hesitate for a minute</u> as she danced her heart out.

_____ **7.** I couldn't <u>afford</u> the time, but I couldn't take my eyes off her. Neither could anyone else.

_____ **8.** She had such <u>composure</u> and stage presence.

_____ **9.** In addition, she was so <u>skilled</u> in her routine.

_____ **10.** As she increased the <u>speed</u>, we all began clapping with her, marking the rhythms, showing our pleasure.

_____ **11.** The joy we felt from her dancing <u>nourished</u> our imagination. For want of an audience, the company even agreed to hold the curtain.

_____ **12.** A special <u>feeling of friendship and loyalty</u> between the spectators and the dancer was created.

_____ **13.** I would've <u>helped</u> her to get a job dancing. I knew that right away. She was a natural! I guess she didn't hear me say, "Come see me after the show." I can still see her running off into the night, and I wonder what happened to her.

EXPAND

1 Study the chart of collocations.

COLLOCATIONS: NOUNS AND VERBS

People work hard to **achieve success** in the arts.

Collocations are combinations of words that are often used together. The noun "success" is frequently used with the verbs "achieve" or "attain."

Nouns	Verbs
degree, diploma	earn, obtain, receive
difficulties	encounter, face, run into
dream	realize, make (a dream) come true
effort	make
goal	achieve, attain, reach
mistake	make
obstacle	encounter, meet
opposition	encounter, face, confront
success	achieve, attain

2 Add pairs of nouns and verbs from Exercise 1 to the sentences to form collocations. There can be more than one correct answer. Compare your answers with a partner's.

1. Rosemary Tejada was able to _____ because she kept trying and never gave up even when she _____.

2. Without hard work, we cannot _____.

3. Teachers hope that the children will stay in school and _____ a high school diploma. They may even go on to a college degree.

4. Persistence is one quality you need in order to _____ because the path is never smooth. Everyone _____.

3 Study the chart of hyphenated adjectives.

HYPHENATED ADJECTIVES

When we use a two-word or compound adjective, or a group of words before a noun, we use hyphens* to link them, and we also make some minor structural changes. Hyphenated adjectives can give texture, exuberance, and poetic feeling to a work of prose.

With descriptions

- a man with sandy hair (light brown or blond) = a sandy-haired man
- a table with three legs = a three-legged table

Measurements in time or space involving plurals

- a child who is two years old = a two-year-old child
- a house with three stories = a three-story house

---

* Many rules of hyphenation are complicated and may be unclear. If you are unsure, look up hyphens in a good grammar handbook.

4 Change the following expressions to hyphenated adjectives.

1. a boy with blue eyes = _____

2. a hat with three corners = _____

3. a woman with thin lips = _____

4. a girl with a broken heart = _____

5. a law that is ten years old = _____

5 Look back at the story "Gotta Dance," and find two sentences that use a number of hyphenated adjectives in the climax of the story (the last six paragraphs). Then rewrite the expressions as hyphenated adjectives.

1. a dance step that tells the audience to wait a minute = _____

_____

2. an ending similar to what a performer in a Broadway musical would do = _____

_____

3. a finish that makes you want to die from happiness = _____

_____

4. a finish that knocks the audience out because it is so good = _____

_____

CREATE

On a separate piece of paper, answer the questions about yourself and other people you know. Use the underlined expressions in your answers.

1. When Katie's relatives criticized her, it <u>lit a fire under</u> her, and she had to do something. What kinds of things make you angry?

   Answer: *When my brother talks back to my mother, it lights a fire under me, and I end up yelling at him about his awful behavior.*

2. When Katie first started to work on her dance routine, it must have seemed like an impossible task, but after she practiced again and again, things started to <u>come together</u> and she did very well. How did you deal with a difficulty that you eventually overcame?

3. Leaving home was not easy for Katie. Saying good-bye to her old room really <u>took it out of her</u>, and she felt drained of energy. What kind of physical or mental activity totally exhausts you?

4. For a long time, Katie was <u>reluctant</u> to start out on her own. But after her brother's death, she decided that she had to follow her dream. Can you think of anything that you were reluctant to do and then found the courage to do?

5. The more Katie danced, the more she <u>nurtured her imagination</u> and became even more creative. What do you do that makes you become more and more creative?

6. Katie's "<u>knock-down, drag-out, could-you-just-die, great big Broadway-baby finish</u>" left the audience speechless. Can you think of something that you or a friend or family member have done that impressed others a great deal?

■■■■■■■■■■■■■■■■■■■■■■■■■■■■■■■■■■ *GO TO* MyEnglishLab *FOR MORE VOCABULARY PRACTICE.*

GRAMMAR

1 Examine these two sentences and discuss the questions with a partner.

- People <u>who are unwilling to risk failure</u> are not capable of achieving big successes.

- The waitress stayed as pleasant the whole time I was there, <u>which was the better part</u> of two hours, so I put down a good tip when I left.

1. In the first sentence, which people are being discussed?

2. In the second sentence, how much time did Katie spend in the restaurant?

3. Which words come at the beginning of the underlined phrases?

4. Do you notice any difference in punctuation in the two sentences?

USING IDENTIFYING AND NONIDENTIFYING ADJECTIVE CLAUSES

Adjective clauses define, describe, or add information about nouns just as adjectives do. These clauses must have a subject and a verb, but they are fragments, not full sentences. The adjective clause can begin with the relative pronouns *who, whom, which, that,* and *whose,* or the relative adverbs *when* and *where. Who* is used for people, *which* is used for things, and *that* can be used for both people and things.

Identifying Adjective Clauses

Identifying adjective clauses give information that is essential to the meaning of the sentence.

- People *who are unwilling to risk failure* are not capable of achieving big successes.

If you take the adjective clause out of this sentence, the sentence itself no longer has any precise meaning. "People are not capable of achieving big successes" is vague and unclear because it implies that no one can ever succeed. The adjective clause is needed because it tells us specifically which people the statement is referring to. Identifying adjective clauses do not have any commas.

Nonidentifying Adjective Clauses

Nonidentifying adjective clauses have a different function in the sentence: They only provide extra or additional information. If nonidentifying adjective clauses are left out, the sentence still retains its basic meaning.

- The waitress stayed as pleasant the whole time I was there, *which was the better part of two hours,* so I put down a good tip when I left.

The significant clauses of this sentence are "The waitress stayed as pleasant the whole time I was there," and "so I put down a good tip when I left." The adjective clause is not essential to the meaning of the sentence. It provides only an additional piece of information about the time.

GRAMMAR TIP: In nonidentifying adjective clauses

- we do not use *that*

- we place commas at the beginning and end of the clause unless the clause comes at the end of a sentence.

2 Underline the adjective clauses in the sentences. Decide whether they are identifying or nonidentifying, and write **I** or **N** on the line. Then add the appropriate punctuation. Note that there is at least one sentence here that could be both I and N.

_____ **1.** People who lack the courage to fail also lack what it takes to achieve big successes.

_____ **2.** Attitudes that help you feel positive about yourself are the key to success.

_____ **3.** Pierre Dulaine who is quoted in the article about kids and ballroom dancing is a British dance champion.

_____ **4.** Children who practice ballroom dances with each other learn good teamwork.

_____ **5.** A college speaker whose exact name I've now forgotten helped us to understand the power of positive thinking.

_____ **6.** A modern idea which I do not share at all is that success can only be measured in financial terms.

_____ **7.** The dance instructor patiently taught his students the steps which he had learned to do so naturally throughout the years.

_____ **8.** Children who work so hard at learning the steps of the various ballroom dances all share the need to excel.

3 Combine each pair of sentences into a single sentence, using relative pronouns and adjective clauses.

1. Katie was a self-taught dancer. She considered herself a "natural."

_____*Katie, who considered herself a "natural," was a self-taught dancer.*_____

2. A young man entered the restaurant hungry. He left it with a full belly.

_____

3. Katie was off to find a new place in the world. Katie's brother had just died.

_____

4. Katie was thinking about a mother. The mother's son had just thrown his hat out the window of the bus.

_____

(continued on next page)

5. Katie waited two hours at a diner. At the diner she had an excellent view of the people lining up for the theater.

_____

6. Tap dancing is an American dance form. It was popularized by Hollywood movies.

_____

■ ■ ■ ■ ■ ■ ■ ■ ■ ■ ■ ■ ■ ■ ■ ■ *GO TO* MyEnglishLab *FOR MORE GRAMMAR PRACTICE AND TO CHECK WHAT YOU LEARNED.*

FINAL WRITING TASK

In this unit, you read the short story "Gotta Dance" and "Kids Learn Poise Through Dance," a passage that describes the advantages of teaching ballroom dancing to children.

*You will **write an essay on the three main qualities that a person must have in order to be successful in life.** Use the vocabulary and grammar from the unit.**

PREPARE TO WRITE: Freewriting

Success can be defined in many ways. Freewrite on a separate piece of paper about a person who is successful in life. It can be a person you know or someone you have read about. Describe how this person's personality helped to overcome the obstacles on the road to success. What character traits were of value in this person's journey?

WRITE: A Topic Sentence, Illustration, and Conclusion

1 Work with a partner. Read the paragraph and discuss the questions.

> People who are unwilling to risk failure are not capable of achieving big successes. The careers of the inventor Thomas Edison and the comedian Charlie Chaplin serve as good examples. Without Thomas Edison, we might still be reading in the dark today. But did you know that Edison discovered the lightbulb after a thousand different attempts? When asked what he had learned from those one thousand mistakes, Edison responded that he had found one thousand ways in which a light bulb could not be made. During his early days in London, people threw things at

_____

* For Alternative Writing Topics, see page 87. These topics can be used in place of the writing topic for this unit or as homework. The alternative topics relate to the theme of the unit, but may not target the same grammar or rhetorical structures taught in the unit.

Charlie Chaplin to make him get off the stage. Would we be enjoying the starring film roles of this famous comedian today if he had taken those audiences' reactions to heart and stopped pursuing his dream to become an actor? Learning to cope with failure makes you strong enough to view every defeat as another step toward success.

1. What kind of information does the first sentence provide?

2. What do the next six sentences have to do with the first sentence?

3. Which sentence does the last sentence refer back to?

2 Read the information in the box and then complete the exercises.

ILLUSTRATION

Illustration, an essential ingredient of effective writing, is used to clarify or support the main idea that has been expressed in the **topic sentence** of a paragraph.

To illustrate an idea, a writer provides clear and concise examples, persuasive explanations, appropriate statistics, and relevant anecdotes (brief stories) that support the topic sentence.

In the example paragraph in Exercise 1, page 82, the writer provides statistics and anecdotes about the lives of Thomas Edison and Charlie Chaplin to show how both these famous people would not have become great successes if they had not risked failure. Thomas Edison's one thousand failed attempts before discovering the light bulb and Charlie Chaplin's experiences of having things thrown at him when he first started to act are two examples that not only convince the reader of the logic of the topic sentence, but also prepare the reader for the **concluding sentence,** which reinforces the main idea of the paragraph.

3 Work with a partner to develop an appropriate topic sentence for the fully developed paragraph on page 84.

Topic Sentence:

_____

_____

(continued on next page)

Both Judy Garland and Marilyn Monroe were wonderful entertainers. Although they died in the 1960s, they are still remembered today for their genius as performers. Judy Garland was a fine actress and singer. There isn't a child who doesn't know her as Dorothy in the classic film *The Wizard of Oz*. Moreover, adults are still buying compact discs of her many record albums. Marilyn Monroe played comic and tragic roles in films and on the live stage. People today still watch videos of *Some Like It Hot, The Misfits,* and *Bus Stop,* her most famous films. Yet both these actresses tried to commit suicide many times. It is not clear if their actual deaths were the result of suicide attempts. What is clear, however, is that despite their great successes, they were not happy people.

4 Develop the idea of the topic sentence below. Write a complete paragraph showing support with illustration and conclusion based on the information in Katie's story. Then, in a small group, compare your paragraphs.

People who decide to follow their dreams sometimes have to be strong enough to go against the wishes of their family.

5 Write an essay that discusses the three main qualities that a person needs to have in order to achieve success. Refer to the work you did in Prepare to Write and Write on pages 82–84 as you organize your thoughts. Pay careful attention to the main elements of a well-constructed paragraph—topic sentence, supporting details, and concluding sentence.

Your well-organized essay will include an introduction culminating in a thesis statement, three body paragraphs (one for each quality) showing support with illustration, and a conclusion. The conclusion should refer back to the main idea contained in the thesis statement, but it must not repeat the idea in the exact words. The conclusion may also express a wish for the future. For more information on conclusions, see Unit 4.

Some Suggestions for Thesis Statements:

There are three main qualities necessary for success: _____, _____, and _____.

Of all the qualities needed for success, _____, _____, and _____ are the most important.

Success cannot be achieved without _____, _____, and _____.

REVISE: Achieving Paragraph Unity

Well-written paragraphs have paragraph unity. There is unity in a paragraph if all sentences focus on the same topic that is introduced in the topic sentence. If other "topics" have been introduced, the paragraph does not have paragraph unity. One topic per paragraph is a good rule to follow: "unity" equals "one."

1 Work with a partner to read the paragraph and answer the questions.

(1) Another trait that people need in order to achieve success is the ability to be passionately enthusiastic about the work they do. (2) Without passion, people won't have the drive or the joy necessary for creative thinking. (3) It is easy to see that the children in the ballroom dance program were passionate about their dancing and committed to upholding the reputation of their team and their school. (4) They also became friends, and their friendships lasted beyond the competition. (5) The students worked enthusiastically, not because they were forced to, but because they loved what they were doing. (6) That quality is the key for many great innovators who made history, not because they were forced to do so, not even because they were thinking of financial rewards, but because they were passionately interested in their work. (7) For example, Steve Jobs, who was a founder of Apple Computer, was never sure he would succeed, and in fact, he failed several times. (8) Yet he never lost the enthusiasm for his ideas. (9) All successful people are passionate about what they are doing. (10) Intelligence is another essential ingredient you will find in all success stories.

1. According to the topic sentence, what is the subject of this paragraph?

2. Which sentences do not belong in this paragraph?

3. What is the best concluding sentence for this paragraph: 8 or 9 or 10?

2 Look at the draft of your essay. Does each of your body paragraphs have paragraph unity? If not, decide what you can do to establish this unity.

--- *GO TO* MyEnglishLab *FOR MORE SKILL PRACTICE.*

EDIT: Writing the Final Draft

Go to MyEnglishLab and write the final draft of your essay. Carefully edit it for grammatical and mechanical errors, such as spelling, capitalization, and punctuation. Make sure you use some of the grammar and vocabulary from the unit. Use the checklist to help you write your final draft. Then submit your essay to your teacher.

FINAL DRAFT CHECKLIST

❑ Is your essay divided into clear paragraphs with one main point in each paragraph?

❑ Are the main points written in topic sentences?

❑ Are all the main ideas well supported through proper illustration?

❑ Are identifying and nonidentifying adjective clauses used to define, describe, or add information?

❑ Have you used new vocabulary and expressions (including hyphenated adjectives) in the essay?

UNIT PROJECT

Success can be defined in many ways: success in careers, in business, in family life, in the arts, in helping others, in spiritual domains. Interviewing successful people can help us all to find ways to achieve the success we want. You may interview a successful person or do research on the Internet about a successful person. Follow these steps:

STEP 1: Work with a partner. Before conducting the interview, decide on the person you want to interview and the reasons why you believe interviewing this person will be helpful. Then come up with questions you would want to use in the interview or as you do research on the Internet.

   1. Write the name of a successful person it would be possible for you to interview:

   _____

   2. Write at least three reasons why you believe understanding this person's success will help you as you strive to realize your dream:

      1. _____

      2. _____

      3. _____

3. Create questions that you want to ask this person. Brainstorm with your partner as you formulate at least five questions in preparation for your interview.

1. _What strategy did you follow to reach your career goals?_

2. _What mistakes did you make, and what did you learn from them?_

3. _____

4. _____

5. _____

STEP 2: When you meet with the person you have chosen to interview, do the following.

1. Explain to the person why you chose to interview him or her.

2. Take notes as you listen to the person's responses to your questions.

STEP 3: After you have conducted the interview or done research on the Internet, work with your partner to write a summary of your findings. Try to use the "language of success" learned in the unit as you discuss the person's insights about success.

1. Examine your notes taken during the interview.

2. Write a summary of the interview. What have you learned? What can be applied to your own career?

3. Prepare a formal presentation to give to the class.

ALTERNATIVE WRITING TOPICS

Write an essay on one of the topics. Use the vocabulary and grammar from the unit.

1. What do you think Katie's life will be like after the end of her story? Explain how certain aspects of her life and personality will influence her future.

2. Read Mary Oliver's poem "The Journey" online. (You can find it on many web sites.) Explain what you believe the poet is expressing, and compare the speaker's "journey" with Katie's in "Gotta Dance."

3. Booker T. Washington wrote, "I have learned that success is to be measured not so much by the position that one has reached in life as by the obstacles which one has had to overcome while trying to succeed." Do you agree or disagree? Booker T. Washington was born into slavery and after emancipation became a great educator and leader. Can you name other people who have overcome many obstacles to achieve success?

■■■■■■■■■■■■■■■ **GO TO** MyEnglishLab **TO WRITE ABOUT ONE OF THE ALTERNATIVE TOPICS, WATCH A VIDEO ABOUT HOW TO BECOME SUCCESSFUL, AND TAKE THE UNIT 3 ACHIEVEMENT TEST.** ■■■■■■■■■■

WHAT IS LOST IN Translation?

1. What are the advantages of living in a multicultural society? What are the disadvantages?

2. What could be "lost in translation" for people who leave one country to live in another?

3. Are there behaviors in your culture that may not be acceptable in another culture? Are there behaviors in another culture that are not acceptable in yours? If so, what are these behaviors?

GO TO MyEnglishLab *TO CHECK WHAT YOU KNOW.*

VOCABULARY

1 Read the passage about Eva Hoffman and Elizabeth Wong, the writers of the two texts you are going to read. See if you can understand the boldfaced words and phrases according to the contexts in which they appear.

Being a teenager is difficult under any conditions. Even in the most normal circumstances, the teenage years are often a **(1) chaotic** period for both children and parents alike. Parents are afraid of losing their **(2) authority.** How much should they **(3) scold** their children? When is **(4) restraint** of any kind advisable? That is, under what circumstances should they loosen or **(5) tighten the reins**? How often should they be **(6) demonstrative** about their love for their children in order to give them the confidence they need to fight life's battles? This kind of normal conflict is all the more dramatic when an immigrant family is **(7) beleaguered** by the tragic memory of its recent past.

Such was the case for Eva Hoffman. Born in Poland in 1945 to Jewish parents who were Holocaust survivors, she left her homeland at age thirteen with her parents and sister to start a new life in Canada. In her autobiography, *Lost in Translation,* she writes about the **(8) grief** they all felt about leaving their old life. This new existence threatened to unravel the **(9) fabric** of their family life. As she **(10) gives vent to** the feelings that she suffered from during this transition, Ms. Hoffman takes us on the journey from Old World Kracow to New World Vancouver; this journey prepared her for her studies at Harvard University, for her literary career at the *New York Times,* and for her work as a well-known author. In her objective and **(11) stoical** tone, Eva Hoffman writes the story of all immigrants. She describes how her Polish identity was transformed into a new Canadian identity as she experienced the physically and emotionally exhausting **(12) challenge** of learning to communicate in English. As the title of her book indicates, during this period Eva Hoffman was "lost in translation," a state that all immigrants may find themselves in, both linguistically and culturally, as they attempt to "translate" their personalities from one language and culture to another.

Although Elizabeth Wong, who was born in Los Angeles, California, in 1958, was not an immigrant herself, she too may have understood Eva Hoffman's feeling of being "lost in translation" as a young girl. In "The Struggle to Be an All-American Girl," she writes how she was torn between two cultures and how she continually resisted her Chinese mother's attempts to get her to learn Chinese and be aware of her cultural background. She did everything in her power to **(13) dissuade** her mother from continuing such efforts so that she would **(14) grant** her a "cultural divorce." Ms. Wong is an award-winning playwright, a teacher of playwriting at several universities, and a writer for television.

These stories show how difficult it is to create an identity in a changing world. Eva Hoffman and Elizabeth Wong give us insight into the difficulties faced by people who must adapt to a new life.

2 Refer to the passage in Exercise 1 as you match the words and phrases in bold with the definitions below. Write the number on the line.

_____ **a.** express   _____ **h.** criticize angrily

_____ **b.** extreme sadness   _____ **i.** uncomplaining

_____ **c.** give   _____ **j.** basic structure

_____ **d.** test   _____ **k.** pressured

_____ **e.** be stricter   _____ **l.** power

_____ **f.** advise against   _____ **m.** showing emotion (emotional)

_____ **g.** confusing   _____ **n.** self-control

GO TO MyEnglishLab *FOR MORE VOCABULARY PRACTICE.*

You are going to read two stories about young girls from immigrant families. Each girl tries to establish her identity in a new country. Before you read, discuss the information and questions with a partner.

The first reading in this section portrays the difficulties of a Polish-Canadian family. This memoir is told from the point of view of Eva, a 13-year-old girl from Poland. Along with her mother, father, and sister, Alinka, she becomes an immigrant to Canada after World War II. The second reading is about a Chinese-American family. This story is told from the point of view of 10-year-old Elizabeth. She and her brother were born in the United States.

1. What do you think these two families will have in common?

2. How might their experiences be different?

Keep your discussion in mind as you read the two texts.

LOST IN TRANSLATION
By Eva Hoffman

1   "In Poland, I would have known how to bring you up, I would have known what to do," my mother says wistfully,[1] but here, she has lost her sureness, her **authority**. She doesn't know how hard to **scold** Alinka when she comes home at late hours; she can only worry over her daughter's vague evening activities. She has always been gentle with us, and she doesn't want, doesn't know how, to **tighten the reins**. But familial bonds seem so dangerously loose here!

2   Truth to tell, I don't want the **fabric** of loyalty and affection, and even obligation, to unravel either. I don't want my parents to lose us, I don't want to betray our common life. I want to defend our dignity because it is so fragile, so **beleaguered**. There is only the tiny cluster, the four of us, to know, to preserve whatever fund of human experience we may represent. And so I feel a kind of ferociousness about protecting it. I don't want us to turn into perpetually cheerful suburbanites, with hygienic[2] smiles and equally hygienic feelings. I want to keep even our sadness, the great sadness from which our parents have come.

3   I abjure my sister[3] to treat my parents well; I don't want her to **challenge** our mother's authority, because it is so easily challenged. It is they who

---
[1] **wistfully:** sadly
[2] **hygienic:** almost antiseptic; figurative: without passion or individuality
[3] **I abjure my sister:** I have made my sister promise

seem more defenseless to me than Alinka, and I want her to protect them. Alinka fights me like a forest animal in danger of being trapped; she too wants to roam throughout the thickets and meadows. She too wants to be free.

4   My mother says I'm becoming "English." This hurts me, because I know she means I'm becoming cold. I'm no colder than I've ever been, but I'm learning to be less **demonstrative**. I learn this from a teacher who, after contemplating the gesticulations[4] with which I help myself describe the digestive system of a frog, tells me to "sit on my hands and then try talking." I learn my new reserve from people who take a step back when we talk, because I am standing too close, crowding them. Cultural distances are different, I later learn in a sociology class, but I know it already. I learn **restraint** from Penny, who looks offended when I shake her by the arm in excitement, as if my gesture had been one of aggression instead of friendliness. I learn it from a girl who pulls away when I hook my arm through hers as we walk down the street—this movement of friendly intimacy is an embarrassment to her.

5   I learn also that certain kinds of truth are impolite. One shouldn't criticize the person one is with, at least not directly. You shouldn't say, "You are wrong about that"—although you may say, "On the other hand, there is that to consider." You shouldn't say, "This doesn't look good on you"—though you may say, "I like you better in that other outfit." I learn to tone down my sharpness, to do a more careful conversational minuet.[5]

6   Perhaps my mother is right after all; perhaps I'm becoming colder. After a while, emotion follows action, response grows warmer or cooler according to gesture. I'm more careful about what I say, how loud I laugh, whether I **give vent to grief**. The storminess of emotion prevailing in our family is in excess of the normal here, and the unwritten rules for the normal have their osmotic effect.[6]

---

[4] **gesticulations:** movements with the arms and hands, usually while speaking
[5] **minuet:** a slow graceful dance of the 17th and 18th centuries
[6] **osmotic effect:** an effect of being gradually absorbed

THE STRUGGLE TO BE AN
All-American Girl

by Elizabeth Wong

1   It's still there, the Chinese school on Yale Street where my brother and I used to go. Despite the new coat of paint and the high wire fence, the school I knew ten years ago remains remarkably, **stoically**, the same.

2   Every day at 5 P.M., instead of playing with our fourth- and fifth-grade friends or sneaking out to the empty lot to hunt ghosts and animal bones, my brother and I had to go to Chinese school. No amount of kicking, screaming, or pleading could **dissuade** my mother, who was solidly determined to have us learn the language of our heritage. Forcibly, she walked us the seven long, hilly blocks from our home to school, depositing our defiant tearful faces before the stern principal. My only memory of him is that he swayed on his heels like a palm tree and he always clasped his impatient, twitching hands behind his back. I recognized him as a repressed maniacal[1] child killer, and that if we ever saw his hands, we'd be in big trouble.

3   We all sat in little chairs in an empty auditorium. The room smelled like Chinese medicine, an imported faraway mustiness,[2] like ancient mothballs[3] or dirty closets. I hated that smell. I favored crisp new scents like the soft French perfume that my American teacher wore in public school. There was a stage far to the right, flanked by an American flag and the flag of the Nationalist Republic of China, which was also red, white, and blue but not as pretty.

4   Although the emphasis at school was mainly language—speaking, reading, and writing—the lessons always began with exercises in politeness. With the entrance of the teacher, the best student would tap a bell and everyone would get up, kowtow,[4] and chant "Sing san ho," the phonetic for "How are you, teacher?"

5   Being ten years old, I had better things to learn than ideographs[5] copied painstakingly in lines that ran right to left from the tip of a *moc but*, a real ink pen that had to be held in an awkward way if blotches were to be avoided. After all, I could do the multiplication tables, name the satellites of Mars, and write reports on *Little Women and Black Beauty*. Nancy Drew, my favorite heroine, never spoke Chinese.

---

[1] **maniacal:** behaving as if you are crazy
[2] **mustiness:** moldy dampness, a smell of decay
[3] **mothballs:** made of a strong-smelling substance; used to keep moths away from clothes
[4] **kowtow:** to bow with respect
[5] **ideograph:** a written sign, for example in Chinese, that represents an idea or thing rather than a sound

6   The language was a source of embarrassment. More times than not, I had tried to dissociate myself from the nagging loud voice that followed me wherever I wandered in the nearby American supermarket outside Chinatown. The voice belonged to my grandmother, a fragile woman in her seventies who could outshout the best of the street vendors. Her humor was raunchy,[6] her Chinese rhythmless, patternless. It was quick, it was loud, it was unbeautiful. It was not like the quiet, lilting romance of French or the gentle refinement of the American South. Chinese sounded pedestrian. Public.

7   In Chinatown, the comings and goings of hundreds of Chinese on their daily tasks sounded **chaotic** and frenzied. I did not want to be thought of as mad, as talking gibberish. When I spoke English, people nodded at me, smiled sweetly, said encouraging words. Even the people in my culture would cluck[7] and say that I would do well in life. "My, doesn't she move her lips fast," they would say, meaning that I'd be able to keep up with the world outside Chinatown.

8   My brother was even more fanatical than I about speaking English. He was especially hard on my mother, criticizing her, often cruelly, for her pidgin speech[8] —smatterings of Chinese scattered like chop suey in her conversation. "It's not 'What it is,' Mom," he'd say in exasperation. "It's 'What is it, what is it, what is it.'" Sometimes Mom might leave out an occasional "the" or "a," or perhaps a verb of being. He would stop her in mid-sentence: "Say it again, Mom. Say it right." When he tripped over his own tongue, he'd blame it on her: "See, Mom, it's all your fault. You set a bad example."

9   What infuriated my mother most was when my brother cornered her on her consonants, especially "r." My father had played a cruel joke on Mom by assigning her an American name that her tongue wouldn't allow her to say. No matter how hard she tried, "Ruth" always ended up "Luth" or "Roof."

10 After two years of writing with a *moc but* and reciting words with multiples of meanings, I was finally **granted** a cultural divorce. I was permitted to stop Chinese school.

11 I thought of myself as multicultural. I preferred tacos to egg rolls; I enjoyed Cinco de Mayo more than Chinese New Year.

12 At last, I was one of you; I wasn't one of them.

13 Sadly, I still am.

---

[6] **raunchy:** obscene
[7] **cluck:** a clicking sound with the tongue showing concern or interest
[8] **pidgin speech:** simplified, uneducated speech

MAIN IDEAS

1 Look again at the Preview on page 92. How did your ideas help you understand the two readings?

2 Work in pairs. Read the statements in the chart about the cultural values expressed in the stories that you have just read. Write down each author's opinion based on your understanding of the reading.

STATEMENTS	HOFFMAN	WONG
1. Parents have more difficulty adapting to a new culture than their children do.	*Eva and Alinka are becoming more like their peers. Their parents are not.*	*Elizabeth's mother maintained Chinese traditions at home and never learned to speak English well.*
2. When people move to another culture, their new language becomes more important to them than their native language.		
3. Parents lose authority over their children when the family moves to another culture.		
4. Families may have trouble maintaining closeness when they must adapt to a new culture.		
5. People who move to a new culture worry about betraying or forgetting their old cultural traditions.		

DETAILS

1 Compare and contrast the cultural customs of Poland and Canada as Eva describes them in *Lost in Translation*. Try to find at least five examples.

POLISH WAYS	CANADIAN WAYS
1. In Poland, Eva was comfortable showing her feelings openly.	1. Eva feels Canadians are more reserved about their feelings.
2.	2.
3.	3.
4.	4.
5.	5.

2 Compare and contrast Elizabeth's attitude toward Chinese things and her attitude toward American things when she was young, as told in "The Struggle to Be an All-American Girl." Try to find at least five examples.

ELIZABETH'S ATTITUDE TOWARD CHINESE THINGS	ELIZABETH'S ATTITUDE TOWARD AMERICAN THINGS
1. Chinese smells are musty, like old mothballs or dirty closets.	1. American smells seem new and crisp, like her teacher's perfume.
2.	2.
3.	3.
4.	4.
5.	5.

MAKE INFERENCES

UNDERSTANDING THE AUTHOR'S MEANING

With a clear understanding of the readings, it is possible to grasp not only what the characters in the story say but also the emotion that drives them to say it.

Look at the example and read the explanation.

Quotation: "In Poland, I would have known how to bring you up. I would have known what to do." (*paragraph 1, Lost in Translation*)

Who: Eva's mother

Explanation: Eva's mother feels lost in the new world. Her authority is weaker because she is unfamiliar with the culture and what is expected of her children.

Go back to the paragraph where each quotation appears. Identify the speaker and explain what the speaker means based on the context. Compare your answers with a partner's.

1. "I want to keep even our sadness, the great sadness from which our parents have come." (*paragraph 2, Lost in Translation*)

   Who: _____

   Explanation: _____

   _____

   _____

2. "My mother says I'm becoming 'English.'" (*paragraph 4, Lost in Translation*)

   Who: _____

   Explanation: _____

   _____

   _____

3. "I was finally granted a cultural divorce." (*paragraph 10, "The Struggle to Be an All-American Girl"*)

   Who: _____

   Explanation: _____

   _____

   _____

4. "At last, I was one of you; I wasn't one of them. Sadly, I still am." (*paragraphs 12–13, "The Struggle to Be an All-American Girl"*)

   Who: _____

   Explanation: _____

   _____

   _____

EXPRESS OPINIONS

Discuss the questions in a small group. Share your group's conclusions with the rest of the class.

1. Eva Hoffman writes about being "lost in translation" culturally and linguistically as she adapts to life in a new country. Is it possible for individuals who grow up in the same country in which they were born to be "lost in translation" for other reasons? Why or why not?

2. Elizabeth Wong says that she was granted "a cultural divorce." Do you think that a cultural divorce is possible? Is it necessary? Does the need for a "cultural divorce" change with age?

3. Eva Hoffman finds that gestures generate emotions, that "emotion follows action, response grows warmer or cooler according to gesture." Do you agree? Why or why not?

▪▪▪▪▪▪▪▪▪▪▪▪▪▪▪▪▪▪▪▪▪▪▪▪▪▪▪▪▪ *GO TO* MyEnglishLab *TO GIVE YOUR OPINION ABOUT ANOTHER QUESTION.*

READING TWO   FROM BAYAMON TO BROOKLYN

READ

1 Look at the boldfaced words and phrases in the reading and think about the questions.

1. What words or phrases do you know the meanings of?

2. Can you use any of the words or phrases in a sentence?

2 Read the passage that follows from the book *Language Crossings. Negotiating the Self in a Multicultural World.* As you read, notice the boldfaced vocabulary. Try to guess the meanings of the words from the context.

FROM BAYAMON TO BROOKLYN
by Rita E. Negrón Maslanek

1   It was a month before my sixth birthday. I remember boarding the plane in San Juan, Puerto Rico, with my mother and three-year-old sister, Lillian. I vividly recall the red-and-white homemade taffeta dresses Lily and I wore. Whenever I am in a fabric store, the unforgettable scent of the material instantly **transports my thought**s to that warm summer night. Within three months of our arrival in New York, my sister and brother joined us in our apartment in Brooklyn.

2   Aided by the **acquisition** of our television set, my English language journey continued uneventfully, for the most part. Because I was a diligent student who loved to read, and perhaps because I was very young when I began to learn a new language, learning English did not prove to be traumatic. This is not to say that there were no difficult moments.

3   One of a few early memories I have of my school days occurred in the second grade. We were learning the poem "Trees" by Joyce Kilmer. I was to read the line, "Poems are made by fools like me, but only God can make a tree." I did not know what "fool" meant,

so I raised my hand and asked the teacher. For some reason unknown to me, my teacher scolded me without answering my question. Then all the kids broke out in laughter. I can still remember the public humiliation and sense of **isolation** I felt when I was trying so hard **to fit in**. That episode taught me that being funny was a ticket to[1] being popular. Apparently, the other children were not laughing at me; they laughed because I had made the teacher angry by asking her to define a "bad" word. To them I was a hero for being a smart aleck, and unlike my teacher, they believed this to be a positive characteristic. So I embarked on my new mission—to be accepted and liked by making others laugh.

4   At the same time I was learning English, I was also learning Spanish. My father's Spanish-only rule at home was strictly enforced until the time came when it was just more natural and easier for my siblings and me to communicate with each other in English. There was also the added advantage that if we spoke fast enough we could actually speak about our parents in their presence without them catching on—well, almost never. Though we had abandoned the Spanish-only rule when speaking with each other, we always spoke in Spanish with our parents. To do otherwise was both unnatural and disrespectful.

5   I have written this chapter in Puerto Rico, where I came to spend Mother's Day with my now widowed mother. In many ways I feel as much a stranger here as I did during my first few years in New York. People who hear me speak for the first time quickly detect my "accent" (which I argue I do not

---

[1] **a ticket to:** a way of; in this case: a way of "being" (or becoming) "popular"

have), that I am from *afuera*, the word used to describe those living in the United States. My errors, which they patiently correct, are often a source for their amusement. Adapting to the tropical heat reminds me of adapting to cold New York winters. The relaxed pace is **in stark contrast to** the rapid pace I have become accustomed to. As I reflect on my language-formation journey, I am reminded that, for me, learning a new language was the easy part. Learning to fit in was/is the bigger challenge.

COMPREHENSION

Read each statement. Decide if it is **T** (true) or **F** (false) according to the reading. If it is false, change it to make it true. Discuss your answers with a partner.

_____ **1.** Learning a new language was hard for Rita because of her age.

_____ **2.** The poem "Trees" reminds Rita of her efforts to "fit in."

_____ **3.** When the teacher scolded her, Rita's feeling of isolation from the other students was temporary.

_____ **4.** Rita and her brother never wanted to speak Spanish.

_____ **5.** Rita's parents encouraged her to speak English at home.

_____ **6.** Culture is harder to learn than a language.

_____ **7.** Rita feels at home in Puerto Rico.

■■■■■■■■■■■■■■■■■■■■■■■■■■■■ *GO TO* MyEnglishLab *FOR MORE VOCABULARY PRACTICE.*

READING SKILL

1 Reread Reading Two. Circle the introductory paragraph and the concluding paragraph. Underline the topic sentences (the first sentences) of the body paragraphs (paragraphs 2, 3, and 4).

CREATING AN OUTLINE: FOCUSING ON THE BODY PARAGRAPHS

When you take notes on an essay, you can remember the information better if you write an outline. This helps you to remember how the writer "took off" (in the introduction) and "landed" (in the conclusion) and what steps were taken on the "journey" itself (in the body paragraphs).

The **topic sentence** is the first sentence of each **body paragraph**. It is the guiding, or unifying, idea of the paragraph because it announces the topic of the paragraph and prepares the reader for the **details** that will provide **support** for that topic.

For example, the topic sentence of paragraph 2 is: "Aided by the acquisition of our television set, my English language journey continued uneventfully, for the most part." We know from this sentence that the writer will be explaining in the rest of the paragraph why her English language journey was relatively "uneventful," or easy.

2 Work with a partner. Complete the outline on the next page by filling in other supporting ideas for the body paragraphs. Use the remaining choices in the box.

- diligent
- ~~example of a difficult moment~~
- fate reversed—other children were laughing with author
- father's Spanish-only rule
- loved to read
- ~~new mission—learn to make others laugh in order to be accepted~~
- poem "Trees" by Joyce Kilmer
- publicly humiliated when trying to fit in
- respecting our parents
- ~~scolded by teacher when asked a question about word "fools"~~
- ~~siblings' communicating with one another in English~~
- ~~very young~~

I. **Paragraph 2**

Topic Sentence: "Aided by the acquisition of our television set, my English language journey continued uneventfully, for the most part."

a.

b.

c. *very young*

II. **Paragraph 3**

Topic Sentence: "One of a few early memories I have of my school days occurred in the second grade."

a. *example of a difficult moment*

b.

c. *scolded by teacher when asked a question about word "fools"*

d.

e.

f. *new mission—learn to make others laugh in order to be accepted*

III. **Paragraph 4**

Topic Sentence: "At the same time I was learning English, I was also learning Spanish."

a.

b. *siblings communicating with one another in English*

c.

3 You circled the introduction and conclusion in Exercise 1. They "frame" the essay because they offer a "before" and "after" view, giving us further insight into the selection. Work with a partner to answer the following questions about the introduction, the conclusion, and the thesis statement.

1. What two time periods in the author's life do the introduction and conclusion refer to? What information does the author give that tells us that her move to America was a successful one for her?

2. This reading is not an academic essay; therefore, it does not have its thesis statement in the first paragraph. Which two sentences in the essay would you identify as the author's thesis?

GO TO MyEnglishLab *FOR MORE SKILL PRACTICE.*

STEP 1: Organize

Work with a partner. Review Reading One (R1) and Reading Two (R2) and consider the people whose names appear in the grid in relation to the categories in the column on the left. Place an X in the boxes where the category relates directly to the person's story.

	R1				R2	
	EVA	EVA'S PARENTS	ELIZABETH	ELIZABETH'S PARENTS	RITA	RITA'S PARENTS
IMMIGRANTS	X	X		X	X	X
EMBARRASSMENT						
CULTURAL CONFLICTS						

STEP 2: Synthesize

The summary below synthesizes some of the main ideas in all three readings. Complete the summary with the sentences in the box. Write the letter of the correct sentence.

---

a. Eva's parents were embarrassed about not knowing the customs of the new country. Elizabeth's mother was ashamed of not being able to speak English clearly.

b. All the children and adults in the readings were immigrants except Elizabeth.

c. All were shaped and molded by struggle or compromise with clashing cultures.

d. Of all the children, Elizabeth was the least concerned with tradition and heritage.

---

(1) _____. The fact that she was born and raised in the United States may explain her attitude toward the past. (2) _____. Only when she grew up did she realize the value of what her mother had been trying to do.

All the children, except for Rita, spoke of being embarrassed about not fitting in. Eva was ashamed of not knowing how to express her feelings. Elizabeth and her brother didn't want to speak Chinese. (3) _____. Only Rita gives no indication of embarrassment. Even when the children laughed at her question in school, she realized the children were laughing at the teacher and, in fact, considered her a hero for embarrassing the teacher!

According to the readings, cultural conflicts were part of the lives of these families who were transplanted to a new environment. Eva moved between her Polish and Canadian identities, Elizabeth rebelled against her Chinese school, and Rita spoke Spanish to her parents out of respect and English to her brother and sister. (4) _____.

GO TO MyEnglishLab TO CHECK WHAT YOU LEARNED.

3 FOCUS ON WRITING

VOCABULARY

REVIEW

Read the thoughts that may have gone through the mind of Alinka, Eva's younger sister. Complete the thoughts with words and phrases from the box. They are synonyms for the items in parentheses.

acquisition	fabric	isolation
beleaguered	fit in	stoical
challenge	giving vent to	tighten the reins
chaotic	grief	transports their thoughts to
dissuade	in sharp contrast to	

These have been very upsetting years for my parents. The _____ of their
                                                 1. (structure)

emotional lives has been made ever so fragile because of their own suffering and their firsthand

knowledge of the terribly tragic circumstances suffered by so many of their loved ones during

World War II. My parents wanted to make a new life for us in Canada despite the difficult

_____ that adapting to life in a new culture would be.
    2. (test)

Although they had hoped that their new home in Canada would provide a safe place for them

from their tragic past, my parents' sense of sorrow and _____ still dominates them.
                                          3. (loneliness)

Despite their _____ appearance, their every gesture is still _____
        4. (self-controlled)   5. (troubled)

by their memories of their violent past. Ironically, the relative safety of their current lives somehow

_____ this traumatic period in their lives at all times.
  6. (makes them recall)

You may think that as the youngest family member of our cluster of four, I have been

untouched by all this. Yet it was not until we moved to Canada that I realized how very trapped I

had been by my parents' _____. I had never realized how simple life could be.
                              7. (sadness)

None of my Canadian friends seems to have a history or to be troubled by the need to understand their family history. Their perpetually happy faces, which my sister sarcastically describes as reflecting not only "hygienic smiles," but also "hygienic feelings," are a welcome relief to me.

While my sister may laugh at my friends and their parents because of their superficiality, I disagree. It is true that our life here in Canada is _____ the life we led in Poland.
8. (totally different from)
However, Eva cannot _____ me from thinking that Canadians are better off than
9. (discourage)
we are. I want more than anything else to _____ with this Disneyland mentality,
10. (blend in)
with this fairy tale of a life where "everyone lives happily ever after."

So, if I am putting a lot of makeup on my face and behaving in ways that make my mother think of the loose girls in our Polish town, be happy for me! As I take advantage of my mother, who has decided not to _____ because she is afraid of losing me, I am doing
11. (impose restraints)
two things at once. I am rebelling as only teenagers know how to rebel, and, in so doing, I am "painting" a new life for myself. Through the _____ of a new identity, not only am
12. (obtaining)
I _____ my frustrations, but I am also liberating myself from the storminess of my
13. (expressing)
family's _____ inner life. I am becoming free!
14. (turbulent)

EXPAND

The suffixes **-ness, -ty, -ity,** and **-ment** mean "the state, quality, or condition of being." When you add **-ness, -ty,** and **-ity** to certain adjectives and **-ment** to certain verbs, you create nouns that relate to the state, quality, or condition of being a particular way.

For adjectives of two syllables or more that end with a *y*, the *y* changes to *i* when *-ness* is added. Other spelling changes may be needed, so you should check your dictionary.

1 Study the chart of suffixes.

ADJECTIVE	SUFFIX ADDED	NOUN
quiet	-ness	quietness (the state, quality, or condition of being quiet)
happy	-ness	happiness (the state, quality, or condition of being happy)
cruel	-ty	cruelty (the state, quality, or condition of being cruel)
authentic	-ity	authenticity (the state, quality, or condition of being authentic)
VERB	**SUFFIX ADDED**	**NOUN**
move	-ment	movement (the state, quality, or condition of moving or being moved)

2 Work with a partner. Read the sentences and write the noun that can be created from the underlined word. Then write a sentence using the noun, without changing the meaning of the original sentence. Other words will have to be changed.

1. Elizabeth likes the <u>refined</u> manner in which Southerners speak English.

    Noun: _refinement_

    Sentence: _Elizabeth likes the refinement of Southerners' speech._

2. Penny does not understand that Eva is being <u>friendly</u> when she shakes her arm in excitement.

    Noun: _____

    Sentence: _____

3. Eva learns that hooking her arm through Penny's as they walk down the street together <u>embarrasses</u> Penny.

    Noun: _____

    Sentence: _____

4. Eva does not want her father, mother, and sister to stop being <u>loyal</u> to one another.

    Noun: _____

    Sentence: _____

5. The Hoffman family's <u>stormy</u> emotional state is far from normal in Canada.

Noun: _____

Sentence: _____

6. Eva is <u>ferocious</u> about protecting her family's common bond.

Noun: _____

Sentence: _____

7. Being able to make her classmates laugh made Rita <u>popular</u>.

Noun: _____

Sentence: _____

CREATE

Work with a partner to complete an imaginary dialogue between Elizabeth Wong and her mother. Elizabeth is young and does not want to go to Chinese school. Her mother is upset and tries to persuade her daughter to respect traditional culture. The daughter wants to be more American than Chinese. In your dialogue, use at least eight words or phrases from the box.

acquisition	friendliness	restraint
challenge	give vent to	scold
chaotic	in sharp contrast to	stoical
demonstrative	isolation	storminess
dissuade	loyalty	tighten the reins
~~embarrassment~~	~~nagging~~	transport one's thoughts to
fit in	refinement	

ELIZABETH: *Why are you always nagging me about going to Chinese school? I hate it*

there.

MOTHER: *It's important for you to learn to speak Chinese. Why does it always*

cause you such embarrassment?

Now go to MyEnglishLab or work on a separate piece of paper to write at least three more exchanges between Elizabeth and her mother.

■■■■■■■■■■■■■■■■■■■■■■■■■■■■■■■■■ *GO TO* MyEnglishLab *FOR MORE VOCABULARY PRACTICE.*

GRAMMAR

1 Examine the sentence from *Lost in Translation* and discuss the questions with a partner.

"You shouldn't say, 'You are wrong about that,' although you may say, 'On the other hand, there is that to consider.'"

1. Is this one sentence or two?

2. Which part of the sentence contains words that are polite to say in Canadian culture?

3. What is the difference between the two parts of the sentence?

4. What is a synonym for *although* in this sentence?

ADVERB CLAUSES OF COMPARISON AND CONTRAST

Adverb clauses can be used to combine two ideas into one sentence. They can be used in the first or second part of the sentence. They provide variety for the sentence and smooth transitions from one idea to another in your paragraphs. The following adverbials used to introduce adverb clauses will be particularly helpful in comparison and contrast essays. Look at the examples carefully to see where commas are needed.

COMPARISON OR SIMILARITY	EXAMPLES
just as	*Just as* Eva is struggling to be accepted in Canada, Elizabeth is struggling to be accepted in the United States.
in the same way that	*In the same way that* many immigrants have chosen to come to the United States, many are choosing Canada as their new home.
CONTRAST OR DIFFERENCE	
whereas	*Whereas* some parents want their children to speak their native language at home, other parents encourage their children to practice English everywhere.
while	Mrs. Wong felt that her daughter Elizabeth needed to learn all about her Chinese traditions *while* Elizabeth rebelled against such instruction.
despite the fact that	*Despite the fact that* Americans accept the use of many immigrant languages, they remain profoundly attached to the English language.
although	*Although* Americans accept the use of many immigrant languages, they remain profoundly attached to the English language.
while	*While* Americans accept the use of many immigrant languages, they remain profoundly attached to the English language.

GRAMMAR TIP: As you can see, *while* can be used in two distinct ways: either as a synonym for *whereas* or as a synonym for *despite the fact that* and *although*. Sentences with *despite the fact that* and *although* often include an unexpected idea or a contradiction. In these sentences, the subject of both clauses is usually the same.

2 For each of the topics, write one or two sentences of comparison and contrast. Use the cues given and **although, despite the fact that, in the same way that, just as, whereas,** or **while.**

1. **Telling the truth**

   Poles / Canadians

   While Poles may prefer to be honest and direct when giving criticism,

   Canadians may choose to be more diplomatic and keep their opinions to

   themselves.

   _____

2. **Cultural identity**

   Elizabeth / Rita

   _____

   _____

   _____

   _____

3. **Respecting one's parents**

   Alinka (Eva's sister) / Rita and her siblings

   _____

   _____

   _____

   _____

(continued on next page)

4. Obedience

Chinese children / Puerto Rican children

_____

_____

_____

_____

5. Independence

Elizabeth / Eva

_____

_____

_____

_____

6. Personal stories

Lost in Translation / "From Bayamon to Brooklyn"

_____

_____

_____

_____

■■■■■■■■■■■■■■■ *GO TO* MyEnglishLab *FOR MORE GRAMMAR PRACTICE AND TO CHECK WHAT YOU LEARNED.*

FINAL WRITING TASK

In this unit you read an excerpt from *Lost in Translation* and "The Struggle to Be an All-American Girl."

You will **write a point-by-point comparison and contrast essay about Eva and Elizabeth.** *Use the vocabulary and grammar from the unit.**

PREPARE TO WRITE: Identifying Similarities, Differences, and Common Categories

1 Fill in the Venn diagram. In the part on the left, write notes about Eva that are true only of Eva. In the part on the right, write notes about Elizabeth that are true only of Elizabeth. In the middle, write notes about what the two of them share.

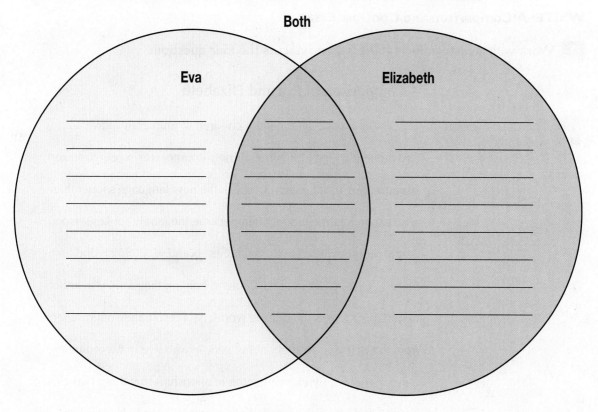

* For Alternative Writing Topics, see page 124. These topics can be used in place of the writing topic for this unit or as homework. The alternative topics relate to the theme of the unit, but may not target the same grammar or rhetorical structures taught in the unit.

2 Look at the Venn diagram. From the similarities and differences that you have noted, identify the categories to which they belong. Place the various ideas under their respective categories. Then fill in the similarities and differences in the chart. Identify one or two more categories to add to the chart.

CATEGORIES	SIMILARITIES	DIFFERENCES
FAMILY LIFE		
CULTURAL IDENTITY		

WRITE: A Comparison and Contrast Essay

1 Work with a partner. Read the essay and discuss the four questions.

A Comparison of Eva and Elizabeth

INTRODUCTORY PARAGRAPH

Whoever once said that the children of immigrants have an easy time adapting to life in their new country was surely mistaken. Because they usually learn to speak the new language sooner than adults, immigrant children often become the family spokesperson. As the oldest children in their families, both Eva Hoffman and Elizabeth Wong play an active role in helping their family members communicate with the outside world. As a result, they often suffer from the pain and frustration that people who live in two cultures can experience. By examining the relationships that these two girls have with their mothers and other important people in their lives, we can see that although Eva and Elizabeth may have certain hopes and feelings in common, they are at the same time very different from one another.

BODY PARAGRAPH 1

Like Eva, Elizabeth wants to be accepted by her peers, and she is embarrassed when she is made to feel different from them. In the same way that Eva becomes self-conscious about expressing her feelings, Elizabeth is ashamed as she wanders through the American supermarket and hears her grandmother calling after her in Chinese. Elizabeth also hates it when her mother speaks English. But, on the surface at least, she does not seem to be as bothered by this as her younger brother. This brings us to another common area of concern. Eva and Elizabeth are both unhappy about the ways in which their brother and sister treat their mother. Just as Eva is angered when her sister Alinka challenges her mother's authority, Elizabeth views her brother's constant criticisms of her mother's English as fanatical and cruel. Both Eva and Elizabeth are more outwardly protective of their mothers' feelings than their brother and sister are.

BODY PARAGRAPH 2

Although Eva and Elizabeth share similar attitudes, they also differ from each other in many respects. Unlike Eva, Elizabeth does not feel that her identity is bound to her family's cultural heritage and history. Whereas Eva embraces her Polish heritage, Elizabeth flees from her Chinese background. While Eva wants to hold on to the memory of the family's sad past, Elizabeth is happy when her mother grants her a "cultural divorce" and says she no longer has to attend the Chinese school. In contrast to Elizabeth, Eva is flexible: She is willing to compromise and accept the best of both cultures. Whereas Eva sees herself becoming bicultural, Elizabeth adores the sights and sounds of everything American and wants only to be an "all-American girl."

(continued on next page)

How could she want anything else if Nancy Drew, her favorite heroine, never spoke Chinese? Of course, all this can be explained by the different ages and the different circumstances of the two girls. Eva is thirteen years old, while Elizabeth is only ten years old. In addition, whereas Eva herself is an immigrant, Elizabeth was born and raised in the United States. Such basic differences in their lives leave a wide gap between them.

CONCLUSION

Eva and Elizabeth have made different adjustments to their cross-cultural experiences. When children like Eva immigrate, they understand the sacrifices their parents have made in order to provide them with a better life because they themselves have participated in the immigration process. However, children like Elizabeth often don't understand the sacrifices their parents have made for them until they become adults. And when they finally do, can it sometimes be too late?

1. Which words and phrases does the writer use to point out similarities and differences?

2. In the body of the essay, can you readily identify the paragraph that deals with the similarities and the paragraph that deals with the differences? Explain how the writer makes this easy for the reader.

3. What does the writer do to connect the two body paragraphs?

4. Are the similarities between the two characters more important than the differences, or are the differences more important than the similarities? Explain.

2 Read the information in the boxes and then complete the exercises.

PURPOSE OF COMPARISON AND CONTRAST ESSAYS

When you write a comparison and contrast essay, the purpose is not just to point out similarities and differences or advantages and disadvantages. The purpose is—as with all essays—to persuade and explain a point of view. The emphasis should be on either the similarities or the differences, and details should be included according to which emphasis is chosen.

The thesis statement of the essay you have just read, the last sentence of the introductory paragraph, tells the reader something about the emphasis that will be developed in the body of the essay. "By examining the relationships that these two girls have with their mothers and other important people in their lives, we can see that although Eva and Elizabeth may have certain hopes and feelings in common, they are at the same time very different from one another." We know by the last sentence of the body of the essay that the differences outweigh the similarities: "Such basic differences in their lives leave a wide gap between them." This point of view is reinforced in the conclusion of the essay.

Patterns of Organization

There are two ways to organize a comparison and contrast essay: through block organization or point-by-point organization.

BLOCK ORGANIZATION	POINT-BY-POINT ORGANIZATION
• Similarities: *Both subjects are discussed (similarities of Eva and Elizabeth).* • Differences: *Both subjects are discussed (differences of Eva and Elizabeth).* OR - All about Eva - All about Elizabeth - Summary of similarities and differences	• Subject One: *Similarities and differences are discussed.* • Subject Two: *Similarities and differences are discussed.* • Subject Three: *Similarities and differences are discussed.*

Block Organization

In a **block organization** essay, the writer discusses each part of the comparison in clearly distinct parts (or blocks) of the essay. For example, the writer could first refer only to Eva and then only to Elizabeth, or, as in the essay "A Comparison of Eva and Elizabeth," the writer could first discuss the similarities between the two girls and then the differences between them.

The paragraph dealing with similarities contains many words and expressions that point out likenesses: *like, in the same way that, just as, both,* and so on. Similarly, the paragraph revealing the differences contains words and expressions that show differences: *unlike, whereas, while, in contrast to,* and so on.

In order to connect one block of the essay to the other, the writer uses a transitional sentence that prepares us for the change in emphasis of the next block: "Although Eva and Elizabeth share similar attitudes, they also differ from each other in many respects."

(continued on next page)

Point-by-Point Organization

In **point-by-point organization,** the writer organizes the development of ideas according to "points," or categories, which are common to both subjects. In each paragraph of the body, a different point is discussed. For example, a comparison of Eva and Elizabeth might (after the introductory paragraph) begin with a paragraph exploring the differences in their *backgrounds*. A second paragraph might discuss the similarities and differences in their *family life,* and so on. It is usually better to limit the categories to three or four. A point-by-point organization is usually chosen when there are many complex aspects to a comparison; a block organization is more suitable for a simpler subject.

The following is an example of a point-by-point body paragraph:

> Eva's and Elizabeth's contrasting backgrounds help us to reflect on the differences between them. As a teenager who directly experienced the tragic history of her family's past, Eva cannot ignore the fact that she is in the middle of two cultures. She holds on to her Polish values while adapting to newly-learned Canadian values. Whereas Eva dips willingly into two cultures and sees herself becoming bicultural, Elizabeth resents her mother's insistence that she learn about her Chinese heritage. Elizabeth was born in America; her mother's native country is not hers. She does not feel bicultural because she is not an immigrant. She adores the sights and sounds of everything American and wants only to fit in and be an "all-American girl." While Elizabeth feels trapped studying about a past she has never known and is too young to appreciate, Eva is mature enough to realize that she must embrace a double identity because of her immigrant status. These basic differences in their situations therefore leave a wide gap between them.

Organizing Information through Outlines

Whether you choose block or point-by-point organization for your comparison and contrast essay, preparing an **outline** can help you to organize your main ideas, topic sentences, and supporting details. After you prepare an outline, you know exactly what you want to write and how you want to write it.

Once you know the topics you want to include in your essay, you will be ready to write the thesis statement. The thesis statement should tell the reader the main idea and announce the topics that will be explored in the body paragraphs. The thesis statement cannot simply state the similarities and differences; it must take a position on the comparison. Are the differences more important than the similarities, or are the similarities more important than the differences?

3 Read the thesis statements with a partner. Give the main idea that is to be emphasized (more similar than different or more different than similar). Then write down the "keywords" (topics and possible focal points) of the supporting body paragraphs.

1. It is easy to overlook the differences in family relationships and childrearing attitudes between Asian and North American parents because of their similar educational aspirations for their children.

    Main Idea: _Differences are more important than similarities._

    Supporting Body Paragraph Topics

    Similarities: _aspirations_

    Differences: _family relationships and childrearing attitudes_

2. Most people believe that Dominicans and Puerto Ricans have a lot in common because of their Caribbean island heritage; however, most people do not know that the Dominicans' love of the *bachata* and the Puerto Ricans' love of *salsa* create a great cultural divide between the two groups on the dance floor.

    Main Idea: _____

    Supporting Body Paragraph Topics

    Similarities: _____

    Differences: _____

3. To fully understand the differences between American and Samoan teenagers' relationships with their parents, you need to look at the differences in the parents' methods of discipline, the amount of time they usually spend with their children, and their expectations for help from their children in their daily lives.

    Main Idea: _____

    Supporting Body Paragraph Topics

    Similarities: _____

    Differences: _____

4. Despite the different modes of transportation used by immigrants today and immigrants who came to America one hundred years ago, immigrants from all over the world still come to America for the same reasons: to escape political oppression and to seek better job opportunities.

    Main Idea: _____

    Supporting Body Paragraph Topics

    Similarities: _____

    Differences: _____

4 Write your thesis statement for the essay on Eva and Elizabeth. Then compare your thesis statement with a partner's.

Thesis Statement:

_____

_____

_____

5 Work with a partner and prepare an outline that will help you to organize your main ideas, topic sentences, and supporting details. Use the following framework as a guide.

Outline: A Comparison of Eva and Elizabeth
(Point-by-Point Organization)

I. Introduction

Thesis Statement: _____

_____

_____

II. Topic Sentence of Body Paragraph 1: _____

_____

   1. Eva: _____

_____

   2. Elizabeth: _____

_____

III. Topic Sentence of Body Paragraph 2: _____

_____

   1. Eva: _____

_____

   2. Elizabeth: _____

_____

IV. Topic Sentence of Body Paragraph 3: _____

_____

1. Eva: _____

_____

2. Elizabeth: _____

_____

V. Conclusion: _____

_____

_____

_____

6 Using what you have learned about organizing a point-by-point comparison and contrast essay, write a comparison and contrast essay about Eva and Elizabeth. Refer to the work you did in Prepare to Write and Write, pages 113–121, to write your first draft.

REVISE: Combining Sentences for Variety

The writer of the body paragraph (page 122) on cultural heritage in a point-by-point comparison and contrast essay has written correct sentences. However, the writing style needs more polish:

- Some sentence patterns are unnecessarily repeated.
- Some sentences conceptually related to each other should be combined either by means of a coordinating conjunction (*and, but*), a cause-and-effect structure (*because, since, however, nevertheless, therefore, consequently*), or a comparison and contrast structure (*both, like, unlike, just as, in the same way that, although, despite the fact that, while, whereas*).

With such revisions, the paragraph should be in good form.

Work with a partner to revise the paragraph. There is more than one correct answer here. After you have finished, check the answer key for suggested answers.

Sergio and Ernest are both loyal to their cultural heritage. Sergio was eight years old when he came to the United States. Ernest was eight years old. Sergio was born in Brazil. Ernest was born in Rwanda. America was a beacon of hope for both their families. They came to America for different reasons. Sergio left Brazil with his parents in search of a better future. Ernest came with his parents to escape the atrocities of the civil war in Rwanda. Their transition to American life was smooth. They both made American friends quickly and had no trouble adapting to American life. They were both able to respond to the challenges of the American dream. They now have successful careers. They have been in America for a long time. They have never forgotten their origins. Sergio goes back to Brazil for Carnival every February. Ernest does volunteer work throughout the year on the Rwandan Relief Fund. Both Sergio and Ernest are successful Americans who maintain close ties with the countries of their birth.

GO TO MyEnglishLab FOR MORE SKILL PRACTICE.

EDIT: Writing the Final Draft

Go to MyEnglishLab and write the final draft of your essay. Carefully edit it for grammatical and mechanical errors, such as spelling, capitalization, and punctuation. Make sure you use some of the grammar and vocabulary from the unit. Use the checklist to help you write your final draft. Then submit your essay to your teacher.

FINAL DRAFT CHECKLIST

❏ Does your essay have an introduction, a body, and a conclusion?

❏ Does the essay follow the point-by-point organizational pattern for comparison and contrast essays?

❏ Does the thesis statement prepare the reader for the topics of the body paragraphs?

❏ Does each body paragraph begin with an appropriate topic sentence and include sufficient support?

❏ Are the adverbials and other comparison and contrast words and phrases in the essay used correctly?

❏ Does the writing have good sentence variety?

❏ Have you used new vocabulary and expressions in the essay?

UNIT PROJECT

In what way has your family been touched by history? Prepare to write an essay in response to this question. Follow these steps:

STEP 1: Interview family members—in person, by mail, or by e-mail—to gather information for your essay. If you don't want to interview family members, you can do Internet research on someone who has decided to learn more about his or her family background and history. Before starting your research, brainstorm with a partner other questions you believe would be worth investigating. Here are some questions to consider.

1. Has your family (or the family of the person you are doing Internet research on) always lived in the same place? What influenced the decision to stay or go?

2. Has the country this family is from undergone any great changes in the last 50 years, such as wars, revolutions, divisions, reunifications, or changes in the political system? What effects have these events had on the family?

3. Have the economic circumstances of the family changed in recent generations? What are the reasons for these changes? How has the family adjusted to changes?

4. Do you think it is important for children to know the history of their family? Why or why not?

(continued on next page)

5. Has this family ever had any secrets that were not immediately told to the younger generation? If so, why were certain facts not discussed in the family?

6. Is there any documentation that you would like to show to illustrate this family's history? This can include photos, newspaper articles, or magazines from the period. (It can include personal items if you and your family agree about using them. If you are doing Internet research, see if there is any additional documentation that you can include.)

STEP 2: When you interview family members or do research, be sure to take good notes. You may want to request permission to record if you are interviewing in person. Ask them if they have any photos, newspaper articles, official announcements, letters, or personal records that you can include with your essay.

STEP 3: Write an essay in which you summarize your findings and explain how this information has affected you. Include relevant documentation. Share the main points of your essay with the class.

ALTERNATIVE WRITING TOPICS

Write an essay on one of the topics. Use vocabulary, grammar, and points of style that you studied in the unit.

1. Have you ever had a friend whose culture, background, talents, or qualities were different from yours? Consider how your similarities and differences contributed to your friendship. Did your friendship grow because you were similar or because you were different?

2. When immigrants arrive in a new country, should they assimilate into the new culture or try to preserve their old culture? In what ways do you think people need to assimilate? What kinds of things do people usually want to preserve from their old culture? What is the risk to the nation if assimilation is too extreme? What is the risk if immigrants do not assimilate?

3. In describing what it meant to be "transplanted" from his Belgian roots in order to live a life in the United States, Luc Sante writes in "Living in Tongues" that he had become "permanently other" because he had "to construct an identity in response to a double set of demands, one from [his] background and one from [his] environment." This feeling of being "other" can be felt by all immigrants who end up living in a place that was not originally theirs. Not only must they get used to their new physical "environment"—that of "another"—but they must also learn to speak a language that was not originally theirs while learning to meet the expectations of a culture that was not originally theirs.

Have you ever had this experience of being "other"? Has the challenge of speaking a new language and adapting to the lifestyle of a new culture made you, like Luc Sante, feel "other"? Why or why not? How do you think Eva Hoffman, Elizabeth Wong, and Rita E. Negrón Maslanek would respond to this question?

■■■■■■■■ GO TO MyEnglishLab TO PRACTICE INTERNET SKILLS, WRITE ABOUT ONE OF THE ALTERNATIVE TOPICS, WATCH A VIDEO ABOUT THE TRADITIONS OF JAPANESE GARDENS, AND TAKE THE UNIT 4 ACHIEVEMENT TEST. ■■■■■■■■■■

SIZE MATTERS IN Business

1. What do you hope to find when you travel? Do you like the comfort of familiar surroundings, or do you enjoy experiencing new things?

2. Are there other stores besides Starbucks® that you can now find all over the world? Why do people like to go to these stores?

3. Multinational chain stores have caused controversy because some people believe that these stores promote the "globalization of culture" (the sameness or the Americanization of culture) all over the world. What do you think about this issue?

■■ GO TO MyEnglishLab TO CHECK WHAT YOU KNOW.

VOCABULARY

Read the advice to future business owners. Try to understand from the context the meanings of the boldfaced words. Then look for their synonyms in the box and write the correct forms on the lines following each piece of advice.

NOUNS	ADJECTIVE	VERBS
generosity	uninteresting	~~be successful~~
permission		contribute to the progress or growth of
problem		go beyond, exceed
salary		imagine, see in the future
special attention		keep
		mention
		pressure those in power for support

Advice on Starting a Business

1. It's not easy to succeed in business. According to the U.S. Department of Commerce, out of every 10 small businesses that opened last year, only seven ***prospered.*** Only two will remain after five years.

   were successful _____

2. How can you get ahead of the competition? First, you need to develop a business plan and clearly ***envisage*** how you will make money, what your expenses will be, and what will make your business unique or superior.

   _____

3. After you develop a strong, thought-out plan, it's time to deal with finances. Best advice: ***Promote*** your business by using your own savings or asking for a loan from the bank.

   _____

4. It's better to scrape together your last cent than to borrow from family or friends, even if they give you ***license*** to do so. (Even if you are able to pay them back, it won't be for years, and this can create conflict.)

   _____

5. If possible, take a partner. Many people find that a partner helps them *retain* their enthusiasm in difficult times and reminds them of what is important. No one can do everything.

_____

6. Location, location, location! Choose your community carefully and, once you are there, steer clear of any *issue* that divides the people of the community.

_____

7. Don't undercharge, but be flexible about pricing. You need to receive appropriate *compensation* for your work in order to make your business pay.

_____

8. Do workers expect health insurance, paid holidays, other benefits? A certain amount of *benevolence* in an employer helps to maintain staff loyalty and efficiency.

_____

9. Don't fail to ask for business benefits! *Lobby* for tax credits and zoning privileges with the local government.

_____

10. Be sure to maintain a positive image of your company. Mindless, *insipid* advertising can make clients turn away.

_____

11. Hire an accountant to help with contracts and taxes. The *emphasis* should be on keeping clear records and saving important papers.

_____

12. Remember that running a business takes long hours, a willingness to learn, and lots of luck. Business studies *cite* many more business flops than successes in current conditions.

_____

13. However, the rewards of success—being your own boss, *surpassing* your own expectations, feeling a sense of accomplishment—are more than worth the risks.

_____

■■■■■■■■■■■■■■■■■■■■■■■■■■■■■■■■■ *GO TO* MyEnglishLab *FOR MORE VOCABULARY PRACTICE.*

You are going to read an article about how an entrepreneur[1] created a successful business. Read the question and discuss your answer with a partner.

Is a CEO with a humanitarian vision more or less likely to succeed in business than a CEO without such a vision?

Keep your discussion in mind as you read this article from *The Economist*.

---

[1] **entrepreneur**: someone who starts a company, arranges business deals, and takes risks in order to make a profit

HOWARD SCHULTZ'S FORMULA FOR STARBUCKS®

The Economist

1   **STARBUCKS®** knows it cannot ignore its critics. Anti-globalization protesters have occasionally trashed[1] its coffee shops. Posh[2] neighborhoods in San Francisco and London have resisted the opening of new branches, and the company is a favorite target of Internet critics. Mr. Schultz is watchful, but relaxed: "We have to be extremely mindful of the public's view of things. . . . Thus far, we've done a pretty good job."

2   The reason, argues Mr. Schultz, is that the company has **retained** a "passion" for coffee and a "sense of humanity." Starbucks® buys expensive beans and pays the owners—whether they are in Guatemala or Ethiopia—an average of 23% above the market price. A similar **benevolence** applies to company employees. Where other corporations try to eliminate the burden of employee benefits, Starbucks® gives all employees working at least 20 hours a week a package that includes stock options

("Bean Stock") and comprehensive health insurance. For Mr. Schultz, raised in a Brooklyn housing project,[3] this health insurance—which now costs the company more than coffee—is a moral obligation. At the age of seven, he came home to find his father, a truck driver, in a plaster cast, having

slipped and broken an ankle. No insurance, no **compensation**, and then no job.

3   Hence, what amounts to a personal crusade. Most of America's corporate chiefs steer clear of the sensitive topic of health care reform. Not Mr. Schultz. He makes speeches, **lobbies** politicians, and has even hosted a commercial-free hour of television,

---

[1] **trashed:** completely destroyed

[2] **posh:** elegant, expensive (e.g., rich people live in "posh" neighborhoods)

[3] **housing project:** an apartment development subsidized by the government for low income families

arguing for the reform of a system that he thinks is both socially unjust and a burden on corporate America. Meanwhile, the company pays its workers' premiums,[4] even as each year they rise by double-digit percentages. The goal has always been "to build the sort of company that my father was never able to work for." By this he means a company that "remains small even as it gets big," treating its workers as individuals. Starbucks® is not alone in its **emphasis** on "social responsibility," but the other firms Mr. Schultz **cites** off the top of his head—Timberland, Patagonia, Whole Foods—are much smaller than Starbucks®, which has 100,000 employees and 35 million customers.

Why Size Matters

4   Indeed, size has been an **issue** from the beginning. Starbucks®, named after the first mate in Herman Melville's *Moby Dick*,[5] was created in 1971 in Seattle's Pike Place market by three hippyish[6] coffee enthusiasts. Mr. Schultz, whose first "decent cup of coffee" was in 1979, joined the company in 1982 and then left it in 1985 after the founding trio, preferring to stay small, took fright at his vision of the future. Inspired by a visit to Milan in 1983, he had **envisaged** a chain of coffee bars where customers would chat over their espressos and capuccinos. Mr. Schultz set up a company he called "Il Giornale," which grew to a modest three coffee bars. Somehow scraping together $3.8 million dollars, he bought Starbucks® from its founders in 1987.

5   Reality long ago **surpassed** the dream. Since Starbucks® went public in 1992, its stock has soared by some 6,400%. The company is now in 37 different countries. China, which has over 200 stores, will be the biggest market after America, and Russia, Brazil, and India are all in line to be colonized over the next three years. The long-term goal is to double the number of American outlets to 15,000—not least by opening coffee shops along highways—and to have an equal number abroad.

6   No doubt the coffee snobs will blanch at[7] the prospect. Yet they miss three points. The first is that, thanks to Starbucks®, today's Americans are no longer condemned to drink the **insipid**, over-percolated brew that their parents endured. The second, less recognized, is that because Starbucks® has created a mass taste for good coffee, small, family-owned coffee houses have also **prospered**.

7   The most important point, however, is that Mr. Schultz's Starbucks® cultivates a relationship with its customers. Its stores sell carefully selected (no hiphop, but plenty of world music and jazz) CD-compilations. Later this year, the store will **promote** a new film and take a share of the profits. There are plans to promote books. Customers can even pay with their Starbucks® "Duetto" Visa card.

(continued on next page)

---

[4] **premiums:** money amounts paid to maintain insurance policies

[5] *Moby Dick*: one of the most famous American novels, written by Herman Melville (1819–1891)

[6] **hippyish:** representative of the "hippy" generation of the 1960s; inclined to be unconventional

[7] **blanch at:** suddenly become "pale" because you are shocked

8   Apart from some health scare that would bracket coffee with nicotine, there is no obvious reason why Starbucks® should fail, however ambitious its plans and however misconceived the occasional project (a magazine called "Joe" flopped after three issues, and the Mazagran soft drink, developed with Pepsi, was also a failure). Mr. Schultz says, "I think we have the **license** from our customers to do more." The key is that each Starbucks® coffee house should remain "a third place," between home and work, fulfilling the same role as those Italian coffee houses that so inspired him 23 years ago.

MAIN IDEAS

1 Look again at the Preview on page 130. How did your ideas help you understand the article?

2 Answer each of the questions in one or two sentences. Share your answers with a partner.

1. How did the family background and experiences of CEO Howard Schultz influence his company's policies?

_____

_____

_____

_____

2. What are two ways that Howard Schultz puts "social responsibility" into practice?

_____

_____

_____

_____

3. How does size influence Starbucks® success?

_____

_____

_____

_____

4. What is the "coffee culture" of Starbucks®?

_____

_____

_____

_____

DETAILS

All the statements below are false. Correct them in the space provided. Then compare your answers with a partner's.

1. Howard Schultz was the founder of Starbucks®.

Howard Schultz joined the company in 1982, 11 years after it was founded.

2. Since he joined the company, Schultz has been its unquestioned leader.

_____

3. Most corporate leaders speak out on the topic of health care reform.

_____

4. All workers in Starbucks® stores get health insurance from the company.

_____

5. Giving employees health benefits does not cost Schultz very much.

_____

(continued on next page)

6. Starbucks® pays $23 more than the market price for coffee beans.

_____

7. The biggest market for Starbucks® is China.

_____

8. There are now 15,000 Starbucks® outlets in the United States.

_____

9. The name Starbucks® comes from the name of one of the founders of the company.

_____

10. Starbucks® is the only U.S. corporation that emphasizes social responsibility.

_____

MAKE INFERENCES

INTERPRETING THE AUTHOR'S INTENTION

When authors put information within dashes, they usually have two possible reasons:

- to provide additional information as support
- to express an opinion related to the focus of the sentence.

Look at the examples and read the explanations.

1. Starbucks® gives a benefits package—including health insurance—even to part-time employees.

    Author's intention: a. to provide additional information   OR b. to praise Starbucks® for giving this package

The answer is *a.* The author is simply providing more information about the package.

2. "The long-term goal is to double the number of American outlets to 15,000—not least by opening coffee shops along highways—and to have an equal number abroad" (*paragraph 5*).

    Author's intention: a. to provide additional information OR b. to show that Starbucks® is very determined to expand

The answer is *b.* It is very unusual to have first-class coffee shops on highways, but opening stores there is an important part of Starbuck's effort to expand.

Read these sentences from the article. Decide what the author's intention is in using dashes. Circle *a* or *b*. Compare your answers with a partner's.

1. "For Mr. Schultz, raised in a Brooklyn housing project, this health insurance—which now costs the company more than coffee—is a moral obligation." *(paragraph 2)*

   Author's intention:

   a. to provide additional facts for the reader

   b. to show how expensive, yet necessary, this moral obligation is

2. "Starbucks® buys expensive beans and pays the owners—whether they are in Guatemala or Ethiopia—an average of 23% above the market price." *(paragraph 2)*

   Author's Intention:

   a. to provide the names of two countries that export coffee beans

   b. to show that Starbucks® doesn't take advantage of poorer countries by paying less for coffee beans

3. "Starbucks® is not alone in its emphasis on 'social responsibility,' but the other firms Mr. Schultz cites off the top of his head—Timberland, Patagonia, Whole Foods—are much smaller than Starbucks®, which has 100,000 employees and 35 million customers." *(paragraph 3)*

   Author's Intention:

   a. to provide examples of other firms that emphasize "social responsibility"

   b. to give publicity to these companies that also demonstrate "social responsibility"

EXPRESS OPINIONS

Discuss the questions in a small group. Share your group's conclusions with the rest of the class.

1. Do you agree that businesses have a responsibility to their employees? Would you like to work for a company like Starbucks®? How important would its social policies be in influencing your decision? What other factors would influence your decision?

2. Do you think employees have a responsibility to the company they work for? If so, explain what kind of responsibility.

3. Starbucks® "diversifies" by selling products other than coffee, such as CDs and books. Do you agree that diversification is a good business practice? Why or why not? Can such a practice have its limitations?

■■■■■■■■■■■■■■■■■■■■■■■■■■■ *GO TO* MyEnglishLab *TO GIVE YOUR OPINION ABOUT ANOTHER QUESTION.*

READ

1 Look at the boldfaced words and phrases in the reading and think about the questions.

1. Which words or phrases do you know the meanings of?

2. Can you use any of the words or phrases in a sentence?

2 Read the article from the *New York Times*. As you read, notice the boldfaced vocabulary. Try to guess the meanings of the words through the context.

SWIPING AT INDUSTRY

Floyd Norris (*New York Times*)

1 Wal-Mart is under attack for paying too little, providing benefits that are too small, and even exploiting illegal immigrants. Laws have been written with Wal-Mart in mind and more are being proposed. The company may not appreciate the honor, but its place in the political debate reflects its revolutionary effect on the American economy. Put simply, the big winners as the economy changes have often been scary to many, particularly to those with a stake in the old economic order being torn asunder. "Twice as many Americans shop in Wal-Mart over the course of a year as voted in the last Presidential election," said H. Lee Scott, Jr. the company's chief executive. Wal-Mart's success reflects its ability to charge less for a wide variety of goods. That arguably has reduced inflation and made the economy more efficient. It has introduced innovations in managing inventory and shipping goods.

2 But Wal-Mart's success has brought pain to others. The company has been blamed for destroying downtown as shoppers desert local merchants for the big-box store. Local newspapers lost some of their best advertisers. "That may not influence news coverage," said Alex Jones, director of the Shorenstein Center on the Press, Politics, and Public Policy at Harvard, "but I don't think you will see many editorials **blasting** the government for **taking on** Wal-Mart." The company's ability to negotiate good deals from suppliers, some of which would probably go out of business if Wal-Mart walked away, has also created anxiety and resentment, both among the suppliers and among merchants who complain that Wal-Mart gets better deals.

3 It has **infuriated** unions by opposing the organization of its employees—even to the point of closing a Canadian store whose workers voted for a union. (The company said the closure was not related to that vote.) In some locations, unions have been forced to agree to reductions in wages and benefits at other stores because they must lower costs to compete with the giant.[1]

---

[1] In the United States, many supermarket employees belong to unions that negotiate collectively with employers for higher wages and better working conditions. Wal-Mart's competitors often have to cut wages in order to compete.

4   Opponents say some Wal-Mart® employees are paid wages so low that they can still qualify for government Medicaid[2] health insurance and call that a government **subsidy** for a company that is forcing down pay for workers at other companies.

5   But the fact that Wal-Mart® has more shoppers than any politician has voters shows that many of those workers—and many people higher on the income scale–find its prices **irresistible**. That group no doubt includes some of the company's critics.

6   Wal-Mart® has been on the defensive in some legislative chambers. Maryland adopted legislation intended to force the company to spend more on health insurance, but that was **struck down** by a federal judge. Chicago passed legislation to force the company to raise its wages.

7   Wal-Mart® is one of the most successful companies in the world, but last week it reported a decline in quarterly profits for the first time in a decade, partly because of problems with its international business and partly because competitors are getting better.

---

[2] **Medicaid:** a government program, paid for by taxpayers, that provides health care to the poor

COMPREHENSION

Complete the sentences based on your understanding of the reading. Then compare your answers with a partner's.

1. Wal-Mart® has been criticized for _____

_____.

2. Wal-Mart® has been able to achieve marketing success because_____

_____.

3. Local newspapers do not support Wal-Mart® because_____

_____.

4. According to Wal-Mart's® opponents, _____

_____.

5. Wal-Mart® may have to reconsider some of its policies because_____

_____.

GO TO MyEnglishLab *FOR MORE VOCABULARY PRACTICE.*

READING SKILL

1 Reread Reading Two. Underline sentences that give reasons why Wal-Mart® is criticized and why Wal-Mart® is successful.

NOTE-TAKING: COMPARING THE POSITIVE AND THE NEGATIVE

Taking notes allows you to identify the important ideas in the reading. It also helps you to review material for future study.

Note-taking is especially helpful when you have a particular focus, such as preparing for a debate about the positive and negative aspects of a company's reputation or for an essay about a company's success and what the company has done to achieve it. This kind of note-taking strategy is especially effective in the preparation of an advantages and disadvantages essay.

Look at the example and read the information.

In what category (**Criticism of Wal-Mart®** or **Evidence of Wal-Mart's® Success**) would you put these notes?

very large customer base / no health insurance for workers / wages too low

Answer:

CRITICISM OF WAL-MART®	EVIDENCE OF WAL-MART'S® SUCCESS
- *no health insurance for workers*	- *very large customer base*
- *wages too low*	

2 Work with a partner. Put the notes from the reading in the proper categories in the chart on the next page.

- hires illegals
- laws can't force them to pay better wages
- anti-union policy
- offers low prices everyone wants
- competition with Wal-Mart® pushing down wages in other companies
- other retailers forced out

- workers so poor they need government aid through Medicaid—taxpayers subsidize Wal-Mart®
- revolutionized the economy
- gets unfair deals from suppliers
- newspapers lose advertising
- innovations in inventory management and shipping

CRITICISM OF WAL-MART®	EVIDENCE OF WAL-MART'S® SUCCESS
wages are too low no health insurance for workers	very large customer base

■■ *GO TO* MyEnglishLab *FOR MORE SKILL PRACTICE.*

CONNECT THE READINGS

STEP 1: Organize

Work with a partner. Review Reading One (R1) and Reading Two (R2) and complete the chart with notes, giving relevant facts for all the categories. Use separate paper if you need more space.

	STARBUCKS® (R1)	WAL-MART® (R2)
COMPANY INNOVATIONS AND DEMAND FOR THE PRODUCT	35 million customers; has increased interest in taste of good coffee	
CRITICISM OF THE COMPANY		exploits illegal immigrants; destroys downtown areas; local stores lose business and have to close; local newspapers lose advertisers; employee organizations angry
RESPONSE TO THE COMMUNITY AND EMPLOYEES	great benefit packages for employees; reaches out to interest of customers by selling CD compilations, promoting new film and great books, and offering Duetto Visa credit card	
FINANCIAL SUCCESS AND SIZE		one of the most successful companies in the world

STEP 2: Synthesize

Work with a partner. You are a financial investment counselor. Your client is interested in investing in either Starbucks® or Wal-Mart® and has asked you for advice. Decide which company would be a better investment. Using the notes you have collected in Step 1, complete a report explaining your decision. Use a separate piece of paper. You can start your report this way:

Dear Client,

You have expressed an interest in investing in one of two companies: either Starbucks® or

Wal-Mart®. Please find below a report explaining why we feel _____ would be a

better addition to your investment portfolio.

There are several reasons why we feel that _____ would be the better choice. ....

Although _____ is also an interesting company, we did not recommend it for the

following reasons. ....

We hope that this analysis will be helpful to you in making your decision. Please feel free to

consult with us at any time. When you have made your decision, we will be glad to help with

your investment needs.

Sincerely,

Chandler and Smith
Investment Counselors

GO TO MyEnglishLab TO CHECK WHAT YOU LEARNED.

VOCABULARY

REVIEW

Fill in the blanks with words from the box.

blasted	infuriated	lobbied	prospering	subsidies
envisaged	license	promote	retain	take on

Corporate Responsibility: The Fall of Enron

How many business students still believe that "morality has nothing to do with business"?

The story of Enron's fall from the seventh largest U.S. corporation to the largest corporate

bankruptcy in U.S. history should make future MBAs more mindful of their responsibilities to

_____ the interests of the community.
     1.

Enron, a Texas energy corporation, overstated its profits, hid its burden of debt, and became

the symbol of a corporate culture of greed and corruption that _____ the public.
                                                        2.

One method Enron used was to make it seem that the company was _____ by
                                                              3.

moving their losses to fake companies that did not appear on the Enron accounts. The company

was determined to _____ its reputation on Wall Street (and a high price for its
                                          4.

stock) at any cost.

One of Enron's worst schemes _____ aggressively using "mark-to-market"
                                                        5.

techniques. If the company made a deal that promised to earn $10 million in ten years, the

executives felt that gave them _____ to mark the money as profit already made.
                                          6.

These often imaginary profits were used as _____ to top executives in the form of
                                                         7.

huge bonuses.

(continued on next page)

Most shocking was the fact that Enron traders dared to _____ the state of
8.
California. They created the California energy crisis to drive up the price of energy, costing

California more than $6 billion in overcharges. Many people blame the California crisis on the

fact that the government in Washington took away the strict regulations that used to control energy

companies. Enron vigorously _____ lawmakers for that deregulation.
9.

In the company's last year, Enron's executives were selling off their stock as fast as they could

to make sure that their personal finances would steer clear of the collapse. CEO Jeff Skilling

made $200 million selling his stock, while at the same time encouraging employees and workers

not to sell. Twenty thousand workers lost their jobs, their pensions, and their savings. When an

employee, Sherrin Watkins, alerted the government, the press _____ the company,
10.
and the courts sent Jeff Skilling to prison.

EXPAND

Go back to the readings to see how the expressions are used. Then read the sentences below,
using those expressions and related expressions, and discuss their meanings with a partner.

1. **steer clear** *(R1, paragraph 3)* / **steering committee** / **steer**

   a. Our company should STEER CLEAR of all wrongdoing.

   b. The STEERING COMMITTEE of our firm has decided to hire four more office employees.

   c. If we are not careful, he will STEER this company in the wrong direction with those dangerous policies.

2. **off the top of his head** *(R1, paragraph 3)* / **top an offer** / **top-down** / **top-drawer**

   a. The company director was able to tell us their profit statistics right OFF THE TOP OF HIS HEAD.

   b. We can TOP THAT OFFER by $500 a share.

   c. This was a TOP-DOWN company, where ordinary workers had no say in policy decisions.

   d. The law firm deals only with TOP-DRAWER clients and provides specialized advice for their lifestyle.

3. **scrape together** *(R1, paragraph 4)* / **scrape / scrape the bottom of the barrel / scrape the surface**

   a. We'll have to SCRAPE TOGETHER every last dime we own to make the debt payments.

   b. This employee is a troublemaker and gets into too many SCRAPES with other employees.

   c. You're SCRAPING THE BOTTOM OF THE BARREL when you bring up such a ridiculous argument.

   d. Your report barely SCRAPED THE SURFACE of the many issues involved in this sale.

4. **swipe / swipe your card / take a swipe at** *(R2, title)*

   a. Don't SWIPE anything from the supermarket because you'll get in trouble for stealing.

   b. Please SWIPE YOUR I.D. CARD as you enter the building.

   c. The author TAKES A SWIPE AT Wal-Mart® for some of its employment practices.

5. **strike down** *(R2, paragraph 6)* / **strike out on one's own / on strike**

   a. The judge decided to STRIKE DOWN the city law against globalization protestors because it went against the Constitution's guarantee of free speech.

   b. I didn't want to work for someone else any more, so I decided to STRIKE OUT ON MY OWN.

   c. When union workers are not satisfied with their working conditions, they can go out ON STRIKE.

CREATE

Howard Schultz of Starbucks® and Rob Walton, the Chairman of the Board of Wal-Mart®, have come to the campus for a discussion about business. Write the script for this interview. Use at least eight of the expressions in the box.

~~benevolent~~	emphasis	issue	scrape together
blasted	envisage	lobby	steer clear of
cite	infuriated	~~prospered~~	surpass
compensation	irresistible	retain	take on

INTERVIEWER: Thank you both for coming here today to speak to our students. Mr. Schultz, you are the leader of a mega-company that has *prospered* with 100,000 employees and more than 35 million customers. Yet you say that your company has to be mindful of its customers and "think small." What do you mean?

SCHULTZ: _____

_____

INTERVIEWER: What about you, Mr. Walton? You are the CEO of Wal-Mart®, the world's largest retailer. How does size matter for your company?

WALTON: _____

_____

INTERVIEWER: Mr. Schultz, you are known as a generally *benevolent* employer. Can you explain to us about "socially responsible business"?

SCHULTZ: _____

_____

GO TO MyEnglishLab *FOR MORE VOCABULARY PRACTICE.*

GRAMMAR

1 Examine the underlined words in the sentences and discuss the questions with a partner.

- Wal-Mart® has the ability <u>to charge</u> less for a wide variety of goods.
- Wal-Mart® is committed to <u>introducing</u> innovations in inventory management.

1. What form is underlined in the first sentence?

2. What form is underlined in the second sentence?

3. Why are these forms used?

COMMON USES OF INFINITIVES AND GERUNDS

The Infinitive

The **infinitive** (*to* + **verb**; *to play, to watch*) is commonly used:

1. When it answers the questions "Why?" or "For what purpose?"
   - Schultz bought Starbucks® **to get** Americans used to good coffee.
2. In certain verb + infinitive + object patterns
   - Employees sometimes **try to force** Wal-Mart® to accept a union.
3. After many adjectives
   - A socially responsible company is more **willing to spend** money for employees' health benefits.
4. After certain expressions

   Many expressions are followed by the infinitive when "*to do* what?" is the answer that the infinitive gives the reader or the listener. In the sentence "He had the opportunity to work in another country," the infinitive *to work* tells us "what" he had "the opportunity *to do*." Here is a list of expressions that follow this pattern:

be ready	have a tendency
be required	have the time
have the ability / have an inability	have the will
have the courage	it is difficult
have the opportunity	it is easy
have the option	it is economical
have the right	it is practical

(continued on next page)

The Gerund

The **gerund** (a verb form ending in *-ing* used as a noun; *playing, watching*) is commonly used:

1. After such verbs as *avoid, consider, enjoy, favor, include, involve, spend*
   - Wal-Mart® should *consider* **changing** its salary scale if it wants to receive less criticism about its policies.
   - Starbucks® now *spends* a lot of time **promoting** music.

2. After all prepositions (for example, ***about, from, in, to, with***)
   - The CEO was concerned *about* **making** a profit.

3. After certain expressions

   Many expressions are followed by the gerund because they end with prepositions (for example, "have a commitment *to going*," "be concerned *about going*," "be interested *in going*"). The rule regarding the use of gerunds after all prepositions is simple to apply if you remember that the preposition is "a part of" the expression. Thus, in the sentence, "He was committed to *going* back to school," the gerund (*going*) is used because the *to* is part of the expression.

   Because it is difficult to remember which expressions end in prepositions, here is a list:

be accustomed to	choose between / among
be committed to / have a commitment to	deal with
be concerned about	have (no) difficulty (in)*
be dedicated to	have (no) experience (in)*
be devoted to	have (no) luck (in)*
be interested in	have (no) trouble (in)*
be involved in	insist on
be responsible for / have the responsibility of	look forward to
	object to
	plan on

*Even when these expressions are used without the preposition, they are followed by the gerund.

2 Read the letter addressed to a management trainee in a large company. Underline the gerunds and the infinitives first. Then list the verbs or expressions on page 148 that take the infinitive and those that take the gerund.

CHANDLER, ADAMS, AND WENTWORTH, ACCOUNTING

Dear Ms. Rachel Smith,

You have been working with our company for two years. During that time, you have provided excellent service to the firm. We are interested in <u>maximizing</u> the potential of our most promising new recruits. It is my pleasure to inform you that you have been chosen to receive one of our management trainee scholarships. We would like you to consider applying to an MBA program dedicated to preparing accounting and financial officers.

We are committed to offering you a full tuition grant for the MBA program of your choice. Because you already have experience working in the business world, we are sure that you will make the most of this opportunity to improve your understanding of the financial field. Please consider applying to schools that offer evening and weekend classes in our area. Prior to entering any program, you will need the approval of our Board of Directors, which reserves the right to advise you on these questions.

We hope you will accept our offer, and we look forward to hearing from you soon.

Sincerely,
Jonathan Weiss
Management Trainee Program

Expressions with Infinitives

1. _____

2. _____

3. _____

Expressions with Gerunds

1. _interested in maximizing_____

2. _____

3. _____

4. _____

5. _____

6. _____

7. _____

8. _____

3 Using the expressions listed on pages 145 and 146 and used in Exercise 2, write seven sentences about why you would or would not like to have a career in business. Use a separate piece of paper.

1. _____

_____

2. _____

_____

3. _____

_____

4. _____

_____

5. _____

_____

6. _____

_____

7. _____

_____

4 Complete the essay with either the gerund or the infinitive of the verb in parentheses.

The Advantages and Disadvantages of Private Business Schools

Students thinking of _____ business careers are required
1. (pursue)

_____ four to five years of work experience in the business world before
2. (have)

they begin an M.B.A. program. When they are ready _____ to school, it is
3. (return)

important for them _____ thorough research on each school that interests them.
4. (do)

Because M.B.A. candidates in the United States can choose between _____
5. (study)

at some excellent public and private institutions, part of the decision-making process involves

_____ whether to enroll in a private or public institution. M.B.A. candidates who
6. (decide)

plan _____ at large multinational corporations should make every effort to attend
7. (work)

a top private school. Despite the high tuition costs of private business schools, they provide more

competitive learning environments and more job placement opportunities in the private sector.

BODY

The disadvantages of private institutions are easy _____. Although private
8. (identify)

schools meet the needs of students who hope _____ for large multinational
9. (work)

corporations, what they offer comes at a great cost. The price of a two-year program at a top

private business school can cost more than $100,000, while an M.B.A. program in a public school

costs less than half that amount. There is no doubt that the very high costs of private business

schools discourage many M.B.A. candidates from _____. Being faced with such
10. (apply)

a large debt is seen as a definite disadvantage despite the advantages of a competitive private

school.

Competition attracts the best students, who compete _____ at the most
11. (enroll)

expensive private business schools. Some of the top private schools can review as many as 8,000

applications in a given year, but no more than 15 percent of the applicants are usually admitted.

(continued on next page)

Connected to this more competitive feature of the student profile is the diversity of the student population. Private institutions devote a lot of time and energy to _____ a diverse
12. (select)
representation of students from all geographic areas of the United States and the world. This international "flavor" is also reflected in the fact that private school students have the opportunity

_____ in a great number of study abroad and internship programs with
13. (participate)
multinational corporations. Studying in a competitive environment with the brightest students, both male and female, from many diverse backgrounds, provides private business students with valuable insights and international experience.

These diverse insights and experiences are appreciated by the multinational corporations who

favor _____ at the top private schools. In a given year, hundreds of recruiters come
14. (recruit)
to private school campuses _____ students. Not only do private school students
15. (interview)
have superb job placement opportunities, but they often receive higher paying job offers: The average starting salary for private school students can go as high as $150,000.

CONCLUSION

Studying for an M.B.A. degree at a top private school provides students with definite

advantages. Students who decide not _____ a private institution because of
16. (select)
the cost alone may be making a serious mistake because they may be able to earn back the initial investment quickly and have a higher-paying job at the same time. After a few years of

_____ for a large multinational corporation, their loans will be paid back, and the
17. (work)
advantages of their choice of a private business school will become clear.

■■■■■■■■■■■■■■■■■■ GO TO MyEnglishLab FOR MORE GRAMMAR PRACTICE AND TO CHECK WHAT YOU LEARNED.

FINAL WRITING TASK

In this unit, you read articles discussing two well-known businesses, Starbucks® and Wal-Mart®.

*You will **write an essay in response to this question: What are the advantages and disadvantages of large chain stores and multinational corporations?** Use the vocabulary and grammar from the unit.**

PREPARE TO WRITE: Brainstorming

1 Work in groups. Write down notes in the chart that point to the advantages and disadvantages of chain stores and large multinational companies. Use examples from the two readings as well as your own ideas.

Advantages

1. can offer many jobs (100,000 in Starbucks®)
2. can help change the culture (support for national health care like Starbucks®)
3.
4.
5.
6.
7.
8.

Disadvantages

1. get trashed by anti-globalization activists
2. often pay employees too little; benefits too small
3.
4.
5.
6.
7.
8.

2 Examine your lists to identify common categories to which your thoughts belong. Group the various ideas under their respective categories. Try to find at least four categories.

1. _Making the economy more efficient_
2. _____
3. _____
4. _____

---

* For Alternative Writing Topics, see page 157. These topics can be used in place of the writing topic for this unit or as homework. The alternative topics relate to the theme of the unit, but may not target the same grammar or rhetorical structures taught in the unit.

WRITE: An Essay Showing Advantages and Disadvantages

1 Reread the essay on pages 149–150 and discuss the questions with a partner.

    1. What is the writer's purpose in this essay?

    2. Underline the thesis statement. According to the thesis statement, will the writer's focus in the essay be on the advantages or on the disadvantages?

    3. Which body paragraph(s) deals with the advantages, and which body paragraph(s) deals with the disadvantages?

    4. In the body paragraphs, what kind of support does the writer provide?

    5. How does the writer show the logical connection between one topic and another?

    6. Is the message in the concluding paragraph expected or unexpected? Why?

2 Read the information in the box and then complete the exercises.

PURPOSE OF ESSAYS SHOWING ADVANTAGES AND DISADVANTAGES

Essays about advantages and disadvantages are similar to comparison and contrast essays, but there are some special points to remember.

- The aim of this kind of essay is to persuade, not simply to inform. You should *not* merely list the positive and negative aspects of the subject in a neutral way. You should take a stand.

- Your thesis statement should therefore take a clear position: Do the advantages outweigh the disadvantages, or are the disadvantages more important than the advantages?

- If the thesis statement states that the advantages are more important, then the body of the essay will devote relatively more space to the advantages. Conversely, if the thesis is focused on the disadvantages, that aspect will take up relatively more space in the essay than the advantages.

- The essay must provide enough support for the thesis so that the main points will be clearly justified and explained. As in all essays, the use of good transitions between the points under discussion ensures this clarity.

Thesis Statement

As you learned in Unit 2, the thesis statement communicates the main idea of the essay. It reflects the writer's focus and point of view, attitude, or opinion, and it also forecasts which aspects of the subject the writer will discuss to support the thesis in the body of the essay.

---

3 Examine the thesis statement from the essay on pages 149–150. Answer the questions.

Despite the high tuition costs of private business schools, they provide more competitive learning environments and more job placement opportunities in the private sector.

1. Is this an adequate thesis statement for an advantages and disadvantages essay? Why or why not?

   _____

   _____

2. The thesis tells the reader that the body paragraphs of the essay will deal with certain subjects. What are they?

   a. _____

   b. _____

   c. _____

4 In your notebook, write an outline for an essay showing the advantages and disadvantages of large chain stores and large multinational corporations. Follow the steps:

   • Use the guidelines for point-by-point outline organization on page 118 (Unit 4).

   • Write your thesis statement.

5 Using what you have learned about writing advantages and disadvantages essays, write an essay about the advantages and disadvantages of large chain stores and multinational corporations. Refer to the work you did in Prepare to Write and Write, pages 151–153, to write your first draft.

REVISE: Using Transitional Sentences

Transitional sentences show the logical connection between topics under discussion. Transitions may be needed within a paragraph ("internal transitions") or between paragraphs. When a transitional sentence connects the ideas of one body paragraph to the ideas of another body paragraph, the transitional sentence can be placed at the beginning of a paragraph (as a topic sentence) or at the end of a paragraph (as a concluding sentence). Transitions are especially important in essays showing advantages and disadvantages because the reader must be able to notice the shift between positive and negative factors.

1 Go back to the essay on pages 149–150. First underline the transitional sentences connecting the body paragraphs in the text. Then underline the internal transitional sentence in body paragraph 2.

2 These two paragraphs come from the first draft of an essay on "The Advantages and Disadvantages of Being Self-Employed." Important transitional sentences are missing. Work with a partner. Review the list of choices on the next page and mark them ✔ (acceptable) or **X** (unacceptable). There can be more than one "acceptable" sentence in each set of choices. Then discuss your answers. Place the letters of your choices for each transitional sentence on the lines provided in these paragraphs in the essay.

Being self-employed permits a certain freedom that supports the development of a free spirit. Because there is no one in authority telling the self-employed person what to do, he or she enjoys a lot of independence. With independence, the individual is more willing to take risks. If a mistake is made, it is not the end of the world; something valuable will be learned from the experience. This passion for experimentation leads to creative undertakings. **(1)** _____. If he or she does not allow room or time for creativity as the business evolves, there will be no opportunity to place an original stamp on the product that is being marketed. Since the self-employed person has agreed to assume sole responsibility for his or her fate, creativity is an essential ingredient for future success.

(2) _____. Because the self-employed person is at the same time both employer and employee, there is no safety net to "catch" him or her if he or she falls, and the financial and psychological stress that may be experienced can be a true test of nerves. That is why the individual must be assertive and yet humble enough to seek advice from financial consultants and mental health care professionals in order to be able to deal with these potential problems. **(3)** _____. Good character in an individual can be seen in his or her strong personality, ethics, positive self-image, willingness to bend and appreciate the value of other people's ideas, along with the determination to work hard and achieve success. Only someone with many such qualities can effectively respond to the challenges that come with being self-employed.

1. Choices for Internal Transition of Paragraph 1

   _____ **a.** Linked, therefore, to the self-employed person's independence is the individual's great potential for creativity.

   _____ **b.** Can anyone doubt that creativity is the next step on the path to success in business dealings?

   _____ **c.** Whether or not these creative urges come to fruition, they are an essential ingredient in success.

2. Choices for Topic Sentence of Paragraph 2

   _____ **a.** Another undeniable problem facing an entrepreneur in the creation of a startup company is the financial burden.

   _____ **b.** But creativity is not enough; a future businessperson must be strong in many other ways.

   _____ **c.** Despite the benefits that accompany independence and creativity, we must not forget that a self-employed person must cope with a great financial and psychological burden.

3. Choices for Internal Transition of Paragraph 2

   _____ **a.** In this sense, going into business for yourself is a true test of character.

   _____ **b.** Undoubtedly, the ability to respond to these stresses requires many positive character traits.

   _____ **c.** Even though independence is a great benefit, being in business is very stressful.

3 Look at the draft of your essay. Does it have transitional sentences to guide the reader from one "topic" to another? If not, revise your essay accordingly.

■■■■■■■■■■■■■■■■■■■■■■■■■■■■■■■■■■■■■■ *GO TO* MyEnglishLab *FOR MORE SKILL PRACTICE.*

EDIT: Writing the Final Draft

Go to MyEnglishLab and write the final draft of your essay. Carefully edit it for grammatical and mechanical errors, such as spelling, capitalization, and punctuation. Make sure you use some of the grammar and vocabulary from the unit. Use the checklist on the next page to help you write your final draft. Then submit your essay to your teacher.

FINAL DRAFT CHECKLIST

❑ Does your essay have an effective introduction, three or more body paragraphs, and a strong conclusion?

❑ Is it obvious from the thesis statement whether the advantages outweigh the disadvantages or the disadvantages outweigh the advantages?

❑ Does the thesis statement forecast the specific topics that are to be covered in the body paragraphs of the essay?

❑ Do the paragraphs have transitional sentences that effectively show the reader the logical connection between topics?

❑ Are the gerunds and infinitives used correctly?

❑ Have you used new vocabulary and expressions in the essay?

UNIT PROJECT

People's attitudes toward business can vary greatly. These attitudes may depend on their own circumstances in life as well as on the state of the economy at a particular moment. A questionnaire can help you find and compare information about people's opinions. Follow these steps:

STEP 1: Create a questionnaire to use in interviewing several people at your school about what they think of business. For instance, you might want the students you interview to consider the following questions:

1. Do people in business have to be aggressive and ambitious?

2. Is corruption a common problem in business?

3. Should businesses be socially responsible to the community?

Work in groups. First discuss what you think of business. Then write at least five *Yes / No* opinion questions that you would like to have in your questionnaire.

NOTE: You may instead do research on the Internet to see what people think about business.

STEP 2: When you conduct your survey, count the *Yes* and *No* responses to each question and take notes on the comments the interviewees (the students you interview) make. You can use the following grid to write your questions, tally responses, and record comments.

QUESTIONS	YES	NO	COMMENTS
Example: Would your family be happy if you went into business?	### ///	###	• Business brings financial security. • People in business have no time for family life.
1.			
2.			
3.			
4.			
5.			

STEP 3: Write a group report on the results of your survey or your Internet research.

1. In the introduction, explain the purpose of the survey and share the questions you asked.

2. In the body, give a summary of the number of yes and no replies you received for each question and the comments the interviewees made.

3. In the conclusion, give your interpretation of the information you collected.

4. Share the results of your research with the class in an oral presentation. You can add research on the Internet that supports your conclusions.

ALTERNATIVE WRITING TOPICS

Choose one of the writing topics. Use the vocabulary and grammar from the unit. Pay special attention to transitions.

1. Do successful businesses have any civic responsibility? Do they have a responsibility to "give back" to the community in terms of jobs; contributions to social causes such as homelessness, medical research, the arts, the environment; and education? Why or why not?

2. Imagine the perfect career pattern for yourself. Would you work for several different companies, or for only one company during the course of your career? Would your career pattern involve building your own company? If so, what business would you create? Explain the steps you would take to create it.

◀▪▪▪▪▪▪▪▪▪▪▪▪■ *GO TO* MyEnglishLab *TO WRITE ABOUT ONE OF THE ALTERNATIVE TOPICS, WATCH A VIDEO ABOUT A GENEROUS BUSINESSMAN, AND TAKE THE UNIT 5 ACHIEVEMENT TEST.* ▪■▪■▪■▪■▪■▪■▪■▪■▶

STAYING
Connected

1. Do you or does someone you know use social media like Facebook, YouTube, Twitter, Google, LinkedIn, Tumblr? In what way can these sites be useful or interesting?

2. In what way can the use of social media add to or take away from the quality of life in the modern world?

3. What are the dangers associated with online communications?

GO TO MyEnglishLab *TO CHECK WHAT YOU KNOW.*

VOCABULARY

Read the definitions. In a small group, try to relate the vocabulary to these categories: **spying, legal matters, privacy,** and **personality.** Put an X in the appropriate column. Some words can fit in more than one category. Explain your choices and try to reach a group consensus.

access: the right to use something or see something	**snoop:** to try to find out private information about someone secretly
comply: to conform to the rules	**survey:** a set of questions you ask to find out people's opinions
draw the line: set a limit	
haunt: to cause problems for someone	**trait:** a particular quality in someone
monitor: to carefully watch, listen to, or examine something	**verify:** to find out if a statement is true
	vet: to check someone's past activities
pry: to find out details of someone's private life	**violation:** an action that breaks a law

	SPYING	LEGAL MATTERS	PRIVACY	PERSONALITY
1. ACCESS				
2. COMPLY				
3. DRAW THE LINE				
4. HAUNT				
5. MONITOR				
6. PRY				
7. SNOOP				
8. SURVEY				
9. TRAIT				
10. VERIFY				
11. VET				
12. VIOLATION				

GO TO MyEnglishLab *FOR MORE VOCABULARY PRACTICE.*

PREVIEW

You are going to read an article about social media and privacy invasion. Discuss the question with a partner.

How can participating in social media lead to an invasion of privacy?

Keep your response in mind as you read "Privacy Invasion and Social Media" by Ms. Smith.

Privacy Invasion and Social Media

HOME

CONTACT

ABOUT US

(Network World Blog, 03/17/12)

By Ms. Smith

(1) Much like a thinly veiled threat, some employers and colleges may suggest you "friend" them on social media—or worse, they may insist on knowing your password to Twitter, to Facebook, Google +, and other social media sites so they can see what you post, your photos, what you say in IMs, and what you chat about.

(2) Sometimes social networking comes back to **haunt** you with privacy invasion such as when attorneys **snoop** on social networks to **vet** jurors, or potential employers **pry** into social media before hiring employees. Sometimes it might be drunken posts or photos that make the difference.

(3) According to a Microsoft **survey** about the negative effects of unwise social media posts, 14% of people surveyed lost out on the college they wanted, 16% lost out on getting a job, and 21% were fired from a job.

(4) Maryland ACLU[1] legislative director Melissa Coretz Goemann stated, "This is an invasion of privacy. People have so much personal information on their pages now. A person can treat it almost like a diary. And (interviewers and schools) are also invading other people's privacy. They get **access** to that individual's posts and all their friends. There is a lot of private information there."

---

[1] **ACLU:** American Civil Liberties Union, a non-profit organization working in the courts, legislatures, and communities to defend the individual liberties guaranteed by the U.S. Constitution.

(continued on next page)

(5) Is it required? Not exactly . . . but in this rough economy people are afraid not to **comply**, afraid they will be denied employment. Whether it is employers or colleges, this type of social media **monitoring** is clearly a **violation** of the First Amendment. "I can't believe some people think it's OK to do this," Bradley Shear, a Washington D.C. lawyer, told MSNBC's Red Tape. "It's not a far leap from reading people's Facebook posts to reading their email. . . . As a society, where are we going to **draw the line**?" Excellent question.

(6) While some employers may use social media monitoring tools like Trackur or SocialIntel, colleges are getting into the act too and demanding "full access" according to Red Tape. Some colleges may use third-party companies like Varsity Monitor and UDiligence to monitor students' social media accounts on the school's behalf. The software offers "a 'reputation scoreboard' to coaches" and sends "'threat level' warnings about individual athletes to the administration."

(7) Student athletes in colleges around the country also are finding they can no longer maintain privacy in Facebook communications because schools are requiring them to "friend" a coach or administrator, giving that person access to their "friends-only" posts.

(8) Of the social media monitoring scholarship providers who answered a recent survey, nearly one-fourth vet students' social networks by searching on "sites such as Google, Facebook, LinkedIn, YouTube and Twitter to check out applicants, primarily just finalists." Of those who do snoop on social media, about 75% "are looking for behavior that could reflect badly on the scholarship provider, such as underage drinking, provocative pictures, illegal drug use, or racial slurs,"[2] reported the *San Francisco Chronicle*. More than 50% want "to know the applicant better or were looking for positive **traits** such as creativity or good communication skills." About 25% want "to **verify** information on the application." And "about one-third have denied an applicant a scholarship, and a quarter have granted an applicant a scholarship because of something they found online."

---

[2] **slurs:** offensive remarks, based on someone's race, religion, nationality, or sexual orientation

(9) The ACLU is supporting Maryland bills to protect civil liberties by restricting "university administrations from checking students' private communications." According to Southern Maryland News, Senator Ronald Young said, "This practice is stepping on constitutional rights. They don't have the right to come into your house and listen to your telephone calls or read your mail. . . . It amounts to a subtle threat." Delegate Shawn Tarrant[3] added, "Students should be able to attend college with a reasonable sense of privacy."

(10) Shear said, "A good analogy for this, in the offline world: Would it be acceptable for schools to require athletes to bug[4] their off-campus apartments? Does a school have a right to know who all your friends are?" Whether it involves employers or universities, this trend to spy via social media is troubling.

---

[4] He ia a delegate to the Maryland House of Delegates.

[3] **bug:** place a concealed microphone (in a room, telephone) to record someone's conversations

MAIN IDEAS

1 Look again at the Preview on page 161. How did your ideas help you understand the article?

2 Check off the main ideas. Share your answers with a partner.

_____ **1.** Lack of privacy on social media can be harmful.

_____ **2.** Colleges are trying to see if students are involved in illegal activities.

_____ **3.** Freedom of speech is being violated.

_____ **4.** Students are being pressured into providing private information.

_____ **5.** Employers can't hire unless they have access to a prospective employee's Facebook page.

DETAILS

For each question there are two correct answers. Cross out the incorrect answer.

1. Why is there a lot of private information on social media?

   a. people post their photos

   b. people chat about their activities

   c. social media sites spy on users

2. Why is social media snooping considered an invasion of privacy?

   a. people are entitled to freedom of speech

   b. a whole network of friends is exposed

   c. people are forced to join social media

3. Who spies on social media?

   a. employers

   b. the government

   c. universities

4. Why do they spy?

   a. to find out about potential jurors

   b. to find out about illegal activities

   c. to find out about political activity

5. How do they do it?

   a. by using companies to spy on Internet activity

   b. by paying people to gain access to their accounts

   c. by intimidating people into giving their passwords

6. According to surveys about colleges and jobs, what are the results of spying?

   a. 25% of people weren't accepted to colleges

   b. 37% of people either lost jobs or weren't hired

   c. more people lost scholarships than gained them

MAKE INFERENCES

ARGUMENT BY ANALOGY

An analogy compares one thing to another, saying they are related or similar.

Look at the example and read the explanation.

"A person can treat [social media] almost like a diary." *(paragraph 4)*

What comparison is the writer making here? What point is made by the comparison?

<u>Analogy</u>: social media = a diary

Just as we wouldn't read personal information in someone else's diary, we shouldn't spy on social media.

With this analogy, the author emphasizes the dangers of social media: People treat it as a diary, but it can be made public. Ms. Smith is highlighting the importance of the problem she is warning about. She wants the reader to realize that if the contents of an individual's most private document—his or her diary—are made public, the most intimate details of a person's life cannot remain private. The analogy therefore shows the danger of losing our right to privacy.

There are several analogies in the reading. For each analogy below, describe what is being compared. Then explain the meaning in the context of the blog article. Check your answers with a partner's.

1. "Much like a thinly veiled threat, some employers and colleges may suggest you 'friend' them on social media—or worse, they may insist on your password to Twitter, to Facebook, Google +, and other social media sites so they can see what you post, your photos, what you say in IMs, and what you chat about." *(paragraph 1)*

   Analogy:

   _____

   Explanation:

   _____

2. "It's not a far leap from reading people's Facebook posts to reading their email." *(paragraph 5)*

   Analogy:

   _____

   Explanation:

   _____

(continued on next page)

3. "A good analogy for this [social media spying], in the offline world: Would it be acceptable for schools to require athletes to bug their off-campus apartments?" *(paragraph 10)*

Analogy:

_____

Explanation:

_____

4. "A good analogy for this [social media spying], in the offline world: . . . Does a school have a right to know who all your friends are?" *(paragraph 10)*

Analogy:

_____

Explanation:

_____

EXPRESS OPINIONS

Discuss the questions in a small group. Share your group's conclusions with the rest of the class.

1. Ms. Smith's blog argues that using social media to find out about people is a violation of their rights. Her blog takes a very clear position, but the other side should be discussed, too. How would people who snoop on the Internet justify their actions and argue that they are doing the right thing?

   - What would scholarship providers say?

   - Universities?

   - Employers?

   What do you think? Which side do you agree with?

2. One point that we can take from the reading is this: What you say may be easily forgotten, but what you write or post can remain for a long time. Do you agree? What do you think people can do to protect themselves on social media?

3. In America, sports events generate a great deal of money for many colleges. Spy companies track the activities of college athletes and send "threat-level warnings" to the college administration when an athlete is getting into trouble over alcohol, driving over the speed limit, or breaking other rules. Should this focus on college athletes be allowed?

■■■■■■■■■■■■■■■■■■■■■■ *GO TO* MyEnglishLab *TO GIVE YOUR OPINION ABOUT ANOTHER QUESTION.*

READ

1 Look at the boldfaced words and phrases in the reading and think about the questions.

1. Which words and phrases do you know the meanings of?

2. Can you use any of the words or phrases in a sentence?

2 Read the passage from "Remár's Report: Using Social Networking Sites Wisely." As you read, notice the boldfaced vocabulary. Try to guess the meanings of the words through the context.

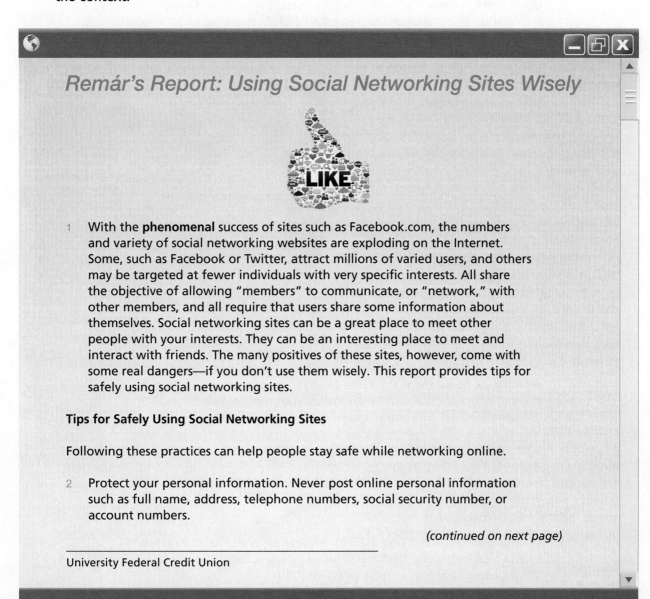

Remár's Report: Using Social Networking Sites Wisely

1   With the **phenomenal** success of sites such as Facebook.com, the numbers and variety of social networking websites are exploding on the Internet. Some, such as Facebook or Twitter, attract millions of varied users, and others may be targeted at fewer individuals with very specific interests. All share the objective of allowing "members" to communicate, or "network," with other members, and all require that users share some information about themselves. Social networking sites can be a great place to meet other people with your interests. They can be an interesting place to meet and interact with friends. The many positives of these sites, however, come with some real dangers—if you don't use them wisely. This report provides tips for safely using social networking sites.

Tips for Safely Using Social Networking Sites

Following these practices can help people stay safe while networking online.

2   Protect your personal information. Never post online personal information such as full name, address, telephone numbers, social security number, or account numbers.

(continued on next page)

University Federal Credit Union

3   Protect your identity. Information that could help someone identify you and where you live should never be posted online. For students, this includes information such as the school they attend, sports team, clubs, where they work, and where they hang out.

4   Choose your screen name carefully. Your screen name shouldn't give away too much information about you. For example, don't use your full name, your age, or your hometown. Someone could combine clues from your screen name and other information in your profile to figure out who you are and where you live.

5   Don't post anything you want to keep private. Before posting any information or material online—an email, instant message, picture, video, or blog—consider whether you want it to be read or seen by everyone. The Net is wide open. Emails can be forwarded to others by the receiver. Instant messages can be saved. Pictures can be saved and **altered**. Even if you delete information or photos, for example, from your page, they may still **reside** on another computer and they may have been posted on another site.

6   A tip: What you post online today can have an impact on your future. Some employers are checking social networking sites and other Internet sites to see what a **prospective** employee may have posted or what may have been posted about them. And an employer doesn't have to tell you if a posting was the reason you weren't hired. Some colleges and universities are also checking out what prospective students have posted.

7   Be careful about adding people to your friends or buddy lists. People you meet online may not be what they claim to be. For example, someone can pretend to be older or younger than they actually are and you have no way of knowing if they are telling the truth. Predators also may seek contact this way.

8   Be **wary** if someone you meet online wants to meet in person. Check the person out thoroughly before you decide to meet them in person. Ask your friends if they know the person. Use a search engine to find out any information about them. If you do decide to meet them, meet them during the day in a public place and with friends you trust. Make sure you tell someone where you're going and when you expect to be back.

9   Check a site's privacy policy. You'll want to review the site's privacy policy to see what they'll do with your information. Some sites may share your email address or other personal information with other sites. If you can't find a privacy policy, don't like what you read, or it's not clear, then don't use that site.

10 The many social networking sites can provide enjoyment and **enhance** communication among friends and among people across the globe with shared interests. Enjoy . . . but protect yourself.

COMPREHENSION

Read each statement. Decide if it is **T** (true) or **F** (false) according to the reading. If it is false, change it to make it true. Discuss your answers with a partner.

_____ **1.** Never meet anyone in person that you have chatted with online.

_____ **2.** Post where you go to school or work, but never where you live.

_____ **3.** Don't use your own name as your screen name.

_____ **4.** Posting photos of your favorite meeting place is OK as long as there are no names.

GO TO MyEnglishLab *FOR MORE VOCABULARY PRACTICE.*

READING SKILL

1 Reread Reading Two. Group paragraphs together with common ideas. How would you label or categorize them?

CREATING SUBHEADINGS FOR NOTE-TAKING AND SUMMARIZING

Subheadings can help you take notes on the important points of a reading because they regroup information on the same topic in a clear way. Once you have taken notes under particular categories, it is easier to summarize the information.

Look at the example and read the information.

"Identity Theft" could be one possible **subheading** for paragraphs 2–4 because all the information in these paragraphs is about protecting your identity: names, addresses, screen names, and so on. To go from note-taking under this subheading to **summarizing,** you would be able to write the following **summary**:

Make sure you don't put anything online that can lead back to you: not your name, your address, the places you frequent, or your screen name. Be careful about photos or any information about your school life.

2 Look at these paragraph clusters and decide which of the suggested subheadings you would use. Match the suggested subheadings with the appropriate paragraph cluster. Then take brief notes under each category.

<u>**Paragraph Clusters**</u>   <u>**Suggested Subheadings**</u>

_____ **1.** Paragraphs 5–6   **a.** Predators

_____ **2.** Paragraphs 7–8   **b.** Embarrassing Information

_____ **3.** Paragraph 9   **c.** Advertisers

Embarrassing Information:

_____

_____

_____

Predators:

_____

_____

_____

Advertisers:

_____

_____

_____

Now compare these subheadings with the labels you gave after grouping paragraphs together with common ideas in Exercise 1. Did you group together the same paragraphs? Why or why not? Would the titles you gave to your categories also work? How were they similar to or different from the suggestions made here?

1 Work with a partner. Write one or two sentences summarizing the information in the reading. To be as brief as possible, you can use the imperative form found in the reading ("<u>Protect</u> your personal information").

_____

_____

_____

GO TO MyEnglishLab *FOR MORE SKILL PRACTICE.*

STEP 1: Organize

Work with a partner. Review Reading One (R1) and Reading Two (R2). Fill in the chart with relevant facts for the dangers of invasion of privacy and for possible ways to protect yourself.

PROBLEM: DANGERS OF SOCIAL MEDIA (R1)	SOLUTION: HOW TO PROTECT YOURSELF (R2)
1. EMPLOYERS: *Employers vet prospective hires on social media and often pressure candidates into giving them passwords.*	1. _____ _____ _____ _____ _____ _____ _____
2. COLLEGE ADMISSIONS: Colleges _____ _____ _____ _____ _____ _____	2. *Be wary about whom you "friend" on your profile pages because information about you can be retrieved from others.*
3. SCHOLARSHIP FUNDS: *Scholarship funds monitor your behavior.*	3. _____ _____ _____ _____ _____ _____ _____

STEP 2: Synthesize

Work with a partner. Complete this brief essay by using the notes from Step 1 to synthesize the information from Readings One and Two.

According to Ms. Smith's blog, one of the most important ways we can protect our privacy online is to recognize that using social media to spy on prospective employees or students is an invasion of privacy. Society should make this behavior illegal. On a more personal level, "Remar's Report" advises us on how we can protect ourselves.

The first point Ms. Smith makes is that some **employers** are using social media to vet job applicants. Sixteen percent of the people responding to a Microsoft survey lost jobs in this way. Thus, "Remar's Report" advises us to _____

_____

_____

Another important point affecting young people is the use of social media for college admissions and scholarships. _____

_____

_____

"Remar's Report" suggests that _____

_____

_____

It is very important that we encourage discussion and debate on this question to clarify the way forward.

GO TO MyEnglishLab *TO CHECK WHAT YOU LEARNED.*

3 FOCUS ON WRITING

VOCABULARY

REVIEW

Complete the sentences with words from the box. Check your answers with a partner's.

access	comply	monitoring	resides	vet
alter	enhance	prospective	~~traits~~	wary

1. Social networking sites can be described as places where people can set up an online profile describing their interests and personality _____*traits*_____.

2. Facebook, Twitter, LinkedIn, Tumblr, or YouTube can _____ your life experience by connecting you with people who share your interests.

3. But they can do more than that; in isolated geographical areas, social networking can provide _____ to other people, who can offer conversation, new ideas, and debate.

4. Although we have to be _____ about how much personal information we provide and _____ all our new friends carefully, social networking can be a great way to break out of isolation and speak to people all over the world.

5. People with limited physical mobility can stay in touch with friends and family by _____ social media.

6. Blogging can be a therapeutic way to _____ feelings of alienation and depression.

7. According to psychological studies, people who _____ with a therapist's instructions to blog show greater success in lifting depression than those who simply write diaries.

8. The difference probably _____ in the fact that people who blog, while preserving their anonymity, have the possibility of receiving sympathetic comments from _____ readers.

EXPAND

Informal Expressions

Many informal expressions are used in blogs and on social media sites. Some of these expressions were used in the readings. You may want to check the readings to see how the expressions are used in the context. Then fill in each blank with the expression from the box that matches the definition in parentheses.

amounts to	getting into the act	not a far leap
check out	hang out with	stepping on
come back to haunt you	~~lose out on~~	thinly veiled

Be careful what you do on the Internet. What you post on social media today as a joke can,

in the future, make you _____ _lose out on_ _____ a job or a college education.
1. (miss the opportunity for)

Employers want to _____ applicants before they commit to hiring
2. (verify)

or accepting people as employees. Employers sometimes ask for your social media password; their

_____ threat is that without access to your social media sites, you
3. (barely hidden)

won't be considered for a job.

Colleges and scholarship funds are also _____. They, too, in
4. (joining the trend)

many cases, wish to have access to your private world. It's _____
5. (not too absurd)

to think that someday students and their friends will have to be vetted for security clearance.

Even buying online or surfing the web can _____. There are
6. (later make you regret what you've done)

hundreds of companies on the web that track not only your purchases, but whatever you click on.

They sell information to advertisers: which novels you read, which political party you contributed

to, how old you are, who you _____. This data collection
7. (spend time with)

_____ surveillance that in government hands would be illegal.
8. (adds up to)

That should make us think: Such intrusive behavior is _____ our
9. (violating)

basic right to privacy.

CREATE

Work in pairs. Create survey questions about students' use of social media that you will ask other students in the class. Three questions are suggested below. You may use these if you want. Then on a separate piece of paper, write five more questions that specifically relate to the issues described in the readings. Include at least five vocabulary words from the unit. Use your questions to survey your classmates.

Survey Question 1: Has a prospective employer ever asked you for **access** to your Facebook page? Did you say "yes" or "no" to this request?

Survey Question 2: Have you ever posted personal information on the web that has **come back to haunt you**?

Survey Question 3: Have you ever had to "unfriend" someone on social media? Why?

■■■■■■■■■■■■■■■■■■■■■■■■■■■■■■■■■■ *GO TO* MyEnglishLab *FOR MORE VOCABULARY PRACTICE.*

GRAMMAR

1 Examine the sentences and the underlined phrases. Then discuss the questions with a partner.

- <u>Because advertisers want to know more and more about us</u>, the trend toward online tracking has grown in recent years.

- Some people share too much personal information about themselves on the Internet; <u>consequently, their privacy can be easily invaded</u>.

- Sites like Facebook and Twitter have seen <u>such great success that many new social networking sites are being created</u>.

1. In the first sentence, what word suggests that a reason is going to be given?

2. In the second sentence, what word suggests that a result is going to be given?

3. In the third sentence, what words suggest that a reason and a result are going to be given?

ADVERB CLAUSES AND DISCOURSE CONNECTORS EXPRESSING CAUSE AND EFFECT

Adverb clauses and **discourse connectors** can be used to link ideas and to express cause and effect. In compound sentences, these **cause-and-effect structures** reveal the connection between the reason for an event or a situation (the *cause*) and the influence this event or situation has on people, places, or things (the *result*, or the *effect*).

Cause: Stating a reason with adverb clauses that begin with *because* and *since*

- *Because/Since* **advertisers want to know more and more about us,** the trend toward online tracking has grown in recent years.
- The trend toward online tracking has grown in recent years *because/since* **advertisers want to know more and more about us.**

PUNCTUATION TIP: When the adverb clause beginning with *because* or *since* comes at the beginning of a sentence, a comma separates the clause from the result.

Effect: Stating a result with the discourse connectors *consequently, thus, therefore,* and *so*

- Some people share too much personal information about themselves on the Internet; *consequently / thus / therefore,* **their privacy can be easily invaded.**
- Some people share too much personal information about themselves on the Internet, *so* **their privacy can be easily invaded.**
- Some people share too much personal information about themselves on the Internet. *Consequently / Thus / Therefore / So,* **their privacy can be easily invaded.**

PUNCTUATION TIP: When using discourse connectors, you may write one sentence and join the other with a semicolon (before *consequently/thus/therefore)* or with a comma (before *so*). If you decide to separate the two sentences with a period, the discourse connectors are capitalized and followed by a comma.

Degree of Effect: *such* and *so . . . that*

Complex sentences using the pattern "*such* (+ noun) or *so* (+ adjective or adverb) . . . *that* . . ." dramatically describe the great degree to which the cause has had an effect (*that* + the explanation) on the situation. This pattern is also used with quantifiers such as "*so many* (+ noun) . . . *that* . . ." and "*so few* (+ noun) . . . *that* . . ."

- Sites like Facebook and Twitter have seen **such** great **success that** many new social networking sites are being created.
- Sites like Facebook and Twitter have been **so successful that** many new social networking sites are being created.
- Facebook and Twitter have **so many members that** they are among the most successful social networking sites in the world.

2 Combine the pairs of sentences to show cause and effect. Write two sentences for each item, one using **because / since** and the other using **consequently / therefore / thus / so**.

1. Jack Dorsey created Twitter in March 2006. He wanted to design a system that would allow his office mates to send each other short status update messages.

   _____

   _____

   _____

2. Dorsey was inspired by the bike messengers, truck couriers, ambulance drivers, and police officers that constantly "squawk" to each other about where they are and what they are currently doing. Twitter now represents this "vehicle dispatch" world of the city in the social, mobile Web.

   _____

   _____

   _____

3. Dorsey believed the word "twitter" was appropriate. His system reflects "a short burst of inconsequential information" and "chirps from birds" that may seem meaningless until they are picked up by the right recipient.

   _____

   _____

   _____

4. Twitter has been adopted as a communication and learning tool in colleges and universities. It can be used as a "backchannel" to promote student interactions, especially in large lecture halls.

   _____

   _____

   _____

(continued on next page)

5. Twitter is also a force for raising social awareness and generating social change. Thousands of people give "journalistic updates" on Twitter of what is happening during and after natural disasters, elections, bombings, and political protests.

_____

_____

_____

6. Twitter is limited to 140-character communications. One has to learn how to be brief and precise when using it.

_____

_____

_____

3 Combine the pairs of sentences with **such / so . . . that** patterns.

1. The impact of Twitter has been extraordinary. It has gone from a neat interoffice messaging tool to a worldwide information exchange system.

_____

_____

_____

2. Twitter is used by a great many people of different nationalities, origins, and walks of life. It has become an international phenomenon.

_____

_____

_____

3. Twitter has gained widespread popularity. It is now one of the ten most visited websites on the Internet.

_____

_____

_____

4. Twitter has a very effective news and information-network strategy. It has changed the question asked to users for status updates from "What are you doing?" to "What's happening?"

_____

_____

_____

4 Work with a partner. Read the descriptions of the situations people found themselves in. After each situation, write a cause-and-effect sentence that summarizes what happened.

1. After the interview, Tanya thought she would definitely get into the college of her choice. But when the admissions officer asked if she could have access to her Facebook account, Tanya thought that her online argument with some friends would come back to haunt her. Tanya was right. After having received positive feedback from the college up to then, her first-choice college rejected her in the end.

_____

_____

_____

2. Jonathan is confined to his house taking care of his sick mother. He sometimes feels isolated and alone, but being able to follow his cousins lives on Facebook and communicate with people all over the world on social media have made a big difference in his life. He has even been in touch with a support group for caregivers, which has helped him find medical information and help.

_____

_____

_____

3. Evelyn Smith was trapped in her home when a hurricane hit her area. By tweeting on social media, rescuers were able to find her before her injuries became too serious.

_____

_____

_____

■■■■■■■■■■■■■ **GO TO** MyEnglishLab **FOR MORE GRAMMAR PRACTICE AND TO CHECK WHAT YOU LEARNED.**

FINAL WRITING TASK

In this unit, you read Ms. Smith's blog "Privacy Invasion and Social Media" and "Remar's Report: Using Social Networking Sites Wisely."

*You will **write a short cause-and-effect essay. Focus on either the positive or negative effects of the Internet and social media.*** *Use the vocabulary and grammar from the unit.*

PREPARE TO WRITE: Listing

1 From the readings and your own experience, write notes about the positive and negative effects of the Internet and social media.

Positive Effects   **Negative Effects**

_____   _____

_____   _____

_____   _____

_____   _____

_____   _____

_____   _____

_____   _____

2 Decide whether you are going to write about the positive effects or negative effects.

---

* For Alternative Writing Topics, see page 187. These topics can be used in place of the writing topic for this unit or as homework. The alternative topics relate to the theme of the unit, but may not target the same grammar or rhetorical structure taught in the unit.

WRITE: A Cause-and-Effect Essay

A cause-and-effect essay most often focuses on either the causes or the effects of an event or a situation. This focus is reflected in the thesis statement of the introductory paragraph.

1 Work with a partner. Read the introductory paragraph of an essay and discuss the questions.

> As a result of the development of the online world of the Internet and social media, our lives have changed for the better. No matter where we are, regardless of the time of day, we can attend to many of our personal needs online. As long as we carry a device that gives us online access, we can do our banking, pay our bills, shop for groceries or clothes, buy tickets for all kinds of events, plan vacations, and, sometimes, even meet the love of our life! In addition to convenience, because the Internet and social media make it easy to connect with family and friends and enrich the experience of globalization all over the world, they have had a positive effect on the present generation.

1. Underline the topic sentence. Does it tell you whether this is an essay about causes or about effects?

2. The first effect concerns convenience. What is the second effect? The third?

3. Underline the thesis statement that will guide the rest of the essay. Will this be an essay about positive or negative effects?

2 The thesis statement gives an idea of the argumentation that is to follow in more detail in the body paragraphs. For each thesis statement, decide whether the essay will be about the positive or negative effects of the Internet and social media. With a partner, discuss the topics that will be developed in the body paragraphs.

1. Social media makes people-to-people contact all the easier: from individuals caught in natural disasters, to support groups bringing people together to help others, to the thousands of people in many countries working for social change.

2. Social media are reducing children's attention span to nanoseconds, creating a platform for immature behavior and exposing young people to online predators.

3. Far from its beginnings as a collection of individual homepages with very little cash, the Internet has become the playground of corporate interests: Consumerism and spyware have created the largest global advertising platform in the history of the world.

4. Social media is a force that can change history: With focused pressure from the Internet and social media, people can change minds and hearts, and all but the most isolated countries are forced to confront the modern world.

3 Read the information in the box and then complete the exercises.

ESSAY ORGANIZATION

Essays about causes or effects must follow a logical pattern of organization. Some common ways of organizing cause-and-effect essays are:

1. *From the personal to the general:* The essay will go from personal experiences to more general and universal statements.

Thesis statement 1 in Exercise 2 on page 181 introduces an essay that will use this pattern.

2. *Immediate versus long-term:* You may want to begin with immediate effects and go on to consider long-range results.

For example, the immediate reaction to social media was great enthusiasm, but now people are concerned about the long-term effects on privacy.

3. *A coherent order of importance:* You may want to begin with the least important causes or effects of an event and work up to the most important. Thesis statement 2 uses this pattern.

Or you may need to begin with the historical background of a situation and then go on to the present-day situation. Thesis statement 3 follows this pattern.

4. *Order of familiarity or interest:* You may want to work from what your readers know or would be most interested in, to what is new and different from what they expect.

The thesis statement of the sample introductory paragraph on page 181 goes from conveniences of the Internet and social media that everyone understands to their more unusual link with globalization.

4 Based on your decision about the focus of your essay, write your thesis statement.

_____

_____

_____

5 Based on what you have read in the Essay Organization box, discuss with your partner the writing strategy you will use in your essay. Will your method of organization be based on "the personal to the general," "immediate versus long-term," "a coherent order of importance," or "order of familiarity or interest"?

6 Read the thesis statement provided. Then study the outline. Write what the focus is for each of the three body paragraphs.

1. Introductory Paragraph

   <u>Thesis statement:</u> "Social media makes people-to-people contact all the easier: from individuals caught in natural disasters, to support groups bringing people together to help others, to the thousands of people in many countries working for social change."

2. Body paragraph 1: _____

   the Red Cross uses social media to identify trouble spots / emergency communications

3. Body paragraph 2: _____

   examples of groups that help the homeless, mentally ill, cancer-patients

4. Body paragraph 3: _____

   the Arab Spring in Tunisia and Egypt

5. Concluding Paragraph

7 Using what you have learned about cause-and-effect essays, write an essay focused on the positive or negative effects of social media. Refer to the work you did in Prepare to Write and Write, pages 180–183, as you organize your notes.

REVISE: Providing Sufficient Supporting Details

The supporting details in your body paragraphs should give the reader complete information about the points you are making. Without the necessary examples, explanations, facts, or reasons, your arguments will not be compelling and the essay will not convince the reader.

1 Read the body paragraph from an essay on social media. Below are supporting details that should be integrated with the paragraph to make it fuller and more complete. Read the supporting details and decide where they should be placed.

(1) Revealing too much about yourself online can lead to serious consequences. (2) Others may steal your identity and rob you of your money and your good reputation. (3) Some photos or posts may at first seem all in fun, but they can become embarrassing all too soon. (4) The information may not even be true, but people neglect to consider social media's lasting "memory." (5) Because of the fast-paced nature of online communications, people can express themselves so quickly and easily on social media that they sometimes do not think before they respond to posts. (6) Unfortunately, these regrettable exchanges may never be totally erased. (7) Evidence of these exchanges can come back to haunt us at the most unexpected moments. (8) Of course, the ultimate danger people face when they sacrifice their privacy goes beyond protecting their identity and personal reputation to putting their physical safety at risk. (9) It stands to reason that we should all be responsible in online media.

1. This embarrassing information can be harmful especially when potential employers or college administrators have access to it.

   BETWEEN SENTENCES _____ AND _____

2. Such "identity theft" can easily occur when people are careless and give their real names, home addresses, and telephone numbers to the strangers that they meet online.

   BETWEEN SENTENCES _____ AND _____

3. This happens when potential predators learn where they live and go to their homes.

   BETWEEN SENTENCES _____ AND _____

4. Even when people cancel their memberships in online communities and delete the contents on their screens, such embarrassing information remains online permanently because it has already appeared on many other people's screens, whether they realize it or not.

   BETWEEN SENTENCES _____ AND _____

2 Look at the first draft of your essay. Are your supporting details effective? Do they include some reasons, facts, examples, and explanations that make your ideas clear? Make any changes needed to improve your supporting details.

GO TO MyEnglishLab FOR MORE SKILL PRACTICE.

EDIT: Writing the Final Draft

Go to MyEnglishLab and write the final draft of your essay. Carefully edit it for grammatical and mechanical errors, such as spelling, capitalization, and punctuation. Make sure you use some of the grammar and vocabulary from the unit. Use the checklist to help you write your final draft. Then submit your essay to your teacher.

FINAL DRAFT CHECKLIST

❏ Does your thesis statement prepare the reader adequately for the focus of the essay, the positive or the negative effects?

❏ Does the thesis statement give the reader a clear idea of the topics that will be discussed in the body paragraphs in support of the thesis?

❏ Do your body paragraphs provide the reader with sufficient supporting details?

❏ Are the adverb clauses and discourse connectors expressing cause and effect used correctly in the essay?

❏ Have you used new vocabulary and expressions in the essay?

UNIT PROJECT

In this chapter, we have discussed the impact of social media on modern society. It would be interesting to learn about a few different social media while examining what they offer their subscribers. Follow these steps:

STEP 1: Start your project by doing Internet research on any three of the following social media: Facebook, Twitter, YouTube, Google, Tumblr, LinkedIn, Yahoo, Outlook. Find the names of the people who have been associated with the initial conceptualization and creation of the site, and write their names here. Next to each of their names, explain what their original intentions were.

_____

_____

_____

_____

_____

_____

STEP 2: Continue your research on the three social media sites you chose. Take notes on as much of the following as you can find:

- what services each site now offers
- how—and why—their current services may no longer reflect their original intentions
- how much it costs them to stay in operation
- where their financial backing comes from
- how many people use their services
- what initiatives they have undertaken to improve their services
- why people use their services and the services of other media
- why—and if—the creators believe people should subscribe solely to the services that they provide
- how prominent their reputation is on the global scene and why that is so

Write down any other questions that you would like to find answers for.

_____

_____

_____

STEP 3: Write a report summarizing your findings and prepare to share your results with the class in an oral presentation.

ALTERNATIVE WRITING TOPICS

Write an essay on one of the topics. Use the vocabulary, grammar, and cause-and-effect style structures from the unit.

1. Some of the prominent people of the Digital Age whose brilliance and creativity have made an impact on our modern lifestyle were college or high school drop-outs. Among them are Bill Gates (Microsoft), Steve Jobs (Apple), David Karp (Tumblr), and Mark Zuckerberg (Facebook).

   Should these people receive honorary college degrees, or better yet, honorary doctorates (Ph.D.s) for what they did? Why or why not?

2. Ms. Smith, the author of "Privacy Invasion and Social Media" (Reading One), explains why the "trend to spy via social media is troubling" and cites Bradley Shear's question: "As a society, where are we going to draw the line?" However, she doesn't seem to give any answers.

   What solutions would you recommend?

3. Critics of social networking state that people who spend so many hours a day communicating with their online "friends" seem not to be fulfilling an important human need—to be in the presence of other people. Do you believe they are right, or has the online world changed the way in which we can respond to our needs? With social media, is it possible that our definitions of intimacy will change? Might "virtual" someday be as real as "real?" Why or why not?

■■■■■■■■■■■■■■■■■■■■■■ *GO TO* MyEnglishLab *TO WRITE ABOUT ONE OF THE ALTERNATIVE TOPICS, WATCH A VIDEO ABOUT SOCIAL MEDIA, AND TAKE THE UNIT 6 ACHIEVEMENT TEST.* ■■■■■■■■■■■■■■■■■

THE
CELLIST OF
Sarajevo

1 FOCUS ON THE TOPIC

1. Through music, people can express many different kinds of emotions. Look at the photo and read the title of the unit. What kinds of emotions do you think the cellist's music might inspire?

2. How do suffering and the creative spirit relate? Can you think of examples where suffering has led to creativity?

3. What creative things do you like to do? Play a musical instrument? Paint? Write? Dance? Design or decorate? Sew? Something else?

GO TO MyEnglishLab *TO CHECK WHAT YOU KNOW.*

VOCABULARY

The boldfaced words are in Reading One. Before you read the passage, read the words and study their meanings.

anticipation: expectation (of something good)

carnage: killing and wounding of many people, especially in a war

~~**cherished:** a cherished memory is one that is very important to you~~

defy: oppose; resist

exuberant: happy and cheerful, and full of energy and excitement

furor: sudden expression of anger among a large group of people; turmoil; rage

haunting: sad but also beautiful and staying in your thoughts for a long time

repertoire: all of the plays, pieces of music, etc. that a performer or group has earned and can perform

solitary: alone

soothe: make someone feel calmer and less anxious, upset, or angry

unassuming: showing no desire to be noticed or given special treatment

Now work with a partner. As you read the background information for the subject of the unit, fill in the blanks with one of the new vocabulary words.

> Whether we are professional artists or not, the creative arts play an important role in our lives. Through the attention that we pay to colors, materials, shapes, and sounds when we select our clothes and decorate our homes, our creative instincts are continually at work. Our visual, auditory, and tactile choices help us to express our identity as we strive to make our mark in the world. They reflect our ___*cherished*___ values, our _____ feelings about
>   1.   2.
> being alive, and even our moments of sadness and grief.

It is also through creativity—through the language of music, for example—that people reach out and connect with each other. Even the loneliest and most _____ among us, 3. those whose shy and _____ personalities never make them the center of attention, 4. experience the power of music. Regardless of the musical _____ people choose 5. to play, music allows them to share emotions and feelings that are common to us all. Music can _____ and comfort us in a harsh world. 6.

One of the harshest realities that people must face is the cruelty and destruction of war. Between March 1992 and November 1995, in the former republic of Yugoslavia, the people of the city of Sarajevo suffered the agony caused by the _____ of war. Once a 7. prosperous, tolerant city, where people of many backgrounds lived together, Sarajevo was torn apart by ethnic conflict. People had to call on all their strength to stay firm in their humanity and _____ the appeals to hatred and violence. Somehow they found the strength 8. to clean up the bloody remains of the _____ in the streets and continue living. 9. In _____ of a peace they hoped would come someday, the people of Sarajevo 10. sought the assistance of the international community, which eventually brought the conflict to an end.

Although the war ended more than a decade ago, people are still deeply upset by the dark, _____ memories of those times. During the war, many artists tried to ease the 11. suffering of the people of Sarajevo by coming to their aid. The first reading in this unit, which combines the beauty of music with the ugly sounds of war, grew out of this struggle.

■■■■■■■■■■■■■■■■■■■■■■■■■■■■■■■■■■ GO TO MyEnglishLab FOR MORE VOCABULARY PRACTICE.

You are going to read a story about the healing power of music. Read the quotation from Georges Braque and answer the question.

The French painter Georges Braque (1882–1963) said, "Art is a wound that becomes light."

1. What do you think this statement means?

2. Write a few sentences in response, and discuss your ideas with a partner.

Keep Braque's statement in mind as you read Paul Sullivan's article.

Yo-Yo Ma

The Cellist of Sarajevo

by Paul Sullivan (from *Reader's Digest*)

1   As a pianist, I was invited to perform with cellist Eugene Friesen at the International Cello Festival in Manchester, England. Every two years, a group of the world's greatest cellists and others devoted to that **unassuming** instrument— bow makers,[1] collectors, historians—gather for a week of workshops, master classes,[2] seminars, recitals, and parties. Each evening, the 600 or so participants assemble for a concert.

2   The opening-night performance at the Royal Northern College of Music consisted of works for unaccompanied cello. There, on the stage, in the magnificent concert hall was a **solitary** chair. No piano, no music stand, no conductor's podium.[3] This was to be music in its purest, most intense form. The atmosphere was supercharged with **anticipation** and concentration. The world famous cellist Yo-Yo Ma was one of the performers that April night in 1994, and there was a moving story behind the musical composition he would play.

---

[1] **bow makers:** people who make the flexible stick used to produce sound by players of the cello and other stringed instruments

[2] **master class:** form of teaching in which a celebrated musician instructs a group of pupils in front of other pupils or a paying audience

[3] **podium:** elevated platform

3   On May 27, 1992, in Sarajevo, one of the few bakeries that still had a supply of flour was making and distributing bread to the starving, war-shattered people. At 4 P.M. a long line stretched into the street. Suddenly, a mortar shell fell directly into the middle of the line, killing 22 people and splattering flesh, blood, bone, and rubble.

4   Not far away lived a 35-year-old musician named Vedran Smailovic. Before the war, he had been a cellist with the Sarajevo Opera, a distinguished career to which he patiently longed to return. But when he saw the **carnage** from the massacre outside his window, he was pushed past his capacity to absorb and endure any more. Anguished, he resolved to do the thing he did best: make music. Public music, daring music, music on a battlefield.

5   For each of the next 22 days, at 4 P.M., Smailovic put on his full, formal concert attire,[4] took up his cello, and walked out of his apartment into the midst of the battle raging around him. Placing a plastic chair beside the crater that the shell had made, he played in memory of the dead Albinoni's *Adagio in G minor*, one of the most mournful and **haunting** pieces in the classical **repertoire**. He played to the abandoned streets, smashed trucks, and burning buildings, and to the terrified people who hid in the cellars while the bombs dropped and bullets flew. With masonry exploding around him, he made his unimaginably courageous stand for human dignity, for those lost to war, for civilization, for compassion, and for peace. Though the shellings went on, he was never hurt.

6   After newspapers picked up the story of this extraordinary man, an English composer, David Wilde, was so moved that he, too, decided to make music. He wrote a composition for unaccompanied cello, "The Cellist of Sarajevo," into which he poured his feelings of outrage, love, and brotherhood with Vedran Smailovic. It was "The Cellist of Sarajevo" that Yo-Yo Ma was to play that evening.

7   Ma came out on stage, bowed to the audience, and sat down quietly on the chair. The music began, stealing out into the hushed hall and creating a shadowy, empty universe, ominous and haunting. Slowly it grew into an agonized, screaming, slashing **furor**, gripping us all before subsiding at last into a hollow death rattle and, finally, back to silence.

8   When he had finished, Ma remained bent over his cello, his bow resting on the strings. No one in the hall moved or made a sound for a long time. It was as though we had just witnessed that horrifying massacre ourselves. Finally, Ma looked out across the audience and stretched out his hand, beckoning someone to come to the stage. An indescribable electric shock swept over us as we realized who it was: Vedran Smailovic, the cellist of Sarajevo!

9   Smailovic rose from his seat and walked down the aisle as Ma left the stage to meet him. They flung their arms around each other in an **exuberant** embrace. Everyone in the hall erupted in a chaotic, emotional frenzy—clapping, shouting, and cheering. And in the center of it all stood these two men, hugging and crying unashamedly: Yo-Yo Ma, a suave, elegant prince of classical music, flawless in appearance and performance; and Vedran Smailovic, dressed in a stained and tattered leather motorcycle suit. His wild, long hair and huge mustache framed a face that looked old beyond his years, soaked with tears and creased with pain. We were all stripped down to our starkest, deepest humanity at encountering this man who shook his cello in the face of bombs, death, and ruin, **defying** them all. It was the sword of Joan of Arc—the mightiest weapon of all.

10   Back in Maine a week later, I sat one evening playing the piano for the residents of a local nursing home. I couldn't help

---

[4] **concert attire:** a tuxedo or formal dark suit worn by musicians at a concert

(continued on next page)

contrasting this concert with the splendors I had witnessed at the festival. Then I was struck by the profound similarities. With his music, the cellist of Sarajevo had defied death and despair and celebrated love and life. And here we were, a chorus of croaking voices accompanied by a shopworn[5] piano, doing the same thing. There were no bombs and bullets, but there was real pain— dimming sight, crushing loneliness, all the scars we accumulate in our lives—and only **cherished** memories for comfort. Yet still we sang and clapped.

11 It was then I realized that music is a gift we all share equally. Whether we create it or simply listen, it's a gift that can **soothe**, inspire, and unite us, often when we need it most—and expect it least.

---

[5] **shopworn:** not in the best condition after years of use

MAIN IDEAS

1 Look again at the Preview on page 192. How did writing about the Braque quote help you understand the article?

2 Work with a partner. Read all the statements and circle the three that represent the main ideas of Reading One. Discuss the reasons for your choices.

1. Involving yourself in what you do best will always help you to emerge victorious from the most difficult situations.

2. Music can help solve political problems.

3. Music can give people the strength they need to soothe both physical and emotional pain.

4. Music can make people sympathize with the suffering of others.

5. Destroying things is not the only way to win a war.

6. Art creates a community of people.

DETAILS

Work with a partner. Number the eight episodes in "The Cellist of Sarajevo" in the order in which they take place.

_____ Yo-Yo Ma plays a cello concert of David Wilde's work at the Royal Northern College of Music in Manchester, England.

__1__ Vedran Smailovic plays the cello with the Sarajevo Opera in the 1980s.

_____ The author plays the piano in a nursing home.

_____ David Wilde reads an article about Smailovic playing the cello in the midst of bombs; Wilde writes a cello composition in Smailovic's honor.

_____ Smailovic plays the cello in the streets of Sarajevo.

_____ The author is invited to perform at the International Cello Festival in Manchester, England.

_____ On May 27, 1992, a breadline in Sarajevo is shelled.

_____ Smailovic embraces Yo-Yo Ma in the concert hall.

MAKE INFERENCES

UNDERSTANDING CHARACTERS' MOTIVATION THROUGH CLOSE READING OF DESCRIPTIONS

Description can tell you not only "what happened" but why. Reading carefully can help you understand the characters' **motivation**.

   Look at the example and read the explanation.

Why did David Wilde write a composition for unaccompanied cello rather than for a whole orchestra? (*Go to paragraphs 6 and 9*: Consider the clause "into which he poured his feelings of outrage, love, and brotherhood with Vedran Smailovic" and the phrase, "the sword of Joan of Arc—the mightiest weapon of all.")

Wilde wrote for a cello alone because he wanted his music to be a tribute to the individual he admired. He also wanted it to be an intense experience for the audience, which focused only on Smailovic's instrument, his fragile "sword."

Work with a partner as you answer the questions. Support each answer by referring to the paragraphs cited.

1. After Yo-Yo Ma's performance, how did the audience know that Ma was asking Vedran Smailovic to come up to the stage? (*paragraphs 8 and 9*) Consider these words and phrases: "stretched"; "beckoning"; "Smailovic rose"; "flung their arms around each other."

   Answer: _____

   _____

   _____

(continued on next page)

2. Why did Yo-Yo Ma remain motionless (without moving) after he finished playing? *(paragraph 8)* Consider the phrase "horrifying massacre."

Answer: _____

_____

_____

3. What was the author's purpose in describing exactly how Yo-Yo Ma and Vedran Smailovic were dressed? *(paragraph 9)* Consider these words: "suave elegant prince" vs. "stained and tattered"; "wild, long hair."

Answer: _____

_____

_____

4. Why does the author begin his article by talking about Sarajevo and end by talking about a nursing home? *(paragraphs 10 and 11)* Consider these words and phrases: "profound similarities"; "defied death and despair, and celebrated love and life"; "soothe, inspire, and unite."

Answer: _____

_____

_____

EXPRESS OPINIONS

Discuss the questions in a small group. Share your group's conclusions with the rest of the class.

1. Some people might say that Vedran Smailovic acted foolishly rather than bravely. What do you think? Was he brave or foolish, or both?

2. Do you agree with the author when he says that music can "soothe, inspire, and unite us" *(paragraph 11)*?

3. Yo-Yo Ma gave a special concert to help the people of Sarajevo. Do you think artists should do this? Can you think of other examples? Why don't they just give money?

■■■■■■■■■■■■■■■■■■■■■■■■■■■■■■ *GO TO* MyEnglishLab *TO GIVE YOUR OPINION ABOUT ANOTHER QUESTION.*

READ

1 Look at the boldfaced words and phrases in the reading and think about the questions.

1. Which words or phrases do you know the meanings of?

2. Can you use any of the words or phrases in a sentence?

2 Read the passage from *The Soloist*. As you read, notice the boldfaced vocabulary. Try to guess the meanings of the words through the context.

The Soloist

by Mark Salzman

1   An idea came to me, and I turned off the lights in the studio. In the darkness, I put the cello's spike into a loose spot on the carpet, tightened the bow, and drew it across the open strings. I took off my shirt and tried it again; it was the first time in my life I'd felt the instrument against my bare chest. I could feel the vibration of the strings travel through the body of the instrument to my own body. I'd never thought about that; music scholars always talk about the **resonating** properties of various instruments, but surely the performer's own body must have some effect on the sound. As I dug into the notes I imagined that my own chest and lungs were extensions of the sound box; I seemed to be able to alter the sound by the way I sat, and by varying the muscular tension in my upper body.

2   After improvising for a while, I started playing the D minor Bach suite, still in the darkness. Strangely freed of the task of finding the right **phrasing**, the right intonation, the right bowing, I heard the music through my skin. For the first time, I didn't think about how it would sound to anyone else, and slowly, joyfully, gratefully, I started to hear again. The notes sang out, first like a trickle, then like a fountain of cool water bubbling up from a hole in the middle of a desert. After an hour or so, I looked up, and in the darkness saw the outline of the cat sitting on the floor in front of me, cleaning her paws and purring loudly. I had an audience again, humble as it was.

(*continued on next page*)

The Cellist of Sarajevo   **197**

3   So that's what I do now with my cello. At least once a day I find time to tune it, close my eyes, and listen. It's probably not going to lead to the kind of **comeback** I'd fantasized about for so long—years of playing badly have left scars on my technique, and, practically speaking, classical musicians returning from **obscurity** are almost impossible to **promote**—but I might eventually try giving a recital if I feel up to it. Or better yet, I may play for Dr. Polk if our date at the concert goes well. Occasionally, I feel a stab of longing, and I wish I could give just one more concert on a great stage **before my lights blink off**, but that longing passes more quickly now. I take solace in the fact that unlike the way I felt before, I can enjoy playing for myself now. I feel relaxed and expansive when I play, as if I could stretch out my arms and reach from one end of the apartment to the other. A feeling of completeness and dignity surrounds me and lifts me up.

COMPREHENSION

Work with a partner. Write your answers to the questions.

1. What did the narrator do for the first time in the darkness (as he practiced playing the cello)?

   _____

   _____

2. Why did the narrator believe that he was finally able to "hear" again?

   _____

   _____

3. What imagery does the narrator use to show that he has come out of his dry spell?

   _____

   _____

4. Why doesn't the narrator anticipate a grand musical comeback?

   _____

   _____

5. Why does the narrator's use of the expression "returning from obscurity" have a double meaning in this passage? (This is an especially clever and ironic use of language for the situation in question.)

_____

_____

6. Why is the narrator happy now?

_____

_____

GO TO MyEnglishLab FOR MORE VOCABULARY PRACTICE.

READING SKILL

1 Reread Reading Two. Underline expressions that you think are good examples of the author's expressive, poetic style.

UNDERSTANDING FIGURATIVE LANGUAGE

Figurative language describes one kind of object in place of another to suggest a likeness. Figurative language stimulates the senses. Writers use it to help the reader see, feel, and hear with more intensity what they are saying.

Readers should look for words that would involve their eyes, ears, or touch. What is the person in the story seeing at the concert? What is he hearing?

For example, in the sentence, "The cello gave a sorrowful wail," the cello is making a human sound. The musical instrument is a symbol for a human being.

2 Work with a partner. Explain the figurative language from Reading Two. First, underline the word that gives a clue to the meaning. Then identify the comparison with the boldfaced word from the choices given. Write what you think the sentence as a whole means.

1. "I <u>dug</u> into the **notes**."
(musical) **notes** = _____ _earth_ _____

a. sky   **b.** ocean   **c.** earth

With the word "dug," the cellist compares his musical instrument, the cello, to

a shovel and the musical composition to the earth. At this time in his life,

playing music is as intensely physical as breaking ground with a shovel.

(continued on next page)

2. "I heard the music through my **skin**."

   skin = _____

   a. feet   **b.** ears   **c.** eyes

   _____

   _____

   _____

3. "The **notes** sang out, first like a trickle, then like a fountain."

   (musical) **notes** = _____

   a. stars   **b.** water   **c.** fire

   _____

   _____

   _____

4. "Occasionally I feel a stab of **longing**."

   longing = _____

   a. pain   **b.** joy   **c.** itch

   _____

   _____

   _____

5. "I wish I could give just one more concert on a great stage before my **lights** blink off."

   lights = _____

   a. eyes   **b.** appetite   **c.** life

   _____

   _____

   _____

GO TO MyEnglishLab FOR MORE SKILL PRACTICE.

STEP 1: Organize

Review Reading One (R1) and Reading Two (R2) and complete this grid by writing notes in the appropriate places. If the information is not specified in the text for a particular category, put an X in the grid.

	INSTRUMENT	LOCATION	CLOTHING	AUDIENCE	EFFECT OF MUSIC
SMAILOVIC (R1)		Sarajevo/ Manchester			
YO-YO MA (R1)			formal concert attire	people in concert hall	
SALZMAN (R2)		apartment		cat	

STEP 2: Synthesize

Work with a partner. Using the notes you took in Step 1, complete the short comparison and contrast essay by filling in each paragraph with the information needed. Use a separate piece of paper or go to MyEnglishLab.

Music is a unifying and healing force for Smailovic, Yo-Yo Ma, and Mark Salzman. Despite the different environments in which they play, music gives each of them the strength needed to face life's challenges.

Undoubtedly, all three artists would agree that they share an infinite love for their instruments. . . .

Where they play is often a question of circumstance. . . .

Regarding the clothing they might wear when they play their music, here, too, the differences, although great, have nothing to do with the respect that they all share for the musical experience. For instance, . . .

Their audiences, whether large or small, are all moved by their performances. . . .

It would, therefore, not be surprising to find that despite all the differences here, music has a similar effect on each of these individuals. . . .

GO TO MyEnglishLab TO CHECK WHAT YOU LEARNED.

3 FOCUS ON WRITING

VOCABULARY

REVIEW

Complete each sentence with one of the words from the box. Check your answers with a partner's.

anticipation	exuberant	obscurity	solitary
comeback	furor	repertoire	soothe
defy	haunting	resonating	

1. The children's _____ was seen in their excited faces as they waited for the concert to begin.

2. The music had a _____ quality because its sad tones made the audience think of their unhappy past.

3. Handel's *Messiah,* Beethoven's *Fifth Symphony,* and Tchaikovsky's *1812 Overture* are all important parts of an orchestra's _____ of Western music.

4. Much of the classical music of the nineteenth century reflected the _____ and violence of revolutionary times.

5. Throughout history, creative artists have had to _____ the standards of society in order to produce new music and art.

6. When people are depressed, listening to music can _____ their pain.

7. The folk music made the people feel so happy and _____ that they became very hopeful about the future.

8. The artist is often a _____ figure, unknown or misunderstood by a society that offers no help.

9. The _____ qualities of the violin vibrated so clearly through the musician's mind that he began to completely identify with his music.

10. People who have grown up in _____ do not easily adjust to becoming "superstars" after their talent has been discovered.

11. Making a _____ after a long time away from the theater can be a difficult task without a first-class manager.

EXPAND

1 Work in a small group. Decide whether each adjective from Reading One listed in the chart expresses the feeling of happiness, sadness, or anger. Some express more than one feeling. Put a check (✓) in the appropriate columns.

	HAPPINESS	SADNESS	ANGER
AGONIZED (paragraph 7)		✓	
EMOTIONAL (paragraph 9)	✓	✓	✓
EXUBERANT (paragraph 9)			
HAUNTING (paragraph 5)			
MOURNFUL (paragraph 5)			
MOVING (paragraph 2)			
OMINOUS (paragraph 7)			
RAGING (paragraph 5)			
SCREAMING (paragraph 7)			
SLASHING (paragraph 7)			
SOLITARY (paragraph 2)			

2 Read the sentences based on the story of the cellist of Sarajevo. Look at the boldfaced adjectives. What is the difference in meaning between **moved** and **moving**? Discuss with a partner.

- The man was **moved** when he heard the cellist's story.

- **Moved** by the cellist's story, the man was close to tears.

- The **moving** story brought tears to the man's eyes.

- **Moving** the man to see the cellist's tragic situation, the story brought tears to the man's eyes.

3 Read the information in the box and then complete the exercises.

PARTICIPLES USED AS ADJECTIVES

The adjective *moved* modifies the noun *man*. The *-ed* suffix shows that the noun it modifies has been affected by something else. In this case, the man was moved by the story. The *-ed* adjective reminds us of the passive voice. It reflects a reaction ("to be moved by").

The adjective *moving* modifies the noun *story*. The *-ing* suffix shows that the noun it modifies has an effect on something else. In this case, the story moves the man. The *-ing* adjective reminds us of the active voice. The *-ing* adjective reflects an action ("the moving story" = "the story that moves us").

4 Complete the paragraph by filling in the blanks with the correct adjective in parentheses.

The audience was settling into their seats, happy because the warm summer evening in Boston

had had a _____ effect on them. But when the refugees came on stage to tell their
      1. (relaxed / relaxing)

stories of war and pain and suffering, the audience was _____. The refugees told
                                   2. (horrified / horrifying)

of _____ brutal soldiers and _____ panicked people running for
  3. (terrified / terrifying)   4. (terrified / terrifying)

their lives.

The audience was _____ by tales of bravery and compassion, but this
           5. (inspired / inspiring)

_____ story of senseless violence remained in their minds for a long time.
6. (haunted / haunting)

5 Complete the sentences based on the context of the paragraph in Exercise 4. There is more than one correct answer for each item.

1. Horrified by the refugees' stories of pain and suffering, _____

_____.

2. Terrifying the panicked people, _____

_____.

3. Inspired by the refugees' tales of bravery and compassion, _____

_____.

4. Haunting the minds of the audience with visions of senseless violence, _____

_____.

CREATE

On a separate piece of paper, write a short paragraph summarizing what Vedran Smailovic did for 22 days in Sarajevo. Use at least eight of the words from the Review and Expand sections.

■■ GO TO MyEnglishLab FOR MORE VOCABULARY PRACTICE.

GRAMMAR

1 Examine the following sentences and discuss the questions with a partner.

- <u>Many people say</u> that music is an international language.
- <u>Music is said to be</u> an international language.
- <u>It is said</u> that music is an international language.

1. Which sentences are in the active voice and which are in the passive voice?

2. In the second and third sentences, who says music is an international language?

3. Is there a difference in meaning among the three sentences?

USING THE PASSIVE VOICE

To Shift Focus

Using the **passive voice** shifts the reader's focus to *the thing being done* or *the process being described*, rather than to the specific agent. For this reason, in academic writing and scientific description, the passive voice is often used.*

- *Active:* A **craftsman dried** and **varnished** the wood for the cello.
- *Passive:* The **wood** for the cello **was dried** and **varnished.**

Using the passive voice relieves the writer of a certain amount of direct responsibility for what is said. For this reason, it is often used in reporting the news when the source of the news is not clear or cannot be told.

- *Active:* An **observer said** that the soldiers came from Sarajevo.
- *Passive:* **It was said** that the soldiers came from Sarajevo.

To Report Ideas and Facts

The passive voice creates a distance between the writer and the idea being communicated. That *impersonal* distance is the reason why the passive is preferred for reporting the ideas of others. The writer is reporting on something without adding his or her personal views, creating a sense of objectivity and impartiality.

- *Impersonal distance:* **Music is said to be** an international language.
- *Greater impersonal distance:* **It is said** that music is an international language.

---

* If there is no specific reason to use the passive, the active voice is preferred in English.

(continued on next page)

GRAMMAR TIP: Because the writer is not interested in identifying the specific agent responsible for this statement, he or she uses the passive voice without *by* or an agent. In this example, "music is said to be an international language" has become a universal truth, and it is not necessary to identify the agent ("by many people," or "by great musicians," or "by experts," and so on).

STRUCTURES COMMONLY USED Two structures can be used to form the passive: **1. Subject + passive form of the verb + *to be*** The agreement of the subject (noun) and verb must be carefully considered. If the subject of the sentence is plural, the verb must be plural. **2. *It* + passive form of the verb + *that*** The second structure uses the impersonal pronoun *it* as well as *that* followed by an independent clause.	*Music is* **said to be** an international language. **Musical *compositions* are said to be** included in the box found in the composer's attic. *It* **is said that *music*** is an international language.

VERBS COMMONLY USED

The verbs ***think, consider, regard, say, allege, believe, claim, know,*** and ***suggest*** are commonly used to report facts, ideas, and beliefs.

2 The sentences below are in the active voice. Rewrite each sentence in the passive voice. Examine both versions of the sentence and decide which is more effective. Give a reason for your decision.

1. Many people say that the arts are essential parts of a child's education.

It is said that the arts are essential parts of a child's education.

This sentence is more effective in the impersonal passive voice because the

agent ("many people") is very vague.

2. The government decided to give money to the school creative arts program.

_____

_____

_____

3. The orchestra will have to dismiss many musicians beginning next week.

_____

_____

_____

4. Sigmund Freud, the father of psychoanalysis, claimed that the imagination is the link to our innermost feelings.

_____

_____

_____

5. Many teachers believe that an education in the arts develops sensitivity.

_____

_____

_____

3 With a partner, read the passage on how the arts are being used to help children. Decide whether the underlined sentences would be more effective if they were in the impersonal passive. (The passive voice is preferred only in specific cases. Most lively writing uses the active voice.) On a separate piece of paper, rewrite the sentences that should be changed.

(1) People say that the creative arts have a healing effect on children. (2) We know that administrators at the Illinois Department of Children's Services are active supporters of this method. Last year, they offered classes in art, theater, dance, and music to help children deal with their inner feelings. (3) The program was so successful that it quickly expanded.

(4) Several hundred children participated in the arts program this year. Children in the Illinois program show an awareness of how the arts are related to feelings. According to their teachers, some children associate a specific color with a particular emotional state: red with anger, orange with happiness, and so on.

(5) Teachers, administrators, and others in the program say that many children are learning how to relieve their tensions by drawing pictures about fighting instead of actually fighting. (6) They also claim that some of the children, noting that Leonardo Da Vinci and Michelangelo expressed both exuberant and mournful feelings in their art, are convinced there is a definite connection between these great artists and themselves. These insights are wonderful moments in building a child's emotional world.

■■■■■■■■■■■■■■■■■ *GO TO* MyEnglishLab *FOR MORE GRAMMAR PRACTICE AND TO CHECK WHAT YOU LEARNED.*

FINAL WRITING TASK

In this unit, you read two narratives demonstrating the value that music can have on our lives. *You will **write a descriptive narrative essay about the effect that a work of art, such as a painting, a play, or a concert, has had on you.** You will place the experience in the context of your life as you explain why your experience with this work of art was so meaningful to you. Use vocabulary and grammar from the unit.**

---

* For Alternative Writing Topics, see page 217. These topics can be used in place of the writing topic for this unit or as homework. The alternative topics relate to the theme of the unit, but may not target the same grammar or rhetorical structures taught in the unit.

PREPARE TO WRITE: Asking Yourself Questions

Asking yourself questions is a prewriting technique that is very useful not only for focusing on your topic but also for narrative writing itself. By questioning yourself and writing brief answers in note form to your questions, you are able to explore your thoughts on the topic. The following questions should give you an idea as to how to follow this exercise. You may add other questions if you think of any. It is really up to you!

Questions		Answers in Note Form
WHAT	kind of work of art will I focus on?	_____
	is the name of the work of art?	_____
	is the artist's message?	_____
	do I want to say in my essay?	_____
	is the purpose of my essay?	_____
WHO	is the artist?	_____
	went with me to see (hear) the work?	_____
WHEN	did I see (hear) the work of art?	_____
	was the work of art created?	_____
WHERE	did I see (hear) it?	_____
WHY	did I want to see (hear) it?	_____
	did I like it?	_____
	do I want to write about it?	_____
	did the artist create it?	_____
HOW	did I feel when I saw (heard) it?	_____

Now freewrite about your topic based on the questions and answers.

WRITE: A Narrative Essay

1 Work with a partner. Refer to the answers in Details, on pages 194–195. Review "The Cellist of Sarajevo" and, on the lines below, place the numbers from that exercise in the order in which they appear in the story's narrative. (Remember that in the exercise, you numbered the events in the order in which they actually took place.) Then answer the questions.

____ > ____ > _2_ > ____ > _6_ > ____ > ____ > ____

(continued on next page)

1. Why is the order of presentation of the events logical for the story that is being told?

2. What does the first paragraph explain? Why do you think the author feels the information he gives here is necessary for the reader to know at this time? How does it help the reader to understand the rest of the narrative?

3. How do the author's closing remarks in the conclusion connect with the information he gives at the beginning of the narrative? How do they permit him to communicate a lesson learned?

2 Go back to *The Soloist*, page 197, and review the order of events. Then answer the questions.

1. How does the author start the narrative?

2. How does the second paragraph connect with the first paragraph?

3. How does the final paragraph give a proper conclusion to the information given in the first two paragraphs? Why is the shift in verb tense significant?

4. Which of the two narratives, "The Cellist of Sarajevo" or *The Soloist,* is more simply constructed? Why?

3 Read the information in the boxes and then complete the exercises.

STARTING NARRATIVES

The first paragraph of a narrative essay should do one of two things:

- Start the story
- Set the scene for the story

Both ways of starting a narrative are effective ways to begin. The story you want to tell should drive your choice of how you start your narrative. Sometimes the story itself will be enough to give the reader sufficient background to understand what is happening. However, at other times, you will need to set the scene for the reader so that you can influence the way the reader understands the characters and events of the story.

When the first paragraph starts the story, the next paragraph usually follows chronologically, in the order of time. Note, however, that this does not mean that the plot has to be told from the first thing that happened to the last, although often that is the easiest way. When the first paragraph sets the scene for the story, the next paragraph is generally where the story starts chronologically.

For example, the author of *The Soloist* **starts the story** immediately. In the first paragraph, his narrator talks about "an idea" that "came to [him]" and tells how he improvised before starting to play the D minor Bach suite, which is the subject of the second paragraph. More specifically, the first and second paragraphs have a cause-effect relationship. In the second paragraph, the narrator shows how the preparation in the first paragraph was the cause of his great performance of the D minor Bach suite in the second paragraph. In the third paragraph, he goes from these past-tense actions to a shift to the present as he explains how he approaches his music NOW because of the experience that he has just shared with us in the first two paragraphs.

THE SOLOIST

INTRODUCTION: STARTING THE STORY

Idea of Playing in the Dark with Cello against Bare Chest ➤

Feeling of Body Becoming Part of the Cello ➤

Improvising ➤

BODY

Playing the D Minor Bach Suite ➤

Return of Musical Ear ➤

Great Performance ➤

Appreciative Audience (Cat Purring) ➤

CONCLUSION

Effect of Experience on Current Attitude towards Performance ➤

Declaration of Importance of Music in his Life

The author of "The Cellist of Sarajevo" **sets the scene** in the first paragraph. It is important for him to tell the reader why he was at the International Cello Festival in Manchester, England. However, immediately thereafter, in paragraphs 2–6, he also has to "set another scene." Before he can tell the moving story of Yo-Yo Ma's performance of "The Cellist of Sarajevo," he must take the reader further back in time with information about how Smailovic reacted to the massacre and how David Wilde was inspired to compose the piece. With the author's return home in the two final paragraphs, he closes the "frame" that the references to his trip provide in the essay, and he shares the lesson that he has learned. Although the narrative structure of "The Cellist of Sarajevo" seems a bit complicated because of its many "layers" in the past, it is so logically put together that it almost seems impossible that it could have been written any other way.

(continued on next page)

"THE CELLIST OF SARAJEVO"

INTRODUCTION: SETTING THE SCENE

The Author's Invitation to Cello Festival in Manchester, England →

Background Information about Vedran Smailovic and Sarajevo →

David Wilde and his composition of "The Cellist of Sarajevo" →

BODY

Yo-Yo Ma's Performance →

Yo-Yo Ma and Vedran Smailovic →

CONCLUSION

The Author's Return to Maine and Visit to Nursing Home →

Closing Remarks

4 Imagine that the first paragraph of *The Soloist* is the first paragraph of the body. Write an introductory first paragraph that sets the scene for the story to follow. Share your paragraph in a small group. Discuss whether you think *The Soloist* is better with or without your introductory paragraphs. Give reasons.

5 Reread "The Cellist of Sarajevo" without the introductory first paragraph. In small groups, discuss the differences in the way the reader would understand the story. Explain which way you think is better. Give reasons.

6 Look back at your notes from Prepare to Write, page 209. Write a brief paragraph explaining the purpose of your essay and how you believe you should organize it, either by starting the story immediately or by first setting the scene.

7 Prepare an outline. Show your strategy for the sequencing of events in the boxes.

INTRODUCTION

Starting the story or *Setting the scene*?

BODY

Telling the main part of the story

CONCLUSION

Closing and communicating the message learned

8 Using what you have learned about writing narratives, write a narrative essay on a work of art that has had a great impact on you. Refer to the work you did in Prepare to Write and Write, pages 209–213, to write your first draft.

REVISE: Using Descriptive Language

1 Read the information in the boxes and then complete the exercises.

DESCRIPTIVE LANGUAGE

Good writers use **descriptive language** when they want to give us the complete picture and to involve us fully in the story that they are telling. Writing without descriptive language just reports facts. This is appropriate when the writer's primary goal is simply to communicate the facts of a situation. But if the goal is to go beyond the facts to move, inspire, and persuade the reader, the writer must use powerful descriptive language. Three ways the writer can create powerful descriptive language are to use well-chosen adjectives, to develop internal rhythms in the sentence by using parallel structure, and to vary sentence structure.

Adjectives

Adjectives can be used to describe feelings, to relate how any of the five senses—sight, smell, taste, hearing, and touch—were stimulated throughout an experience, and to report simple facts. They can also be used to reflect the writer's values and judgment.

(continued on next page)

Adjective phrases can also be used in descriptive writing. Adjective phrases begin with present participles ("-*ing*" forms of verbs) or with prepositions (*for, with, like,* and so on) and modify a noun just as adjectives do.

- "[Smailovic walked] into the midst of the battle *raging* <u>around him</u>."

Adjective clauses are also found in descriptive writing. They begin with *that, who,* and *which*.

- "He played . . . to the terrified people *who* <u>hid in the cellars</u> . . ."

Parallel Structure

Powerful descriptive passages have a certain music-like quality that is achieved when paragraphs have good internal sentence structure. Musical sentence rhythms are created by using **parallel structure**—repeating patterns or sequences of action verbs, adjectives, nouns, adverbs, prepositional phrases, or adjective-noun pairs in one sentence. By threading sequences of images together—as a film editor does with the frames of a film—the writer is able to paint a complete picture and draw the reader into the world he or she is describing.

- ". . . <u>for</u> human dignity, for those lost to war, <u>for</u> civilization . . ."

Varied Sentence Structure

Varied sentence structure also contributes to good descriptive writing. The repetition of word patterns can be effective within the sentences themselves, but the repetition of the same grammatical sentence structure is not effective. Good writing should never have all the sentences in a paragraph starting in the same way. When this happens, the writing is very boring. Sentences should be both long and short, both simple and complex.

2 Work with a partner. Examine the paragraph from Paul Sullivan's "The Cellist of Sarajevo," and discuss the questions.

For each of the next 22 days, at 4 P.M., Smailovic put on his full, formal concert attire, took up his cello, and walked out of his apartment into the midst of the battle raging around him. Placing a plastic chair beside the crater that the shell had made, he played in memory of the dead Albinoni's *Adagio in G minor,* one of the most mournful and haunting pieces in the classical repertoire. He played to the abandoned streets, smashed trucks, and burning buildings, and to the terrified people who hid in the cellars while the bombs dropped and bullets flew. With masonry exploding around him, he made his unimaginably courageous stand for human dignity, for those lost to war, for civilization, for compassion, and for peace. Though the shellings went on, he was never hurt.

1. Why is the following brief summary less interesting and effective than the whole paragraph on page 214?

Despite the bombs, a man named Smailovic played the cello in the streets of Sarajevo in memory of the dead.

2. Give examples of how the author makes a great effort to describe actions, places, and objects very carefully. Circle all the adjectives, adjective phrases, and clauses, and identify each one's purpose. Do they make facts more precise; communicate sights, sounds, or smells; tell about feelings; or communicate the author's value judgments?

3. Do you see examples of repeating patterns in Sullivan's language? Underline all the parallel structures that give a certain music-like quality to the language.

4. Study the sentence structure in the paragraph. How many sentences start in the same way? Which sentence is the only one in the paragraph that begins with a subject-verb pattern? Why do you think this is the only sentence that starts in this way?

3 Work in a small group. Using the techniques you have just learned, analyze the descriptive language in the paragraph from *The Soloist*.

1. Underline the adjectives and adjective phrases.

2. Circle the repetitive patterns and parallel structures.

3. Discuss the variety of sentence structures in the passage.

After improvising for a while, I started playing the D minor Bach suite, still in the darkness. Strangely freed of the task of finding the right phrasing, the right intonation, the right bowing, I heard the music through my skin. For the first time I didn't think about how it would sound to anyone else, and slowly, joyfully, gratefully, I started to hear again. The notes sang out, first like a trickle, then like a fountain of cool water bubbling up from a hole in the middle of a desert. After an hour or so I looked up, and in the darkness saw the outline of the cat sitting on the floor in front of me, cleaning her paws and purring loudly. I had an audience again, humble as it was.

4 Look at the first draft of your essay. Have you used descriptive language to inspire the reader about the story you are telling? Did you include adjectives, adjective clauses, and parallel and varied sentence structures to make your writing more interesting?

GO TO MyEnglishLab *FOR MORE SKILL PRACTICE.*

EDIT: Writing the Final Draft

Go to MyEnglishLab and write the final draft of your essay. Carefully edit it for grammatical and mechanical errors, such as spelling, capitalization, and punctuation. Make sure you use some of the vocabulary and grammar from the unit. Use the checklist to help you write your final draft. Then submit your essay to your teacher.

FINAL DRAFT CHECKLIST

❏ Does the introduction of your essay set the scene in an interesting and effective way?

❏ Is there a logical connection between the introduction and the body?

❏ Does the conclusion bring the essay effectively to an end and readily communicate your message?

❏ Is the role of art in the essay clear?

❏ Are the elements of descriptive language—parallel structure, varied sentence structure, adjective clauses—correctly integrated into the style?

❏ Is the passive voice used to report ideas and facts?

❏ Are –ed and –ing adjectives used correctly?

❏ Have you used new vocabulary learned in the unit? Are some words or expressions used figuratively?

UNIT PROJECT

The character in *The Soloist* was haunted by the loss of his musical ear and the exuberant feeling of accomplishment that he used to have when he gave concerts to audiences that cherished his flawless performances. We leave him on a positive note as he seems to have rediscovered his musical gift. He now anticipates the possibility of playing for new audiences, either on the concert stage or in the privacy of his own home.

For this project, you will conduct an interview and write a summary. Follow these steps:

STEP 1: Work with a partner. Interview a professional musician, if possible, to find out how he or she feels about the instrument he or she plays. If you cannot interview a professional musician, you can interview someone for whom music is a serious hobby, or a rock guitarist who plays in a student band—someone who plays an instrument all the time, even though he or she is not a professional. You can also do Internet research to find information about a musician and how the musician feels about his or her instrument.

Before conducting the interview, or to guide you in your Internet research, brainstorm with your partner to come up with questions to use in the interview. In addition to your own questions, you may want to consider the following questions.

1. What was your first experience with the instrument?

2. At what age did you first take lessons?

3. How do you feel about the instrument?

4. What feelings do you have when you play for an audience and when you play for yourself?

5. Which do you enjoy more—playing with other musicians or playing alone?

STEP 2: To find a musician, consider the following possibilities:

1. Ask friends to introduce you to a professional musician or someone who plays an instrument.

2. Consult the orchestras or the music schools in your area.

3. Contact the host of a local radio program who interviews musicians on the air.

Talk with your partner and consider what other resources may be available to you.

STEP 3: After you have conducted the interview or done your Internet research, work together and write a summary of your findings. Use descriptive language as you explain how the person you interviewed feels when he or she plays an instrument, either in public or at home.

ALTERNATIVE WRITING TOPICS

Write an essay on one of the topics. Use the vocabulary and grammar from the unit.

1. What role does music play in your life? Is it a source of comfort or help in difficult times? What other emotions does music evoke for you?

2. Choose one of the quotes below, and write an essay explaining what it means to you. Use examples from your own life or your reading to explain your understanding. Say whether you agree or disagree with the quote.

"Music expresses that which cannot be put into words and that which cannot remain silent."
— Victor Hugo

"Art is a human activity having for its purpose the transmission to others of the highest and best feelings to which men have risen."
— Count Leo Tolstoy

■■■■■■■■■■■■■■ ■ *GO TO* MyEnglishLab *TO WRITE ABOUT ONE OF THE ALTERNATIVE TOPICS, WATCH A VIDEO ABOUT AN ART ACADEMY, AND TAKE THE UNIT 7 ACHIEVEMENT TEST.* ■■■■■■■■■■■■■■■■■■■■■■

THE END OF
Poverty

1 FOCUS ON THE TOPIC

1. Look at the title of the unit and the photo. What difficulties do these children face?

2. The GDP, or gross domestic product,* of developed countries is approximately $45,000 while the GDP of the poorest countries is around $500. How do you think these differences relate to the quality of life in these countries, from childhood to old age?

3. What do you think poor countries need to do in order to "catch up" to the developed nations?

---

* GDP = the total value of all the goods and services produced in a country, except for income received from abroad.

GO TO MyEnglishLab *TO CHECK WHAT YOU KNOW.*

VOCABULARY

Work with a partner. Read the sentences and circle the correct synonyms for the boldfaced words. Use the context of the sentences to help determine the meaning of the words. Then use a dictionary to check your work.

1. Each year more than eight million people around the world face the **prospect** of dying because they are too poor to stay alive.

   a. possibility   **b.** hope   **c.** sight

2. Without enough food to eat and adequate health care, their deaths are **inevitable**.

   a. unavoidable   **b.** uneventful   **c.** untimely

3. Some economists fear that any plans to help the poor are just **fanciful** solutions that will never work out.

   a. expensive   **b.** practical   **c.** imaginary

4. Others are convinced that today's global prosperity makes it **feasible** to offer more help to the world's poorest people.

   a. probable   **b.** impossible   **c.** likely to work

5. They believe that it will take a **concerted** effort to solve some of the problems of poor countries; one nation cannot do it alone.

   a. careful   **b.** collective   **c.** clever

6. During the Cold War, more than $1 trillion was spent on aid to poor countries, but since the end of the Cold War, political interest has **waned**.

   a. decreased   **b.** increased   **c.** remained the same

7. The Bill Gates Foundation, set up by the founder of Microsoft, has given billions of dollars to **zero in on** health care in poor countries.

   a. look into   **b.** take away   **c.** concentrate on

8. Reducing the spread of tropical diseases would be a big step in the **eradication** of extreme poverty in the world.

   a. excusing   **b.** ending   **c.** establishing

9. Lack of basic education is a factor that can **inhibit** a country's economic development.

   a. hold out   **b.** hold on to   **c.** hold back

10. In the opinion of some economists, foreign aid is an essential **spur** to economic growth in today's developing world because developing countries lack capital for investment.

    a. stimulus   **b.** service   **c.** statistic

11. The uneven development typical of our economic system means that the difference between the most **affluent** and the poorest countries is growing bigger all the time.

    a. ancient   **b.** wealthy   **c.** humble

12. The United States is experiencing the largest gap between rich people and **impoverished** people in a hundred years.

    a. depressed   **b.** very poor   **c.** wealthy

13. It seems that important initiatives should be **undertaken** in order to address the potential consequences of this trend.

    a. launched   **b.** processed   **c.** responded

14. Even small changes can make a **dramatic** difference in the lives of many people.

    a. spectacular   **b.** conservative   **c.** meaningless

GO TO MyEnglishLab *FOR MORE VOCABULARY PRACTICE.*

PREVIEW

You are going to read an article about poverty in developing countries, its causes and possible solutions. Read the following paragraph and discuss the information and the question with a partner.

Jeffrey Sachs, author of *The End of Poverty,* is Director of the Earth Institute at Columbia University and Special Advisor to the United Nations on the Millennium Development Goals. These goals, agreed on in 2000, focus on the hope of eliminating extreme poverty in the world.

Look at the title of the essay. Do you believe extreme poverty can be eliminated? Why or why not?

Keep the main points of your discussion in mind as you read Jeffrey Sachs's essay.

Can Extreme Poverty Be Eliminated?

By Jeffrey Sachs (from *Scientific American*)

1   For the first time in history, global economic prosperity has placed the world within reach of eliminating extreme poverty altogether. This **prospect** will seem **fanciful** to some, but the **dramatic** economic progress made by China, India, and other low-income parts of Asia over the past 25 years demonstrates that it is realistic. Although economic growth has shown a remarkable capacity to lift vast numbers of people out of extreme poverty, progress is neither automatic nor **inevitable**. Market forces and free trade are not enough. Many of the poorest regions are caught in a poverty trap; they lack the financial means to make the necessary investments in infrastructure,[1] education, health care systems, and other vital needs. Yet the end of such poverty is **feasible** if a **concerted** global effort is **undertaken**, as the nations of the world promised when they attended the United Nations Millennium summit. The Millennium Project published a plan to halve the rate of extreme poverty by 2015 (compared to 1990). A large-scale public investment effort could, in fact, eliminate this problem by 2025. This hypothesis is controversial, and I am pleased to have the opportunity to respond to various criticisms that have been raised about it.

2   Public opinion in affluent countries often blames extreme poverty on faults within the poor themselves—or at least with their governments. Culture was once thought to be the deciding factor: religious divisions and taboos, caste[2] systems, a lack of entrepreneurship, gender inequalities. Such theories have **waned** as societies of an ever-widening range

of religions and cultures have achieved relative prosperity. Moreover, certain supposedly unchangeable aspects of culture (such as fertility choices and gender and caste roles) do, in fact, change, often dramatically, as societies become urban and develop economically.

3   Most recently, commentators have **zeroed in on** "poor governance," or corruption. They argue that extreme poverty persists because governments

---

[1] **infrastructure:** a support system including roads, power, and ports, as well as health care and legal systems
[2] **caste:** division of society based on class differences of birth, rank, rights, profession, or job

fail to open up their markets, provide public services, and eliminate bribe taking. Developmental assistance efforts have become largely a series of good governance lectures. It is no good lecturing the dying that they should have done better with their lot in life. Although the debate continues, the weight of the evidence indicates that governance makes a difference, but it is not the sole determinant of economic growth. According to surveys conducted by Transparency International, business leaders actually perceive some fast-growing countries to be more corrupt than some slow-moving African ones.

4   A second common misunderstanding concerns the extent to which corruption is likely to eat up the donated money. Some foreign aid in the past has indeed ended up this way. That happened when the funds were provided for political reasons during the Cold War. When assistance has been targeted at development rather than political goals, the outcomes have been favorable, ranging from the Green Revolution[3] to the **eradication** of smallpox and the recent near-eradication of polio. Aid packages would be directed towards those countries with a reasonable degree of good governance. The money would not be merely thrown at them. It would be provided according to a detailed and monitored plan, and new rounds of financing would be delivered only as the work actually got done. Much of the funds would be given directly to villages and towns to minimize the chances of their getting diverted by central governments.

5   Geography—including natural resources, climate, topography, and proximity to trade routes and major markets—is at least as important as good governance. As early as 1776, Adam Smith argued that high transportation costs **inhibited** development in the inland areas of Africa and Asia. Other geographic features, such as the heavy disease burden of the tropics, also interfere. Tropical countries saddled with[4] malaria have experienced slower growth than those free of the disease. The good news is that technology can offset[5] these factors: drought can be fought with irrigation systems, isolation with roads and mobile telephones, malaria with bed nets and insecticide, and other diseases with prevention and therapy.

6   Another major insight is that although the most powerful mechanism for reducing extreme poverty is to encourage overall economic growth, a rising tide does not necessarily lift all boats. Average income can rise, but if the income is distributed unevenly, the poor may benefit little, and pockets of extreme poverty may persist. Moreover, growth is not simply a free-market phenomenon. It requires basic government services: infrastructure, health, education, and scientific and technological innovation. Government spending, directed at investment in critical areas, is itself a vital **spur** to growth, especially if its effects are to reach the poorest of the poor.

7   Adding it up, the total requirement would be 0.7 percent of the combined gross national product (GNP) of the **affluent** donor nations, which is what all donor nations have long promised but few have given. If rich nations fail to make these investments, they will face famine, epidemics, regional conflicts, and the spread of terrorist havens. They will condemn not only the **impoverished** countries but themselves as well to chronic political instability, humanitarian emergencies, and security risks. As the UN Secretary-General wrote: "There will be no development without security, and no security without development."

---

[3] The *Green Revolution* of the 1960s and 1970s in Asia introduced high-yield grains, irrigation, and fertilizers, which ended the cycle of famine, disease, and despair.

[4] **saddled with:** burdened with a heavy responsibility or a difficult problem

[5] **offset:** to make up for, balance

MAIN IDEAS

1 Look again at the Preview on page 221. How did your ideas help you understand the article?

2 On the lines provided under "Objections to Sachs's Proposals" and "Sachs's Answers to Critics," summarize in one sentence the information required, based on your understanding of the reading. Compare your answers with a partner's. After you have answered the questions in Express Opinions on page 227, you will be asked to come back to this section and give "Your Opinion."

OBJECTIONS TO SACHS'S PROPOSALS	SACHS'S ANSWERS TO CRITICS	YOUR OPINION
1. *The poor have only themselves to blame; their culture, habits, and attitudes are not appropriate.*		
2. _____	*Even if governments were excellent, they could not get their countries out of the poverty trap all alone. Aid money should be targeted directly to the villages rather than to the central governments and be carefully monitored.*	
3. _____		
4. *The free market is enough. You don't need government or international aid.*		

DETAILS

Circle the best answer to complete each statement.

    1. For impoverished countries, free trade _____.

        a. is not an important factor

        b. will bring prosperity for all

        c. is only part of the solution

2. People's cultural practices _____.

    a. never change because people respect their traditions

    b. may change with economic progress

    c. are not important for economic growth

3. Corruption is _____ a factor in economic decline.

    a. always

    b. sometimes

    c. never

4. _____ is NOT an example of targeted aid as Jeffrey Sachs proposes.

    a. The eradication of smallpox

    b. Giving political support

    c. Bringing better seeds, fertilizer, and irrigation to Asia

5. Aid will be given to countries _____.

    a. that can show they need it

    b. that have reasonably good government

    c. that are entirely free of corruption

6. _____ is a consequence of geography that CANNOT be helped by technology.

    a. The high cost of transportation

    b. Climate

    c. The lack of natural resources

7. Government spending _____.

    a. is necessary for investment in the infrastructure

    b. is not a good idea because it interferes with free trade

    c. should be avoided because of corruption

8. A good deal of the funds of the Millennium Project will be given _____.

    a. to governments

    b. to villages

    c. to aid agencies

MAKE INFERENCES

UNDERSTANDING THE AUTHOR'S PURPOSE

An author's purpose can be understood through a close examination of how the arguments are presented.

Look at the example and read the explanation.

"Culture was once thought to be the deciding factor [in why countries are poor]: religious divisions and taboos, caste systems, a lack of entrepreneurship, gender inequalities" (*paragraph* 2).

What is the author's purpose in presenting this argument? Select the correct answer.

   a. He agrees with the statement.

   b. He wants people to know about culture.

   c. He wants to express people's wrong ideas so he can answer them.

The answer is **c.** By writing that culture "was **once** thought to be the deciding factor," the author indicates that he does not agree with the statement. In fact, he devotes the rest of the paragraph to refuting it. He is not interested in explaining culture. His purpose is to express openly the objections people may have to helping poor countries. In this way, he can answer these objections.

Work with a partner as you answer the questions. For each of the quotes given, select the statement that best explains Sachs's purpose. Go back to the paragraph in the essay where the quote appears and reread it in context as you consider the author's purpose. Then give your reasons for the answer you chose.

   1. "A second common misunderstanding concerns the extent to which corruption is likely to eat up the donated money. Some foreign aid in the past has indeed ended up this way." *(paragraph 4)*

   What is the author's purpose in presenting this argument?

   a. He thinks that we shouldn't donate money after all.

   b. He concedes that corruption has been a problem.

   c. He never admits that corruption is a problem.

   2. "Geography—including natural resources, climate, topography, and proximity to trade routes and major markets—is at least as important as good governance." *(paragraph 5)*

   What is the author's purpose in presenting this argument?

   a. To show that good governance is not the most important factor.

   b. To show the meaning of difficult geography.

   c. To show that good governance is not important at all.

3. "As the UN Secretary-General wrote: 'There will be no development without security, and no security without development.'" *(paragraph 7)*

What is the author's purpose in presenting this argument?

a. He disagrees with the U.N. Secretary-General.

b. He wants to show people in affluent countries that if they want to be safe, they must pay.

c. He wants to show people that the U.N. Secretary-General is concerned about development, not safety.

EXPRESS OPINIONS

What do you think of Sachs's proposal? Discuss with the members of your group what the political, economic, and moral reasons to help impoverished countries are. Then go back to Main Ideas, page 224, and, under "Your Opinion," rank Sachs's responses to the critics using a scale from **1** (least convincing) to **4** (most convincing). Discuss why you ranked each idea as you did. Then share your group's opinions with the rest of the class.

■■■■■■■■■■■■■■■■■■■■■■■■■ *GO TO* MyEnglishLab *TO GIVE YOUR OPINION ABOUT ANOTHER QUESTION.*

READING TWO MAKING ENDS MEET

READ

The following excerpt is taken from a review of a book by Barbara Ehrenreich entitled *Nickel and Dimed: On (Not) Getting By in America.* "To nickel and dime" is an idiom. Nickels and dimes are very small coins that are worth very little. "To nickel and dime" people is to pay them very little or have contempt for them. Another related meaning is to be petty or small-minded, particularly about money. Barbara Ehrenreich, a writer and social activist, went undercover for three months and lived in three different American cities to find out what it's like to be earning a minimum wage.

1 Look at the boldfaced words and phrases in the reading and think about the questions.

1. Which words and phrases do you know the meanings of?

2. Can you use any of the words or phrases in a sentence?

2 Read the passage that follows from a *New York Times* book review. As you read, notice the boldfaced vocabulary. Try to guess the meanings of the words through the context.

MAKING ENDS MEET

From a *New York Times* book review written by Dorothy Gallagher

1   In Key West, Florida, Ehrenreich found a job as a waitress at an inexpensive family restaurant. Her shift ran from 2:00 P.M. to 10:00 P.M. Salary: $2.43 an hour plus tips. To find an **affordable** rent, she had to move 30 miles out of town, a 45-minute commute on a crowded two-lane highway. How did her coworkers manage housing? One waitress shared a room in a $250 a week flophouse;[1] a cook shared a two-room apartment with three others; another worker lived in a van parked behind a shopping center.

2   "There are no secret economies that nourish the poor," Ehrenreich writes. "If you can't put up the two months' rent you need to get an apartment, you end up **paying through the nose** for a room by the week. If you have only one room, with a hotplate at best, you can't save by cooking up huge stews that can be frozen for the week ahead. You eat hot dogs and the styrofoam cups of soup that can be microwaved at a convenience store." Without health insurance from work, you risk a small cut becoming infected because you can afford neither a visit to the doctor nor antibiotics.

3   In the summer tourist slump, Ehrenreich found her salary with tips dropped from about $7 an hour to $5.15. At this rate, the only way to pay her rent was to get a second job. So, for a while she worked 8:00 A.M. to 2:00 P.M. and then rushed to her regular shift at the first restaurant—a 14-hour day of brutal physical labor, as anyone who has waitressed for a living knows. With such a schedule, she could not, of course, keep her decent housing so far from town. Ehrenreich's new home was an eight-foot-wide trailer parked among others "in a nest of crime," where "desolation rules night and day . . . There are not exactly people here but what amounts to canned labor, being preserved between shifts from the heat."

4   Moving to Maine, Ehrenreich took two jobs to make ends meet—a weekend job in a nursing home and a full-time job in a house-cleaning service. At Merry Maids, the cleaning service, the economics were as follows: The customer pays the service $25 an hour per cleaning person; the service pays $6.65 an hour to each cleaner. "How poor are my co-workers?" Ehrenreich asks. Half bags of corn chips for lunch; dizziness from **malnutrition**; a toothache requiring frantic calls to find a free dental clinic; worries about makeshift childcare arrangements because a licensed day-care center at $90 a week is beyond any cleaner's budget; no one sleeping in a car, but everyone crowded into housing with far too many others, strangers or family; "signs of real difficulty if not actual misery."

5   Soon, Ehrenreich starts having money troubles even with two jobs. Housing is the

---

[1] **flophouse:** a very rundown, shabby place that rents you a bed or a small room by the night

killer. She foresees a weekend without food unless she can find charitable help. More than an hour on the phone with various private charitable agencies (cost of phone calls: $2.50) nets her a severely **restricted** food voucher[2]— no fresh fruits, vegetables, chicken or cheese— worth $7.02.

6   Minneapolis is Ehrenreich's last stop. In this city, as in the other two, affordable housing was the major problem. Across the nation, the supply of housing for low-income families was decreasing: 36 units **available** for every 100 families in need. The old rule that one should pay no more than 30 percent of income for rent has become impossible. For most poor renters, the figure is more than 50 percent. In the Minneapolis-St. Paul region, where the minimum living wage for a parent and one child was calculated to be $11.77 an hour, Ehrenreich has a job at Walmart® paying $7 an hour. Many of her fellow workers, even those with working spouses, work two jobs.

7   What does Ehrenreich conclude from her experiences? No surprises here. Even for a worker holding two jobs, wages are too low, housing costs too high, for minimally decent survival in the life of America's working poor.

---

[2] **food voucher:** a coupon given to you by the government that you can exchange for food at no cost to you

COMPREHENSION

Read the questions and select the best answers. In some cases there is more than one correct answer. Discuss your answers in a small group.

1. Which of the following jobs did Barbara Ehrenreich have?

    a. waitress, cook, tourist guide, store employee

    b. cook, waitress, housecleaner, store employee

    c. waitress, housecleaner, nursing home attendant, store employee

    d. nursing home attendant, cook, tourist guide, housecleaner

2. Based on Ehrenreich's description of the trailer park in Key West, what are living conditions like for the working poor?

    a. dangerous

    b. congested

    c. depressing

    d. hot

(continued on next page)

3. What conclusions can we draw about Ehrenreich's job as a housecleaner?

    a. Homeowners pay the cleaning company $50 an hour for two cleaners.

    b. Only about 25 percent of the money goes to the cleaners; 75 percent goes to the cleaning company owners.

    c. Cleaning houses provides Ehrenreich with enough money to live on.

    d. The cleaning workers eat nourishing lunches.

4. What can we conclude about Ehrenreich's attempt to get help from private charities?

    a. She was successful in getting some food.

    b. It was easy to get help from charities.

    c. The charities provided the food she wanted to eat.

    d. The food voucher was really worth only $4.52 to her.

5. "There are not exactly people here [in the trailer park] but what amounts to canned labor, being preserved between shifts from the heat." What does this mean?

    a. The workers are treated well.

    b. Life in the trailer park is not fit for humans.

    c. Workers are housed only so that they can continue working.

    d. Employers use robots.

GO TO MyEnglishLab *FOR MORE VOCABULARY PRACTICE.*

READING SKILL

1 Reread Reading Two. Pay special attention to the places where Barbara Ehrenreich did her research. Put circles around the names of the places that are mentioned as you consider the jobs Ehrenreich took and the difficulties she encountered in each location.

SCANNING A TEXT FOR SPECIFIC INFORMATION

When you **scan** a text, you are reading it quickly in search of specific information.

Scanning can help you improve your focused reading and note-taking skills. You often scan the Internet when there is something you want to find out. Your scanning skills also come into play on a timed reading examination. This kind of "close concentration" can be valuable when you are doing research on a particular issue and you need to respond to a particular question. As you practice scanning, you develop a more expert "eye" that can locate information in a text readily and efficiently.

Read the example.

If you want to find information on the first job Barbara Ehrenreich took while doing her research, you will look at Paragraph 1, which is about Key West, Florida, the first location referred to in the reading. You will immediately see "found a job as a waitress in an inexpensive family restaurant" in the first sentence. After locating this information, you will then be able to find other relevant information connected with the first job: the rent, the commute, etc.

2 Work with a partner to fill in the chart. Find the information requested and identify the paragraph where you have found it.

FIND . . .	ANSWER	WHERE THE INFORMATION WAS FOUND
1. how much Ehrenreich was paid at her first job.		
2. what Merry Maid co-workers ate for lunch.		
3. why Ehrenreich had to get a second job in Key West.		
4. what the old rent-salary "rule" was.		
5. how large Ehrenreich's second home in Key West was.		
6. why Ehrenreich needed a food voucher in Maine.		
7. where Ehrenreich worked in Minneapolis.		
8. how much a licensed day-care center in Maine costs per week.		

GO TO MyEnglishLab *FOR MORE SKILL PRACTICE.*

STEP 1: Organize

Review Reading One and Reading Two and complete this grid by putting notes in the appropriate places. Share your answers with a partner.

	PROBLEMS WITH POVERTY	SOLUTIONS TO POVERTY
DEVELOPING COUNTRIES	- disease	- government investment in the infrastructure
	- lack of capital to invest	- directed aid packages
	-	-
	-	-
DEVELOPED COUNTRIES	- low wages	-
	- lack of affordable health care	-
	-	-
	-	-

STEP 2: Synthesize

Work with a partner. Complete the two paragraphs using the information in Step 1. Compare and contrast the problems of poverty in developed and developing countries and possible solutions to those problems.

The Experience of Poverty

The experience of not being able to live a decent life is something that poor people share no

matter what country they live in. Nevertheless, there are significant differences between poverty in

developed countries and developing countries. In developed countries, _____

_____

_____

In developing countries, the situation may be more desperate_____

_____

_____

GO TO MyEnglishLab TO CHECK WHAT YOU LEARNED.

3 FOCUS ON WRITING

VOCABULARY

REVIEW

Complete the paragraphs with the words from the boxes. Check your answers with a partner's.

| feasible | impoverished | prospect |

The desire to help correct the worst injustices of the economic system in our own countries also leads us to reach out to help _____ people in other lands. What makes
1.
such an effort _____ today is the fact that so much of what people suffer
2.
from is preventable with science and technology. However, not every economist supports the

_____ of more foreign aid. Some criticize Jeffrey Sachs for exaggerating the role of
3.
donor aid.

| dramatic | restricted | spur |

William Easterly at New York University severely criticizes what he calls Sachs's "Big Plan"
to make a _____ difference in Africa's ills. He believes that despite his good
4.
intentions, Sachs's results will be _____ to creating only small pockets of success
5.
because of the United Nations' inefficient and wasteful bureaucracy.

Even Sachs's assurance of careful monitoring of all aid money does not convince some critics.

They see Sachs as a technocrat who gives technical solutions to what are essentially unsolvable

human and political problems. Paul Collier in *The Bottom Billion* agrees with many of Sachs's

points, but emphasizes the role of trade as a _____ to economic development.
6.

(continued on next page)

affordable	eradicate	inhibit

To show what can be done, Sachs's Millennium Project has set up 12 "research villages" in 10

African countries, with 66 more villages grouped around them. Each village has received $250

per person in aid over five years. The money is carefully supervised by village councils and aid

agencies to _____ any tendency to corruption. The Project is trying to show how
              7.

a few _____ reforms like cleaner water and better fertilizer and seeds, which do
         8.

not require a great deal of money, can improve people's lives. For the price of a cup of coffee in

New York, a child can be free of disease for a year. Free bed nets may not _____
                                                                            9.

malaria completely, but in Sauri, Kenya, for example, they have reduced its incidence from 50 to 8

percent.

concerted	malnutrition	zeroing in on

A _____ effort from everyone in a village is the best solution. For example,
     10.

after helping farmers to grow better crops, the Sauri village council asked the farmers to give one

free meal of maize and beans to every young child in school to fight _____. The
                                                                      11.

result? With full stomachs, Sauri's children went from 108th in district exam results to 2nd. By

_____ the idea of villagers taking responsibility for the innovations, villagers say
     12.

that now everyone can find at least a little to eat.

affluent	available	fanciful

Is it _____ to think that these few villages will be enough to make a difference
13.
on a whole continent? Will this make Africa too dependent on money from _____
14.
foreigners? For many economists, making help _____ to poor countries so that
15.
they can climb onto the ladder of economic growth is the challenge of this generation. How to do

this is the subject of a great debate.

EXPAND

1 Work with a partner. Choose the sentences that best express the meaning of the
underlined words and phrases. Refer to Reading Two to see how the words and phrases
are used.

1. Are you able to <u>put up</u> the rent, or do you need to borrow some money?

   a. Can you change the money?

   b. Are you able to afford the rent?

   c. Can you excuse this high rent?

2. If you don't have health insurance, you have to pay <u>through the nose</u> to see a doctor or a
dentist.

   a. You have to pay cash.

   b. You have to pay less.

   c. You have to pay a lot.

3. We can't afford a regular babysitter, so we have <u>makeshift</u> childcare arrangements with
neighbors and family.

   a. We use temporary solutions.

   b. We are able to use better childcare arrangements.

   c. We have to spend a lot of money.

(continued on next page)

The End of Poverty 235

4. Many people come here in the summer, but the winter tourist <u>slump</u> is badly affecting the economy of our city.

    a. Tourists are not coming at all.

    b. Fewer tourists are coming.

    c. Tourists are too fearful to come.

5. It is very difficult <u>to make ends meet</u> when you earn only $7 an hour.

    a. It is hard to meet others.

    b. It is hard to work in such conditions.

    c. It is hard to earn enough to cover your expenses.

2 The words in each pair have approximately the same meaning, but one has a positive connotation, while the other has a negative connotation. Write **P** next to the more positive word and **N** next to the one with the more negative connotation.

1. _____ **a.** stubborn   _____ **b.** determined

2. _____ **a.** economical*   _____ **b.** miserly

3. _____ **a.** scrawny   _____ **b.** slender

4. _____ **a.** foolhardy   _____ **b.** brave

5. _____ **a.** average   _____ **b.** mediocre

6. _____ **a.** self-satisfied   _____ **b.** self-confident

7. _____ **a.** statesmen   _____ **b.** politicians

8. _____ **a.** malnutrition   _____ **b.** diet

_____

* NOT a synonym for "economic" (relating to trade and industry)

3 Circle the word that best completes each sentence. Pay special attention to connotation and context.

1. Despite criticism, the United Nations is convinced of the need to make a (*stubborn / determined*) effort to reach the Millennium Goals.

2. Mothers in traditional societies are not so (*stubborn / determined*) that they will refuse new customs like vaccinations if it means saving the lives of their children.

3. A researcher who is (*self-satisfied / self-confident*) is full of conceit and arrogance.

4. We need to appear (*self-satisfied / self-confident*) when we speak in front of an audience at a professional conference.

5. A child who doesn't get enough food to eat is (*scrawny / slender*) and malnourished.

6. Healthy people want to appear (*scrawny / slender*).

7. (*Diet / Malnutrition*) and exercise can help people maintain a reasonable weight.

8. (*Diet / Malnutrition*) is the result of severe food shortages.

9. The (*average / mediocre*) American earns about $45,000 a year.

10. Because a lot of foreign aid during the Cold War was directed to the military, it brought at best only (*average / mediocre*) results in raising ordinary people's standard of living.

11. Jeffrey Sachs feels that giving aid to developing countries is the (*economical / miserly*) thing to do because the money spent now will save huge sums on security or immigration in the future.

12. It is difficult to get all countries to contribute their fair share to development goals because some are very (*economical / miserly*) with their money.

13. Millennium Project volunteers are (*brave / foolhardy*) people who travel far away to help the impoverished.

14. It would be (*brave / foolhardy*) to simply send money to needy areas without strict monitoring procedures.

15. (*Politicians / Statesmen*) do only what brings them popularity in the short term.

16. (*Politicians / Statesmen*), on the other hand, may defend unpopular or difficult causes because they know these causes are morally right.

CREATE

Write a dialogue between Barbara Ehrenreich and Jeffrey Sachs about poor people and what they need. Use six vocabulary words, two idioms, and two more words with either negative or positive connotations. Use a separate piece of paper or go to MyEnglishLab.

BARBARA EHRENREICH: I am pleased to be able to meet you at last. I think that we are very concerned about the same kind of problem: the people who live in poverty. One big problem is that people don't seem to care about the poor. How can we get them to pay attention?

JEFFREY SACHS:

GO TO MyEnglishLab FOR MORE VOCABULARY PRACTICE.

GRAMMAR

1 Examine the underlined clauses in the sentences and discuss the questions with a partner.

- What Jeffrey Sachs hopes to see by 2025 is the end of extreme poverty in the world.
- That our advanced science and technology can help us to make the achievement of this goal possible is being considered seriously by whoever wants to improve the human condition.
- Critics of Jeffrey Sachs point to what the results of past humanitarian aid efforts clearly show: a failure to use the financial aid properly because of corruption.
- Nevertheless, despite past failures, what Jeffrey Sachs says, that there are now new ways to eradicate extreme poverty in the world, is probably true.

1. Does each clause have a subject and a verb? If so, what are they?

2. What words do these clauses start with?

3. What is the subject-verb word order in each of these clauses?

4. In the last sentence, there are two clauses underlined. How does the second clause "clarify" the first clause? What is the subject of this sentence?

USING NOUN CLAUSES IN ARGUMENTATIVE ESSAYS

Noun clauses are like nouns in a sentence. Noun clauses can be subjects, objects of verbs or prepositions, or complements. The following words often introduce noun clauses: *what, that, who, whom, whether, why, where, how, whatever, whoever, whomever, wherever, however.*

Noun clause as SUBJECT	**What Jeffrey Sachs hopes to see by 2025** is the end of extreme poverty in the world.
Noun clause as OBJECT	We must consider seriously **what Jeffrey Sachs hopes to see by 2025.**
Noun clause as COMPLEMENT	This is **what Jeffrey Sachs hopes to see by 2025.**

Noun clauses can also be placed **in apposition** with each other (alongside each other):

What Jeffrey Sachs says, that there are now new ways to eradicate extreme poverty in the world, is probably true.

This sentence is a combination of these two sentences:

SUBJECT

What Jeffrey Sachs says is probably true.

SUBJECT

That there are now new ways to eradicate extreme poverty in the world is probably true.

Pattern for Noun Clauses in Apposition

What "X" insists,   that + opinion or idea being discussed, is probably true.

(comma) *(that + complete sentence)* *(comma)*	
asserts	is indisputable.
suggests	does not make sense.
implies	is worthy of consideration.
etc.	etc.

Combining the two noun clauses in one sentence permits writers or speakers to clarify exactly what they are referring to. This is a good technique to use when writing a persuasive or argumentative essay or participating in an oral debate.

GRAMMAR TIP: Like all clauses, noun clauses must have a subject and a verb. In noun clauses that start with a question word, the word order is not the inverted subject-verb word order that is used in questions. In all noun clauses, the subject comes before the verb. Note that sometimes the question word itself is the "subject" of the noun clause, as in "whoever wants to improve the human condition."

2 Fill in the blanks first with **what, that, who, why, where, how,** or **whoever.** Then add the subject and/or the correct form of the verb in parentheses to complete this story.

How a Goat Fed a Young Girl's Dream

Who would ever think that a goat could dramatically change the course of a person's life?

This is _____ *what happened* _____ to a Ugandan woman by the name of Beatrice
                              1. (happen)
Biira. When she was nine years old, her parents could not afford to send her to school.

_____, in the small village of Kisinga, in the western part of
                2. (the family / live)
Uganda, there were not enough jobs and not enough food to eat. Beatrice and her family were

hungry. _____ eating cassava and sweet potatoes every day was
              3. (the young girl / survive)
almost a miracle.

_____ Beatrice even at that young age understood that her
             4. (know)
hunger was for education as well as for food. Her luck changed when Beatrice's family, one of the

poorest in her village, was among 12 families chosen to receive a goat from Heifer International,

a charity in Little Rock, Arkansas. Beatrice's parents were finally able to send her to the local

school when she was ten years old. Understanding _____
              5. (one goat / able to provide)
this opportunity for Beatrice is not difficult. Because Heifer goats produce a great deal of milk,

Beatrice's mother was able to sell enough milk to send Beatrice to school.

Right from the start, with a combination of _____ her passion
              6. (reflect)
for an education and her intelligence, Beatrice impressed her teachers in the local school. As a

result, she won a scholarship to a high school in Kampala, the country's capital. Soon after, she

went to a private high school in New England, in the United States, and eventually received a

bachelor's degree from Connecticut College and a master's degree from The Clinton School of

Public Service.

It is in _____ using the education she has received that makes
7. (Beatrice / envisage)
this young woman special. Beatrice will never forget _____.
8. (she / come from)
_____ now as a Community Engagement Officer for Heifer
9. (she/do)
International is to engage volunteers in New York City and other urban areas in the fight against

poverty in Africa. With this job and a previous one she held with the Millennium Promise

Alliance, she is living her dream of giving back to her community.

Beatrice's story should make _____ skeptical about donating
10. (be)
aid to impoverished countries think again about the question. Just as the people in her village

celebrate "Passing on the Gift" by giving newborn goats to other families, Beatrice is passing on

the gift of her education to her countrymen in need.

Surely, _____, _____
11. (Beatrice's story / prove)   12. (providing aid to people in poor countries / be)
sometimes very beneficial, cannot be overlooked.

3 Do the following with the statements below.

- Make each statement part of a noun clause-in-apposition pattern as you show whether it is likely to be made by Jeffrey Sachs or one of his critics.

- Give your stand on the issue at the end of the noun clause-in-apposition pattern.

- Develop your argument further by adding a few sentences with examples and evidence that clarify your position.

1. There are now ways to eradicate extreme poverty in the world.

  What Sachs insists, that there are now ways to eradicate extreme poverty in the

  world, is probably true. We have the scientific training and the technical

  know-how to provide the impoverished around the world with enough food to eat.

  However, I question how we will make this happen. This can be a costly process.

(continued on next page)

2. Foreign aid in the past has been eaten up by corruption.

_____

_____

_____

_____

_____

3. The geography of a country can inhibit its development.

_____

_____

_____

_____

_____

4. Free trade market forces will not resolve the problems of poverty in some countries.

_____

_____

_____

_____

_____

5. Poverty on a large scale is a threat to world peace.

_____

_____

_____

_____

_____

■■■■■■■■■■■■■■■■■ *GO TO* MyEnglishLab *FOR MORE GRAMMAR PRACTICE AND TO CHECK WHAT YOU LEARNED.*

FINAL WRITING TASK

In this unit, you read Jeffrey Sachs's essay "Can Extreme Poverty Be Eliminated?" and Dorothy Gallagher's review of Barbara Ehrenreich's book, *Nickel and Dimed: On (Not) Getting By in America.*

*You will **write an argumentative essay in response to the following question: Should affluent countries assume the financial burden of eliminating extreme poverty in the world, according to the proposal made by Jeffrey Sachs in his essay?** Use the vocabulary and grammar from the unit.* *

PREPARE TO WRITE: Make a List

Work with a partner. Write a list of arguments FOR and AGAINST expecting affluent countries to assume the financial burden of eliminating extreme poverty in the world, according to the proposal made by Jeffrey Sachs in his essay.

For	Against
1.	1.
2.	2.
3.	3.
4.	4.
5.	5.

Examining the list, determine which arguments you believe are more logical to your way of thinking. State here the position you are going to take in your essay:

_____

_____

WRITE: An Argumentative Essay

1 Reread the introductory paragraph from Reading One. Then discuss the questions with a partner.

(1) For the first time in history, global economic prosperity has placed the world within reach of eliminating extreme poverty altogether. **(2)** This prospect will seem fanciful to some, but the dramatic economic progress made by China, India, and other low-income parts of Asia over

(continued on next page)

---

* For Alternative Writing Topics, see page 253. These topics can be used in place of the writing topic for this unit or as homework. The alternative topics relate to the theme of the unit, but may not target the same grammar or rhetorical structures taught in the unit.

The End of Poverty 243

the past 25 years demonstrates that it is realistic. **(3)** Although economic growth has shown a remarkable capacity to lift vast numbers of people out of extreme poverty, progress is neither automatic nor inevitable. **(4)** Market forces and free trade are not enough. **(5)** Many of the poorest regions are caught in a poverty trap; they lack the financial means to make the necessary investments in infrastructure, education, health care systems, and other vital needs. **(6)** Yet the end of such poverty is feasible if a concerted global effort is undertaken, as the nations of the world promised when they attended the United Nations Millennium summit. **(7)** The Millennium Project published a plan to halve the rate of extreme poverty by 2015 (compared to 1990). **(8)** A large-scale and targeted public investment effort could, in fact, eliminate this problem by 2025. **(9)** This hypothesis is controversial, and I am pleased to have the opportunity to respond to various concerns that have been raised about it.

1. What kind of information do sentences 1 through 5 give the reader?
2. Why is sentence 6 important?
3. How do sentences 7 and 8 reinforce the statement made in sentence 6?
4. What purpose does sentence 9 serve?

2 Read the information in the box and then complete the exercises.

ARGUMENTATIVE ESSAYS

Introduction and Thesis Statement

The aim of an **argumentative essay** is to convince the reader to agree with the author's point of view or opinion. An argumentative essay tries to be very persuasive by appealing to *reason* and *logic*.

An argumentative essay must introduce and explain the background to the issue or problem. The background information presents the issue and leads to the thesis statement. In the thesis statement, the author must take a stand and present his or her point of view *strongly* and *clearly*. Most commonly, this is done through the use of modals such as *should (not), must (not), would be better if . . . , would like you to . . . .*

For instance, in the introduction to his essay, "Can Extreme Poverty Be Eliminated?" Jeffrey Sachs gives us the necessary background information in the first five sentences. Without this information, the reader would not be prepared to consider his thesis statement, which begins in sentence 6: "Yet the end of such poverty is feasible if a concerted global effort is undertaken, as the nations of the world promised when they attended the United Nations Millennium summit."

He furnishes more background information to accompany his thesis in sentence 7. However, in sentence 8—"A large-scale and targeted public investment effort could, in fact, eliminate this problem by 2025"—he completes the thesis statement that he started in sentence 6. In sentence 9, Sachs gives us the procedure he will follow in supporting his thesis.

Sachs does not force the issue on his readers. He presents the arguments without the use of words *must (not), should (not),* etc. Instead, he wisely calls his idea a "hypothesis," which is something that needs to be proven, and calls the arguments against his proposal the "concerns that have been raised about it." In so doing, he encourages the reader to join him in a necessary dialogue with the hope that people will eventually accept the challenge of helping him to prove his theory. This reflects his optimism about what "could" happen if people all over the world took his hypothesis seriously.

Supporting Your Views

In most good argumentative essays, the writer's point of view is obvious in the first paragraph. However, an essay is not a mere opinion. The body of the essay should provide support or reasons for the author's point of view: factual details, explanations, examples, and even, in appropriate cases, anecdotes from personal experience.

Refuting Opposing Points of View

Writing an argumentative essay is like taking one side in a debate, either for or against. The writer must not only show that his or her ideas are correct, but also that opposing views are wrong. Refuting an opponent's views involves showing why the opponent's arguments, or "counterarguments," are incorrect. To be effective, an argumentative essay must contain a point-by-point **refutation** of the main arguments of the opposing view.

Concession

If an opponent has a valid point or expresses an idea that is true, the writer must, in honesty, concede it. It is very rare that the arguments on one side are *all* bad and on the other *all* good. After admitting that the opposition may have a good point, the writer can go on to show that, overall, his or her reasons are superior to the opponent's views.

Every argumentative essay should have at least one concession to show some understanding of the ideas of the opposite side. The concession should not appear in the conclusion. Nor can it be allowed to change the main idea or divert attention from the thesis statement of the essay.

In paragraph 4, Jeffrey Sachs makes a concession. He agrees that corruption has been an obstacle to charitable aid efforts in the past. However, by offering his recommendation for a new method of giving by means of a "detailed and monitored plan" that would only be "directed towards those countries with a reasonable degree of good governance," he hopes to answer the objections of his critics.

Conclusion

The **conclusion** should follow logically from the arguments in the essay. It summarizes the main ideas and reaffirms the thesis. It may also offer further suggestions for consideration. For instance, in his conclusion, Jeffrey Sachs actually suggests that *we must eliminate extreme poverty in the world if we want to live relatively secure lives.*

As you develop your arguments and refute opposing points of view, you can organize your essay in one of three ways:

1. Make your own arguments, followed by the counterarguments and refutations.

2. Alternate between your own arguments and the relevant counterarguments and refutations.

3. Discuss the counterarguments and refutations. Then follow with your own arguments.

For instance, in paragraph 3 of his essay, Sachs goes from a reference to the *counterargument* ("poverty persists because governments fail to . . . ") to his own *argument* ("the weight of the evidence indicates that governance makes a difference but it is not the sole determinant of economic growth") to a *refutation* ("According to surveys conducted by Transparency International, business leaders actually perceive some fast-growing countries to be more corrupt than some slow-moving African ones").

3 Work with a partner. Review Reading One and underline the counterarguments Sachs deals with. Then evaluate his refutations. Discuss whether or not Sachs has done a good job in refuting the criticisms of his position.

4 Write an outline for your essay. Circle your thesis here:

"Affluent countries **should assume the financial burden of** eliminating extreme poverty in the world."

"Affluent countries **should not assume the financial burden of** eliminating extreme poverty in the world."

Now write in complete sentences your arguments, counterarguments, and refutations here:

Arguments:

_____

_____

Counterarguments:

_____

_____

Refutations:

_____

_____

Write at least one concession here:

Concession:

_____

_____

_____

You should try to have at least three arguments, with their respective counterarguments and refutations.

5 When you have finished, share your plan with a partner. Discuss which of the three organizational patterns described above will be best for you to follow.

6 Using what you have learned about writing argumentative essays, write an essay in response to the question asked at the beginning of Final Writing Task, page 243. Refer to the work you did in Prepare to Write and Write, pages 243–247, as you organize your notes into logical patterns.

REVISE: Using the Language of Concession

There should be at least one concession in your essay where you acknowledge a good point in your opponent's argument.

The following phrases can introduce concessions:

CONCESSION	WRITER'S ARGUMENT
It is true that / I concede that / I agree that corruption has been a major challenge to individuals or institutions that have tried to give aid to countries suffering from extreme poverty.	**Nevertheless,** this should not stop us from looking for ways to help people whose lives depend on our support.
Undoubtedly, / Admittedly, poor countries also suffer from civil wars, bad leadership, and ethnic conflicts.	**However,** donors should not use problems as an excuse to do nothing.

In each concession sentence, the writer concedes an opposing point. He then continues to pursue his main argument with a transitional discourse connector.

Concessions can also be made with the contrastive conjunctions, **although** and **even though,** which contrast two opposite ideas in the same sentence. The argument appears in the main clause, NOT the subordinate clause. The concession comes in the subordinate clause (the clause with **although** and **even though**). The argument can come before or after the concession: "Although the most powerful mechanism for reducing extreme poverty is to encourage overall economic growth, a rising tide does not necessarily lift all boats." (Jeffrey Sachs, "Can Extreme Poverty Be Eliminated?")

(continued on next page)

CONCESSION	WRITER'S ARGUMENT
Although the most powerful mechanism for reducing extreme poverty is to encourage overall economic growth,	a rising tide does not necessarily lift all boats. (overall growth doesn't help every country or every person)

WRITER'S ARGUMENT	CONCESSION
A rising tide does not necessarily lift all boats	**even though** the most powerful mechanism for reducing extreme poverty is to encourage overall economic growth.

1 Work with a partner. Refer to Main Ideas, page 224, where you have outlined "Objections to Sachs's Proposals" (AGAINST Jeffrey Sachs's proposals) and "Sachs's Answers to Critics" (FOR Jeffrey Sachs's proposals). Using the language of concession shown above, choose two additional arguments for each point of view and write sentences that include a main argument and a concession.

For Jeffrey Sachs's Proposals

1. _Although the corruption of centralized governments prevented financial aid from going to where it was needed most in the past, future financing will be closely monitored and sent in installments directly to the villages where people will be working on important development projects._

2. _____

    _____

    _____

3. _____

    _____

    _____

Against Jeffrey Sachs's Proposals

1. _It is impossible to believe there will be no corruption in the villages where people live with so many basic needs, even though the close monitoring of future financial aid has been promised._

2. _____

_____

_____

3. _____

_____

_____

2 Examine the model paragraph of a Concession and Refutation. Work with a partner to answer the questions that follow as you consider how the kinds of sentences you have practiced in the previous exercise and in Exercise 2 of the Grammar section, pages 240–241, can contribute to a well-developed concession / refutation paragraph.

It is true that the desire for survival is a force that can quickly change into dangerous rage. **What Jeffrey Sachs suggests,** that terrorism will increase on a global scale if attempts are not made to eradicate extreme poverty, **may be correct.**

Concession →

Main Argument

(Refutation)

People who are trapped in one way or another eventually rebel if they are kept from improving their condition. **However, even though the security of the world may be at risk if nothing is done to help people of poor countries,** affluent countries should not be expected to send large amounts of financial aid to impoverished nations. Solving poor countries' problems this way will not be easy because finding countries in Africa that demonstrate good governance seems difficult. For instance, people who live in Ethiopia, Somalia, Eritrea, the Sudan, and Darfur are not only the victims of hunger but also of the horrors of regional conflicts and civil war. Because of this situation, even sending skilled administrators,

(continued on next page)

teachers, engineers, health, and agricultural workers to these countries, which would be a better idea than sending them money, is not possible at this time. Undoubtedly, Jeffrey Sachs knows that his argument is a bit weak when he uses the words "*a reasonable degree* of good governance" (italics added). How "reasonable" would it be for donor countries to expect a good return on their investment? In the current climate, it is hard to believe it would be very reasonable at all.

1. A concession / refutation paragraph has three main parts: a part that **states** the ideas of an opponent, a part that **refutes** most of the ideas of the opponent, and a part that **agrees** with some aspects of an opponent's ideas. Where do these parts appear in the paragraph?

   First: _____

   Second: _____

   Third: _____

2. Underline the sentence that has a noun clause-in-apposition format. Which of Jeffrey Sachs's opinions does the writer refer to there? How does the writer react to that viewpoint?

3. In what sentence does the writer start to disagree with Sachs? Why does the writer's tone in that sentence seem to be diplomatic and tactful?

4. What is the writer's main opinion in the paragraph? Does the writer support this opinion well? Why or why not?

GO TO MyEnglishLab *FOR MORE SKILL PRACTICE.*

EDIT: Writing the Final Draft

Go to MyEnglishLab and write the final draft of your essay. Carefully edit it for grammatical and mechanical errors, such as spelling, capitalization, and punctuation. Make sure you use some of the vocabulary and grammar from the unit. Use the checklist to help you write your final draft. Then submit your essay to your teacher.

FINAL DRAFT CHECKLIST

❑ Does your introduction give the necessary background information and thesis statement?

❑ Does the thesis statement clearly reflect the writer's stand on the issue?

❑ Are the arguments, counterarguments, and refutations presented in a logical manner?

❑ Does the essay have at least one concession / refutation paragraph?

❑ Does the conclusion restate the thesis and offer the reader other ways to consider the problem?

❑ Did you use noun clauses and noun clauses in apposition effectively in the essay?

❑ Have you used new vocabulary, expressions, and positive and negative connotations in the essay?

UNIT PROJECT

In preparing to write her book, Barbara Ehrenreich went under cover to investigate the living conditions of America's working poor. Ironically, in the United States, the richest nation in the world, there are still many people who live in poverty. The same is true for people who live in other developed nations. For this project, you will research data about the poor in developed nations. Follow these steps:

STEP 1: Work with a partner. Identify at least five developed countries and list them here.

1. _____

2. _____

3. _____

4. _____

5. _____

STEP 2: Do the following in conducting your research:

- Find data on the Internet about the poor in these five countries: what percentage of the population they represent; how many of them work and how many of them do not work; what the poverty line is in each country; what services the poor are given from the government in order to survive; where they live; and so forth.

- Choose one of the countries. Find an issue that is now being argued in this country about the treatment of the poor. Using the Internet, read about the arguments that are dividing people on ways in which to address this issue.

STEP 3: When you have found the information you need, write a summary of the results of your research. Evaluate your findings by referring to data that you thought was surprising and data that you thought was "expected." Give your opinion about the issue that is now being argued in the country that you did specific research on. Include whatever recommendations you may have to improve the conditions in this country and the others covered in your report.

ALTERNATIVE WRITING TOPICS

Write an essay on one of the topics. Use the vocabulary, grammar, and argumentative essay structures from the unit.

1. *"If a free society cannot help the many who are poor, it cannot save the few who are rich."*
   —John F. Kennedy, President of the U.S.

   What do you think President Kennedy meant by this quote? Does it apply only to people in one country? Does it apply to the world in general? Do you agree or disagree with this idea? Give examples to illustrate your point of view. Remember to include at least one concession and refutation.

2. Some people feel that "charity begins at home." What is the meaning of this quote? Do you agree or disagree? How would that apply to Jeffrey Sachs's proposals?

3. As an investigative journalist, Barbara Ehrenreich wrote *Nickel and Dimed* by living the lives of the people she was writing about—in this case, America's working poor. What kind of investigative journalism would you like to do, and how would you do it?

▪▪▪▪▪▪▪▪▪▪▪▪▪▪▪▪▪▪ *GO TO* MyEnglishLab *TO WRITE ABOUT ONE OF THE ALTERNATIVE TOPICS, WATCH A VIDEO ABOUT A TEEN WORKING TO END POVERTY, AND TAKE THE UNIT 8 ACHIEVEMENT TEST.* ▪▪▪▪▪▪▪▪▪▪

GRAMMAR BOOK REFERENCES

NorthStar: Reading and Writing Level 5, Fourth Edition	Focus on Grammar Level 5, Fourth Edition	Azar's Understanding and Using English Grammar, Fourth Edition
Unit 1 Past Unreal Conditionals	**Unit 22** Conditionals; Other Ways To Express Unreality **Unit 23** More Conditions	**Chapter 20** Conditional Sentences and Wishes: 20–4
Unit 2 Double Comparatives	_____	**Chapter 9*** Comparisons *From Fundamentals of English Grammar, Fourth Edition
Unit 3 Identifying and Nonidentifying Adjective Clauses	**Unit 12** Adjective Clauses: Review and Expansion **Unit 13** Adjective Clauses with Prepositions; Adjective Phrases	**Chapter 13** Adjective Clauses
Unit 4 Adverb Clauses of Comparison and Contrast	**Unit 19** Adverb Clauses **Unit 20** Adverb and Adverbial Phrases **Unit 21** Connectors	**Chapter 17** Adverb Clauses: 17–4, 17–5 **Chapter 19** Connectives that Express Cause and Effect, Contrast, and Condition: 19–6
Unit 5 Specific Uses of Gerunds and Infinitives	**Unit 16** Gerunds **Unit 17** Infinitives	**Chapter 14** Gerunds and Infinitives, Part 1 **Chapter 15** Gerunds and Infinitives, Part 2

(continued on next page)

NorthStar: Reading and Writing Level 5, Fourth Edition	Focus on Grammar Level 5, Fourth Edition	Azar's Understanding and Using English Grammar, Fourth Edition
Unit 6 Adverb Clauses and Discourse Connectors	**Unit 19** Adverb Clauses **Unit 21** Connectors	**Chapter 17** Adverb Clauses: 17–3 **Chapter 19** Connectives that Express Cause and Effect, Contrast, and Condition: 19–1, 19–2, 19–3, 19–4
Unit 7 Reporting Ideas and Facts with Passives	**Unit 14** The Passive Voice **Unit 15** The Passive to Describe Situations and to Report Opinions	**Chapter 11** The Passive: 11–1, 11–3
Unit 8 Noun Clauses	**Unit 10** Noun Clauses: Subjects, Objects, and Complements	**Chapter 12** Noun Clauses: 12–1, 12–2, 12–3, 12–4, 12–5

UNIT WORD LIST

The Unit Word List is a summary of key vocabulary from the Student Book. Words followed by an asterisk* are on the Academic Word List (AWL).

UNIT 1

affective*
anomaly
conduct*
display*
empathy
hailed
impact*
in a vacuum

orchestrate
overboard
revelation*
simulation*
skeptical
transmit*
validate*

UNIT 2

artful
betrayal
conscience
cover up
creativity
cunning
deception
delusions
empirical*
false stories
feverish
foolproof
get around
   (something or
   someone)
lie

magic
malicious
manipulate*
outright
persuade
plagued by
pretend
promptly
quest
sleight of hand
spot (verb)
tall tales
throw a veil over
   (something)
trickery

UNIT 3

back (verb)
camaraderie
civility
come together
dim (adjective)
discretion*
miss a beat
nurture
pace
poise
proficient
reluctant*
spare (something)
take it out of
   (someone)

Collocations

achieve* / attain*
   success
achieve / attain / reach
   a goal*
earn /obtain* / receive
   a degree
encounter* / face /
   confront opposition
encounter / face / run
   into difficulties
encounter / meet / an
   obstacle
make a mistake
make an effort
realize a dream / make
   a dream come true

UNIT 4

acquisition*
authority*
beleaguered
challenge*
chaotic
demonstrative*
dissuade
fabric
fit in
give vent to
grant*
grief
in stark contrast to*
isolation*
restraint*
scold
stoical
tighten the reins
transport* one's
   thoughts

Suffixes
Changing an adjective
   to a noun: -ness, -ty,
   -ity
Changing a verb to a
   noun: -ment

authentic, authenticity
cruel, cruelty
embarrass,
   embarrassment
ferocious, ferocity
happy, happiness
loyal, loyalty
move, movement
popular, popularity
quiet, quietness
refine, refinement*
stormy, storminess

(continued on next page)

UNIT 5

benevolence
blast (verb)
cite*
compensation*
emphasis*
envisage
infuriated
insipid
irresistible
issue
license*
lobby
off the top of one's head
on strike
promote*
prosper
retain*
scrape

scrape the bottom of the barrel
scrape the surface
scrape together
steer
steer clear of
steering committee
strike down
strike out on one's own
struck down
subsidy*
surpassing
swipe
swipe a card
take a swipe at
take on
top an offer
top down
top drawer

UNIT 6

access*
alter*
amounts to
check out
come back to haunt you
comply
draw the line
enhance*
getting into the act
hang out with
haunt
monitor*
(not) a far leap

prospective*
pry
reside*
snoop
stepping on
survey*
thinly veiled
trait
verify
vet (verb)
violation*
wary

UNIT 7

agonized
anticipation*
before my lights blink off
carnage
cherished
comeback
defy
emotional
exuberant
furor
haunting
mournful
moved
obscurity
ominous
phrasing

raging
repertoire
resonating
screaming
slashing
solitary
soothe
unassuming

Participles as Adjectives
haunted, haunting
horrified, horrifying
inspired, inspiring
moved, moving
relaxed, relaxing*
terrified, terrifying

UNIT 8

affluent
affordable
available*
concerted
dramatic*
eradication
fanciful
feasible
impoverished
inevitable*
inhibit*
make ends meet
makeshift
malnutrition
paying through the nose
prospect*
put up
restricted*
slump
spur

undertaken*
waned
zero in on

Connotations
average
brave
determined
diet
economical*
foolhardy
malnutrition
mediocre
miserly
politician
scrawny
self-confident
self-satisfied
slender
statesman
stubborn

TEXT CREDITS

UNIT 1

"Do Mirror Neurons Give Us Empathy?" greatergood.berkeley.edu. Used with permission. All rights reserved.

"From the Kindness of Strangers: Penniless Across America," © 1996, 2010 Mike McIntyre. Reprinted by permission.

UNIT 2

"Looking for the Lie." This article appeared originally, in longer form, in *The New York Times Magazine,* Feb 5, 2006. Copyright © 2006 by Robin Marantz Henig. All rights reserved. Reproduced by permission.

"On The River," *The Adventures of Huckleberry Finn* by Mark Twain.

UNIT 3

"Gotta Dance" by Jackson Jodie Daviss—Reprinted with permission from the author from *Story,* Summer 1992.

"Kids Learn Poise Through Dance," CBS News. Reprinted by permission.

UNIT 4

"Exile," from LOST IN TRANSLATION by Eva Hoffman, copyright © 1989 by Eva Hoffman. Used by permission of Dutton, a division of Penguin Group (USA) Inc.

"The Struggle to Be an All-American Girl," by Elizabeth Wong. Reprinted by permission of the author. www.elizabethwong.net

"From Bayamon to Brooklyn," reprinted by permission of the Publisher. From Karen Ogulnick, Editor, *Language Crossings,* New York: Teachers College Press. Copyright © 2000 by Teachers College, Columbia University. All rights reserved.

UNIT 5

"Howard Schultz's Formula for Starbucks®," © The Economist Newspaper Limited, London (February 23, 2006) Reprinted by Permission.

"Swiping at Industry" From *The New York Times,* August 20, 2006 © 2006 *The New York Times.* All rights reserved. Used by permission and protected by the Copyright Laws of the United States. The printing, copying, redistribution, or retransmission of this Content without express written permission is prohibited.

UNIT 6

"Privacy Invasion and Social Media," used with permission of Networkworld.com. Copyright © 2013. All rights reserved.

"Using Social Networking Sites Wisely." Copyright © Remar Sutton. www.foolproofme.com of The Fool Proof Foundation.

UNIT 7

"The Cellist of Sarajevo" by Paul Sullivan. Used by permission of the author and River Music. www.rivermusic.com.

"The Soloist" by Mark Salzman. Reprinted by permission of Donadio & Olson, Inc. Copyright 1994 Mark Salzman.

UNIT 8

"Can Extreme Poverty be Eliminated?" originally published in *Scientific American* by Jeffrey Sachs. Copyright 2005 by Jeffrey Sachs, used by permission of The Wylie Agency LLC.

"Making Ends Meet" from *The New York Times,* May 13, 2001 by Dorothy Gallagher © 2001 *The New York Times.* All rights reserved. Used by permission and protected by the Copyright Laws of the United States. The printing, copying, redistribution, or retransmission of this Content without express written permission is prohibited.

PHOTO CREDITS

Cover photo credits: (top left) al1center/Fotolia, (top right) Comstock Images/Getty Images, (middle left) Hill Street Studios/Blend Images/Corbis, (middle right) Comstock Images/Getty Images, (bottom left) Lou Linwei/Alamy, (bottom right) monika3steps/Shutterstock.

Page xii (top) ABC News; p. 2 EpicStockMedia/Fotolia; p. 5 Aurora Photos/Alamy; p. 15 Everett Collection Inc/Alamy; p. 24 davidevison/Fotolia; p. 28 Presselect/Alamy; p. 48 NASA/UPI/Newscom; p. 50 JPL-Caltech/MSSS/NASA; p. 52 NASA Images; p. 57 NASA/JPL/NASA Images; p. 74 Phase4Photography/Fotolia; p. 76 Jupiterimages/Photolibrary/Getty Images; p. 84 (left) imagebroker/Alamy, (middle) Eddie Gerald/Alamy, (right) FER737NG/Fotolia; p. 100 Radius Images/Alamy; p. 102 Monkey Business Images/Shutterstock; p. 104 Pixsooz/Fotolia; p. 105 JDC/LWA/Corbis/Glow Images; p. 110 wavebreakmedia/Shutterstock; p. 128 John Warburton-Lee Photography/Alamy; p. 132 maurice joseph/Alamy; p. 136 staphy/Fotolia; p. 137 Keren Su/China Span/Alamy; p. 138 BMJ/Shutterstock; p. 152 Ariadne Van Zandbergen/Alamy; p. 156 Jon Arnold Images Ltd/Alamy; p. 161 Nga Nguyen/Flickr Select/Getty Images; p. 176 al1center/Fotolia; p. 179 (top) razlomov/Fotolia, (middle) roca83/Fotolia, (bottom) egd/Shutterstock; p. 181 (left) cobaltstock/Fotolia, (right) David Sprott/Shutterstock; p. 194 Lane Erickson/Fotolia.

THE PHONETIC ALPHABET

Consonant Symbols

/b/	be	/t/	to
/d/	do	/v/	van
/f/	father	/w/	will
/g/	get	/y/	yes
/h/	he	/z/	zoo, busy
/k/	keep, can	/θ/	thanks
/l/	let	/ð/	then
/m/	may	/ʃ/	she
/n/	no	/ʒ/	vision, Asia
/p/	pen	/tʃ/	child
/r/	rain	/dʒ/	join
/s/	so, circle	/ŋ/	long

Vowel Symbols

/ɑ/	far, hot	/iy/	we, mean, feet
/ɛ/	met, said	/ey/	day, late, rain
/ɔ/	tall, bought	/ow/	go, low, coat
/ə/	son, under	/uw/	too, blue
/æ/	cat	/ay/	time, buy
/ɪ/	ship	/aw/	house, now
/ʊ/	good, could, put	/oy/	boy, coin